THE CORPORATE IDEAL

IN THE LIBERAL STATE: 1900–1918

THE CORPORATE IDEAL

IN THE LIBERAL STATE:

1900–1918

by James Weinstein

BEACON PRESS

BOSTON

First published by Beacon Press in 1968

First published as a Beacon Paperback in 1969

Beacon Press books are published under the auspices of
the Unitarian Universalist Association

Printed in the United States of America

89 88 87 86 85   15 14 13 12 11 10 9

The author gratefully acknowledges permission to reprint in slightly revised and retitled form: "Organized Business and the Commission and Manager Movements," which was first published in *The Journal of Southern History*, Volume XXVIII, Number 2, May 1962, copyright © 1962 by the Southern Historical Association and reprinted by permission of the Managing Editor; and "Big Business and the Origins of Workmen's Compensation," which was first published in *Labor History*, Volume VIII, Number 2, Spring 1967.

Library of Congress Cataloging-in-Publication Data

Weinstein, James, 1926–
    The corporate ideal in the liberal state,
1900–1918.

    Includes index.
    1. United States–Politics and government–20th
century.   2. Progressivism (United States politics)
3. Business and politics–United States–History–
20th century.   I. Title.
E743.W44   1985   973.91   68-12846
ISBN 0-8070-5457-7

TO ANNE

ACKNOWLEDGMENTS

WORKING WITH MARTIN J. SKLAR made this book possible. Many of the ideas I explore here were taken from him or emerged in discussions with him. His work, most of it unpublished, has been invaluable in helping to develop my mode of thought and in supplying insights and information. Warren I. Susman also discussed the underlying concepts of the book with me, as well as many specific subjects. In addition, he read and criticized several chapters of the manuscript. His generous encouragement and useful suggestions are deeply appreciated.

William Appleman Williams' books and articles made me aware of many of the problems posed by the liberalism of the large corporations. His critical reading of the manuscript increased my debt to him. Gabriel Kolko's *The Triumph of Conservatism* has also been an important source of ideas and stimulation. Several others have read all or parts of the manuscript and have criticized its content and style. I am particularly grateful to Ronald Radosh for his careful reading of parts of the manuscript and for many leads and pieces of information which he shared with me from his own research. David W. Eakins discussed many of the themes of the book at an early stage of its evolution and read the manuscript when it was almost completed. Others who read major parts of the manuscript and whose comments and suggestions were useful include James B. Gilbert, James O'Connor, and Anne Farrar. I am thankful to each of them and hope that the book justifies the efforts they have made to improve it.

Finally, I also thank the Louis M. Rabinowitz Foundation for a grant that made possible the completion of this book.

J.W.

INTRODUCTION

THE TWO MAIN THESES of this book run counter to prevailing popular opinion and to the opinion of most historians. The first is that the political ideology now dominant in the United States, and the broad programmatic outlines of the liberal state (known by such names as the New Freedom, the New Deal, the New Frontier, and the Great Society) had been worked out and, in part, tried out by the end of the First World War. The second is that the ideal of a liberal corporate social order was formulated and developed under the aegis and supervision of those who then, as now, enjoyed ideological and political hegemony in the United States: the more sophisticated leaders of America's largest corporations and financial institutions.

This book is not based upon a conspiracy theory of history, but it does posit a conscious and successful effort to guide and control the economic and social policies of federal, state, and municipal governments by various business groupings in their own long-range interest as they perceived it. Businessmen were not always, or even normally, the first to advocate reforms or regulation in the common interest. The original impetus for many reforms came from those at or near the bottom of the American social structure, from those who benefited least from the rapid increase in the productivity of the industrial plant of the United States and from expansion at home and abroad. But in the current century, particularly on the federal level, few reforms were enacted without the tacit approval, if not the guidance, of the large corporate interests. And, much more important, businessmen were able to harness to their own ends the desire of intellectuals and middle class reformers to bring together "thoughtful men of all classes" in "a vanguard for the building of the good community." [1] These ends were the stabilization, rationalization, and continued expansion of the existing political economy, and, subsumed under that, the circumscription of the Socialist movement with its ill-formed, but nevertheless dangerous ideas for an alternative form of social organization.

There are two essential aspects of the liberal state as it developed in the Progressive Era, one tightly and sometimes indistinguishably intertwined with the other, but both clearly different. The first was the need of many of the largest corporations to have the government (usually the federal government) intervene in economic matters to protect against irresponsible business conduct and to assure stability in marketing and financial affairs. Gabriel Kolko has examined this aspect in his *The Triumph of Conservatism*,[2] and I will deal with it only peripherally. The second was the replacement of the ideological concepts of laissez faire, or the Darwinian survival of the fittest, by an ideal of a responsible social order in which all classes could look forward to some form of recognition and sharing in the benefits of an ever-expanding economy. Such a corporate order was, of course, to be based on what banker V. Everitt Macy called "the industrial and commercial structure which is the indispensable shelter of us all." [3]

The key word in the new corporate vision of society was responsibility, although the word meant different things to different groups of men. To most middle class social reformers and social workers—men such as Frank P. Walsh of Kansas City, or Judge Ben B. Lindsey of Denver, or Walter Weyl of the *New Republic*, or Jane Addams of Hull House, responsi-

[1] Sidney Kaplan, "Social Engineers as Saviours: Effects of World War I on Some American Liberals," *The Journal of the History of Ideas*, XVII (June 1956), 347.

[2] New York, 1963.

[3] Speech to the 17th Annual Meeting of the National Civic Federation, January 22, 1917, Box 187, National Civic Federation papers, New York Public Library.

bility meant, first of all, the responsibility of society to individual Americans or to underprivileged social classes. To the corporation executives it meant, above all, the responsibility of all classes to maintain and increase the efficiency of the existing social order. Of course some middle-class reformers, like *New Republic* editor Herbert Croly, understood that progressive democracy was "designed to serve as a counterpoise to the threat of working class revolution." [4] But even for them the promotion of reform was not an act of cynicism: they simply sought a way to be immediately effective, to have real influence. Their purpose was not only to serve as defenders of the social system, but also to improve the human condition. In the most profound sense they failed, and badly; yet they were a good deal more than simply lackeys of the capitalist class.

The confusion over what liberalism means and who liberals are is deep-seated in American society. In large part this is because of the change in the nature of liberalism from the individualism of laissez faire in the nineteenth century to the social control of corporate liberalism in the twentieth. Because the new liberalism of the Progressive Era put its emphasis on cooperation and social responsibility, as opposed to unrestrained "ruthless" competition, so long associated with businessmen in the age of the Robber Baron, many believed then, and more believe now, that liberalism was in its essence anti big business. Corporation leaders have encouraged this belief. False consciousness of the nature of American liberalism has been one of the most powerful ideological weapons that American capitalism has had in maintaining its hegemony. An intellectual tradition has grown up among liberal ideologues that embodies this false consciousness. Arthur M. Schlesinger, Jr., intellectual in residence of the Kennedys, for example, writes that "Liberalism in America has been ordinarily the movement on the part of the other sections of society to re-

[4] Kaplan, "Social Engineers," pp. 354–355.

strain the power of the business community."[5] Consistent with this assertion is the popular image of movements for regulation and social reform—the Pure Food and Drug Act, the Federal Trade Commission, workmen's compensation, social security, unemployment insurance, the poverty program —as victories of "the people" over "the interests." In one sense this is true. Even so, Schlesinger's pronouncement is misleading. It is not only historically inaccurate, but serves the interests of the large corporations by masking the manner in which they have exercised control over American politics in this century.

Both in its nineteenth and twentieth century forms, liberalism has been the political ideology of the rising, and then dominant, business groups. Changes in articulated principles have been the result of changing needs of the most dynamic and rapidly growing forms of enterprise. Thus in the days of Andrew Jackson, liberalism's main thrust was against monopoly (and Arthur Schlesinger tells us this meant it was antibusiness). But more recent scholarship has shown that it was the new business class, made up of individual small entrepreneurs (as well as threatened and declining farmers and artisans), that fought state chartered monopoly. Rising entrepreneurs struggled to free business enterprise of the outmoded restrictions of special incorporation and banking laws and to end what was then an overly centralized control of credit. Their laissez faire rhetoric in opposition to "unnatural" or artificial privilege was that of the common man, but their achievements—general incorporation and free banking laws, the spread of public education and popular suffrage—created the conditions for unfettered competition and rapid industrial growth. Half a century later that competition and industrial expansion had led to the development of new forms of monopoly, grown so powerful that a relative handful of merged cor-

[5] Arthur M. Schlesinger, Jr., *The Age of Jackson* (Boston, Little, Brown, 1946), p. 505.

porations came to dominate the American political economy. Thereafter, liberalism became the movement for state intervention to supervise corporate activity, rather than a movement for the removal of state control over private enterprise.

To achieve conditions suitable for free competition during the Age of Jackson, the rising entrepreneurs and their political representatives had to believe in, and promote, ideals of equality of opportunity, class mobility, and noninterference by the government with individual initiative (although, even then, government subsidy of such necessary common services as railroads and canals was encouraged where private capital was inadequate to do the job). At the turn of the century the new trust magnates also pressed for reform in accordance with their new political, economic, and legal needs. The nature of the ideals and the needs in the two periods were different. In the first, the principles of competition and individual efficiency underlay many proposed reforms; in the second, cooperation and *social* efficiency were increasingly important. But in each case the rising businessmen—or, at least, many of them— helped promote reforms. In both instances, business leaders sponsored institutional adjustment to their needs, and supported political ideologies that appealed to large numbers of people of different social classes in order to gain, and retain, popular support for their entrepreneurial activity. In the Progressive Era, and ever since, corporation leaders did this by adapting to their own ends the ideals of middle class social reformers, social workers, and socialists.

My main concern in this book is not with the social reformers, men and women who might be called ordinary liberals. Instead I will focus on those business leaders (and their various political and academic ideologues) who saw liberalism as a means of securing the existing social order. They succeeded because their ideology and their political economy alone was comprehensive. Radical critics of the new centralized and manipulated system of social control were disarmed and absorbed by the corporate liberals who allowed potential opponents to participate, even if not as equals, in a process of adjustment, concession, and amelioration that seemed to promise a gradual advance toward the good society for all citizens. In a formal democracy, success lay in evolving a social vision that could be shared by most articulate people outside the business community. Corporate liberalism evolved such a vision. More than that, it appealed to leaders of different social groupings and classes by granting them status and influence as spokesmen for their constituents on the condition only that they defend the framework of the existing social order.

As it developed, the new liberalism incorporated the concepts of social engineering and social efficiency that grew up alongside of industrial engineering and efficiency. The corollary was a disparagement of "irresponsible" individualism and localism. On the municipal level, as Samuel P. Hays has observed, the drama of business-led reform lay in competition between two systems of decision-making. One was based upon ward representation and traditional ideas of grass-roots involvement in the political process; the other, growing out of the rationalization of social life made possible by scientific and technological developments, required expert analysis and worked more smoothly if decisions flowed from fewer and smaller centers outward toward the rest of society. The same competition went on at the federal level, although formal changes in the political structure were more difficult to make and, therefore, less extensive. In general, however, the Progressive Era witnessed rapid strides toward centralization and a decline in importance of those institutions which were based upon local representation, most obviously in the decline of Congress and the increasing importance of the executive branch in the shaping of policy and in the initiation of legislation. As Hays concludes, this development constituted an accommodation of forces outside the business community to political trends within business and professional life.[6]

The process of developing social reform through extra-political negotiation between various social groupings went on most consistently in the early years of the century in one organization, the National Civic Federation. It is, therefore, central to this study. The National Civic Federation was primarily an organization of big businessmen, although it established the principle of tripartite (business-labor-public) representation in public affairs. Founded in 1900, it was the leading organization of politically conscious corporation leaders at least until the United States entered the First World War. I will, in addition, look at the circumstances under which small businessmen acted like big businessmen—that is, when they played the role of class-conscious political reformers, capable, if necessary, of transcending their most immediate, or apparent, interests or traditions. And I will examine the role of leaders of the major political parties during the Progressive Era (1900 to 1920), to explore their relationship to particular business groupings, but, more important, the manner in which they assimilated and translated into legislation the social and institutional principles talked about and advocated by business leaders in the Civic Federation and other organizations. In short, this book will attempt to show that liberalism in the Progressive Era—and since—was the product, consciously created, of the leaders of the giant corporations and financial institutions that emerged astride American society in the last years of the nineteenth century and the early years of the twentieth.

[6] Samuel Hays, "The Politics of Reform in Municipal Government in the Progressive Era," *Pacific Northwest Quarterly*, LV, 4 (October 1964), 168–169.

CONTENTS

THE CORPORATE IDEAL

IN THE LIBERAL STATE: 1900–1918

CHAPTER ONE

THE NATIONAL CIVIC FEDERATION
AND THE CONCEPT OF CONSENSUS

THE PROGRESSIVE ERA—the years from 1900 to 1920—was a period of social turmoil and intense competition among different social groupings and classes for political power and influence in the United States. By 1918 the leaders of the large corporations and banks emerged secure in their loose hegemony over the political structure. They did so by accepting, and unobtrusively leading, a new politics which we will call corporate liberalism, but that was known then by such names as the New Nationalism and the New Freedom. Underlying all, or most, of the new politics of these years was an awareness on the part of the more sophisticated business and political leaders that the social order could be stabilized only if it moved in the direction of general social concern and social responsibility. Dissatisfaction with the increasing polarization of American society and with the apparent decline in the influence of some social classes created a climate for change. In that climate many movements grew. The one that was truly conservative triumphed; it did so in the name of liberalism.

Of course, since the end of the Civil War, commercial and industrial interests had enjoyed an informal control of American politics. But that control had not gone unchallenged. In the 1880's and 1890's a wide variety of radical critics agitated against what they considered to be the corruption of American politics by various business groups. The best known of these were the Populists, who functioned outside of the major

3

parties from 1890 to 1896, but there were many other groupings of middle class and working class radicals: Single Taxers,
Edward Bellamy Socialists, Christian Socialists, Knights of Labor, Socialist Laborites, anarchists. Labor troubles were common and severe in these years despite the absence of a stable
center of trade unionism, such as the American Federation of
Labor would become in the late 1890's and early 1900's. Among
the more violent and serious strikes were the railroad strike of
1877, the strikes in Chicago in 1886 that culminated with the
Haymarket bombing, the Homestead strike of 1892 that was
brutally suppressed by Andrew Carnegie's subordinate, Henry
C. Frick, and the Pullman strike of 1894, led by Eugene V.
Debs of the American Railway Union and broken by the Attorney General of the United States.

By the time of the Spanish-American War in 1898 all of
these movements and groups had been broken up or reduced
to insignificance. Yet the contest was not over. The new century saw a number of political realignments and consolidations
that gradually took on the shape of politics as they have been
known for most of the last 50 years. In the industrial and
financial world a polarization occurred between the larger
corporations, railroads, and the various banks that financed
them (particularly the House of Morgan) on one side, and
the small and middle-range manufactures and merchants on
the other. In general, as we will see, the smaller businessmen
were tied much more immediately to the market than were
many of the larger corporations. Their attitudes toward trade
unions, working conditions, and wages were more rigid and
uncompromising. This was so because their financial positions
and profit margins were generally poorer and because their
relative provincialism kept many of them from an awareness
of the larger problems of interclass harmony and social (as
opposed to purely individual) efficiency posed by the growth
of the unions, the radical insurgents in both major parties,
and by the Socialist Party of America.

The smaller businessmen, organized in various merchants

4

associations and in the National Association of Manufacturers (NAM), formed an opposition from the right to the new liberalism that developed in cooperation between political leaders such as Theodore Roosevelt, William Howard Taft, and Woodrow Wilson and financial and corporation leaders in the National Civic Federation (NCF) and other organizations. The NAM certainly was not an enemy of the business system. On the contrary, it was the upholder of the traditional, or laissez faire, values. But as the unions and the more socially conscious radicals grew in strength the traditional values of dog-eat-dog capitalism, in which the worker and consumer had little hope for gain, became an increasing impediment to political stability.

Radicalism in the Progressive Era took two forms: socialism and neopopulism. As if to symbolize the changes taking place in American politics, the Socialist Party ran its first presidential candidate in 1900 and was formally organized a few months later in 1901. The new party was a coalition of Bellamy Socialists, Christian Socialists, elements of the old Populist Party, former Single Taxers, former members of Debs' American Railway Union, and a faction of the old Socialist Labor Party. The new Socialist Party never achieved major proportions as compared to the Democratic or Republican parties. But it did attain a membership of well over 100,000, at one time had 1,200 officeholders in some 340 municipalities, and controlled about one third of the organizations in the American Federation of Labor. More important, the socialist critique of American capitalism was widely discussed beyond the confines of the party membership, particularly since the Socialists alone had a view of an alternative form of social organization that approached being comprehensive. Other criticism might be absorbed through a process of political conciliation and compromise. Socialism, as a vision of a new mode of social existence, had to be aborted, or, at least narrowly circumscribed.

Neopopulism was far less ideological than socialism, and

5

far less clearly distinguishable from the new liberalism. A movement of middle class reformers, midwestern farmers and small businessmen, and of skilled workers, it had leaders in both major parties. Known as insurgent progressives, most of the political figures were Republicans. Best known of them was Robert M. La Follette of Wisconsin. La Follette was antimonopoly and hoped to restore an earlier era of free competition by and for small businessmen and farmers—through government dissolution of trusts and regulation of railroads. In this respect he was not far from the businessmen in the NAM, but he differed in his attitude toward organized labor and in his sponsorship of social reform. Like most neopopulists, La Follette rarely, if ever, attacked the basic structure of the corporation-dominated system. Speaking in the interest of the small entrepreneur and the free market, he pressed for a redress in the power relationships between the small producer and the large corporations and their financiers. He consistently and courageously attacked special privileges that corporations had wrested from state or federal government, but he had no fear of government intervention to regulate "natural" monopolies, or to destroy "artificially" created trusts. If La Follette had had his way the American political economy would have been returned to a condition like that existing prior to the emergence of the large corporation. In that, he was not unlike the NAM, and for that reason his critique did not offer a primary threat to the underlying principles or values of a business society.

The National Civic Federation stood in opposition to what it considered its twin enemies: the socialists and radicals among workers and middle class reformers, and the "anarchists" among the businessmen (as it characterized the NAM). Before the First World War the Civic Federation was the most important single organization of the socially conscious big businessmen and their academic and political theorists. There were a number of other organizations which helped to develop the new liberalism and its concepts of the welfare state —the American Association for Labor Legislation, for example—but the NCF concerned itself with the widest range of problems and questions and took the lead in educating businessmen to the changing needs in political economy that accompanied the changing nature of America's business system. In its membership the National Civic Federation originated the principle of tripartite representation that was later to become a feature of various government boards and agencies. The Federation was organized in three nominal divisions, representing business, labor, and an undefined public. Business leaders were of central importance, but the leading trade unionists of the day were members, as were professionals (particularly corporation lawyers), political leaders, university presidents, newspaper publishers and editors, and leaders of conservative farm organizations. Under a fairly rigid public ideology of free enterprise and the denial of class interests, the corporation leaders in the Federation sought to establish an extra-political system of rationalization, conciliation, and reform based on cooperation with representatives of organized workers, farmers, academics, and reformers. These men considered and sometimes sponsored a number of legislative and regulatory proposals designed, as they put it, to restore "that habitual normal sense of social solidarity which is the foundation stone of democracy." [1]

The National Civic Federation was organized in 1900 by Ralph M. Easley, a former school teacher and journalist whose experience with Kansas Populists and Chicago Socialists converted him into a crusader for better relations between capital and labor. A staunch Republican and self-styled conservative, Easley sought to preserve the good things in the old order. To do so, he set out to build a widely representative organi-

---

[1] Quoted in Gordon M. Jensen, "The National Civic Federation: American Business in an Age of Social Change and Social Reform, 1900–1910" (unpublished Ph.D. dissertation, Princeton University, 1956), p. 90.

7

zation of the top leaders of the business and labor worlds. His experience in the Chicago Civic Federation in the late 1890's gave him the organizational knowledge and the personal contacts to make a start. The conference of the Chicago Federation on the trust problem in 1899 gave him confidence, bolstered by widespread acclaim from the press. When Easley set out to organize the National Civic Federation he had powerful support and enjoyed quick success.

From the beginning big businessmen led and dominated the National Civic Federation. Marcus A. Hanna was its first president. Others among its early leaders were utilities magnate Samuel Insull, Chicago banker (and later Secretary of the Treasury), Franklin MacVeagh, Charles Francis Adams, Andrew Carnegie, Consolidated Gas president George B. Cortelyou, and several partners in J. P. Morgan and Company. By 1903 there were representatives in the NCF of almost one third of the 367 corporations with a capitalization of more than $10,000,000 and representatives of sixteen of the sixty-seven largest railroads in the United States. Labor was also represented by its top leaders. Samuel Gompers was the original First Vice President of the Federation and retained that position until his death in 1924. John Mitchell of the United Mine Workers was an active member, co-chairman of the Trade Agreements Department from 1904 to 1908, and its full-time head from 1908 to 1911. The heads of the major railroad brotherhoods and many AFL international unions were also on the executive committee. The members of the executive committee representing the public at one time or another included Grover Cleveland, William H. Taft, Charles J. Bonaparte (Roosevelt's Attorney General), Nicholas Murray Butler, Charles W. Eliot, Benjamin Ide Wheeler (President of the University of California), and many other men prominent in politics and the professions.[2]

The leaders of the Civic Federation, particularly its busi-

[2] Jensen, "National Civic Federation," pp. 30, 35, 50.

ness members, viewed the problem of the relationship between capital and labor as central to the political and economic stability of the emerging system of large corporations.
In its initial years—until 1905—the Federation saw its main
role to be that of a direct mediator in labor disputes. During
the 1902 coal strike, for example, the NCF was quietly active
in trying to bring together the coal operators and the union
men. As Marcus A. Hanna commented in 1903, he aimed to
establish through the Civic Federation a relation of mutual
trust between the laborer and the employer that would "lay
the foundation stone of a structure that will endure for all
time." [3] Similarly, George W. Perkins, a partner of J. P. Morgan and Company and a director of both the United States
Steel Corporation and the International Harvester Company,
often spoke of the need to spread the benefits of the new trust
system to the workers. For labor, John Mitchell concurred.
He was "glad to be a part of this peace movement," as he
called the National Civic Federation. To him, and, he asserted, "to every observant person," it was obvious that relations between capital and labor had "become strained almost
to the breaking point" in some industries. As a good citizen
who "cares for the progress and the perpetuity of this republic," Mitchell believed it was his duty to help "bring into
closer and more harmonious relation these two apparently
antagonistic forces." [4]

Easley summed up this initial purpose at an early annual
dinner. Pointing to Samuel Gompers, who presided, and to
August Belmont, banker and traction magnate, who had been
elected president upon the death of Marcus A. Hanna, Easley
observed that "in no other country in the world could such
a gathering be brought together." Only the democracy of

[3] Marcus A. Hanna to a dinner of the Executive Committee of the National Civic Federation, May 13, 1903. *National Civic Federation Monthly
Review*, VI, 2 (June 1903), p. 7.

[4] John Mitchell to the Annual Dinner of the NCF, December 15, 1904,
NCF Review, I, 10 (January 1, 1905), p. 6.

American institutions "made possible the comingling in un-conscious equality and in conscious co-operation" of repre-sentatives of "billions of capital, millions of wage earners, of scholarship and letters, of the bar, the press, the platform and the church." [5] The official and public view of the Civic Fed-eration in its earliest years was that compared to the "labor problem" all others were secondary. "The very foundations of prosperity," a Federation conference on conciliation concluded in 1901, rested upon "the relations existing between the em-ployer and employee classes . . . Here it seems everything in the industrial world begins and ends." [6]

Yet even at this early stage of the Civic Federation's de-velopment, its leaders were concerned with more than the immediate, or direct, relationship between the employer and his workers. That is, the business leaders who participated in the activities of the NCF had transcended a narrow interest-consciousness and were emerging as fully class conscious. In 1910, George W. Perkins explained that "the officers of the great corporation instinctively lose sight of the interest of any one individual and work for what is the broadest, most en-during interest of the many." Their situation at the "com-manding heights" of American industrial life enabled them to view matters "from the point of view of an intelligent, well-posted and fair arbitrator." What this meant was that the businessman was merging "into the public official." "No longer controlled by the mere business view," he was more and more acting "the part of the statesman." [7] Frank A. Van-derlip, president of the National City Bank, shared Perkins' view. "We should demand," he wrote to Ralph Easley, that leadership in business be "accompanied by a more thorough spirit of service to the community at large." [8]

[5] *Ibid.*, p. 1.
[6] Quoted in Jensen, "National Civic Federation," p. 101.
[7] Quoted in *NCF Review*, III, 10 (September 1910), p. 7. Cited in Jen-sen, p. 64.
[8] Quoted in Jensen, "National Civic Federation," p. 87.

Of course, not all businessmen were capable of taking the progressive view of the NCF leaders. Even in the trusts there was division, both on broad policy matters and on attitudes toward the unions. As Ralph Easley informed Senator Joseph L. Bristow in 1909, Frank Vanderlip and George W. Perkins had only recently come to view unions favorably. It was, he explained, "almost an individual question. There are no corporations but what are themselves divided in opinion. Take the United States Steel Corporation: Judge Gary, George Perkins, and Henry Phipps are friendly to our work, whereas Henry C. Frick and W. E. Corey hate the Federation and believe it is doing great harm by recognizing the labor leaders. They would smash every union in the country if they could. In fact, our enemies are the Socialists among the labor people and the anarchists among the capitalists." [9]

In the large corporations, such as United States Steel, the "anarchists" tended to be those men who came from the manufacturing end of the business—the old steel men—while the progressives were usually those who represented the banks, or who were second-generation managers. But even these progressives only partially supported unionism. They understood the need to mold the character and direction of the labor movement, to help the conservative unionists against the militants and Socialists, but they never sought to encourage the movement's growth. In the minds of many financial and corporation leaders there existed a constant tension between their general and particular interests. Many NCF leaders accepted the necessity of conservative unionism as an abstract principle, but opposed unions in their shops. Outstanding among these were Cyrus McCormick, George W. Perkins, Elbert H. Gary, Henry W. Phipps, and Henry P. Davidson of International Harvester and United States Steel. These men were among the most generous contributors to the Federation and par-

---

[9] Ralph M. Easley to Joseph L. Bristow, New York, July 17, 1909, Box 46, National Civic Federation Papers (New York Public Library).

11

ticipated fully in its activities, but their companies became more anti-union between 1904 and 1910;[10] United States Steel remained a bastion of anti-unionism until the early days of the New Deal.

As president of the National Civic Federation from Hanna's death in 1904 to the accession of Seth Low in 1908, August Belmont typified these apparent ambiguities. Samuel Gompers, John Mitchell, and William D. Mahon, president of the Amalgamated Association of Street and Electric Railway Employees had insisted that Belmont succeed Hanna. They did so, according to Easley, because they wanted a man at the head of the Civic Federation "who would largely outclass David M. Parry," president of the open-shop NAM.[11] But despite this support and an attitude of cordiality toward the union leaders, Belmont did not welcome unionization of his Interborough Rapid Transit Company. Quite the contrary. He did settle one strike in 1904 after arbitration by the Civic Federation, but in 1905 a strike of the Amalgamated Association was broken with the help of Gompers, Mitchell, and Mahon because the strikers included among their own demands some of those of the motormen, for whom the Brotherhood of Locomotive Engineers had a three-year contract.

Thereafter, Belmont would have no dealings with the union, despite occasional pleas by Gompers, Mitchell, and others.[12] In 1916 he explained that he had been opposed to unionization of the New York transit companies because the corporation, as a franchise holder, was under state and mu-

[10] See correspondence between Ralph M. Easley, Isaac N. Seligman, Gertrude Beeks, Charles D. Lithgrow, and William Corwine for lists of contributors to the NCF in 1909 (Box 47, NCF papers); also see Ralph M. Easley to J. G. Schmidlapp, New York, March 24, 1913, Box 50, NCF papers, for list of contributors in 1912.

[11] Easley to Bristow, New York, July 17, 1909, Box 46, NCF papers; Philip S. Foner, *The Policies and Practices of the American Federation of Labor, 1900–1909* (New York, International Publishers, 1964), p. 102.

[12] For details of this strike see Foner, pp. 103–106.

nicipal supervision, but its employees were not. Belmont would recognize the union only when the state laws were changed "so that a man entering a public service corporation would ipso facto be entering a personal contract with the State or City" and be "held to strict accountability for what he might do." [13]

Other NCF employers were less ambivalent. William C. Brown, senior vice president of the New York Central Railroad, wrote in 1908 that "organized labor has done a tremendous work for labor," and, at the same time, "by raising the standard of intelligence," had been "beneficial to all interests." Certainly, Brown concluded, "this is true so far as it relates to organized railroad labor." [14] Mark Hanna, and through his influence many coal operators, had also recognized unions and come to agreements with them in their organized capacity. [15]

In general, in its early years, the NCF focused on the need to come to terms with the trade union movement as a permanent institution in American life. Business leaders in the Federation were flexible. They did not often recognize unions unless compelled to do so, but they did not greatly fear dealing with conservative unions when the workers demonstrated that they had the strength and determination to carry through militant actions. After the successful strike of the Industrial Workers of the World, in Lawrence, Massachusetts, in 1912, John Golden, president of the conservative AFL Textile Workers wrote Easley that many of the manufacturers there had gained "a very rapid education" in the benefits of con-

[13] Belmont to Easley, New York, August 3, 1916, Box 188, NCF papers. Belmont's suggestion was similar to the Condon-Wadlin Act in New York State, adopted in 1940, and now unenforceable.

[14] William C. Brown to Easley, Paul Smith's, New York, August 19, 1908, Box 30, NCF papers. Brown later became president of the NYCRR.

[15] Samuel Gompers, opening remarks, Minutes of the Executive Committee of the NCF, May 6, 1904, Box 188, NCF papers; Hanna, NCFMR, VI, 2 (June 1903), p. 7.

servative unionism, and that "some of them are falling all over themselves now to do business with our organization." Golden claimed that since the strike his union had been able to form seven new locals in Lawrence, and that the union had also won wage increases in a strike at mills in New York.[16]

This aspect of business ideology within NCF had been symbolized in 1904 by the formation of a Trade Agreements Department under the joint chairmanship of Francis L. Robbins of the Pittsburgh Coal Company and John Mitchell of the United Mine Workers (UMW). Most of the trade agreements of this period were concluded between employer groups and unions with representatives in the NCF. Among them were the New York Clothing Trades agreement, the National Founders Association—Iron Moulders agreement, the bituminous operators—UMW agreement, and agreements between the Erie Dock Managers and the Longshoremen, the Newspaper Publishers Association and the Typographical Union and Pressmen, the New York Metal Trades Association and the Boilermakers, the United States Steel Corporation and the Metal Workers, and the Theatrical Managers and the Musicians Protective Association.[17]

In contrast to the attitude of the business leaders in the National Civic Federation toward the trade union movement, the small and middle-range manufacturers who led the National Association of Manufacturers after 1902 were adamantly hostile to organized labor in any form. The NAM neither accepted the trade union movement as a permanent force in American life, to be dealt with and molded, nor did most of its members recognize unions in their plants, except when

---

[16] John Golden to Ralph M. Easley, Fall River, Mass., April 24, 1912, Box 49, NCF papers. The IWW strikers won wage increases of from five to twenty-five percent for the unskilled workers in Lawrence. Golden's Textile Workers organized only the relatively few skilled workers in the mills. See Paul F. Brissenden, *The I.W.W.* (New York, Russell & Russell, 1957), pp. 284–294.

[17] Jensen, "National Civic Federation," pp. 125–126.

14

forced to do so by bitterly fought strikes. Organized in 1895, the NAM was initially concerned almost entirely with the expansion of foreign trade. Theodore Search, the Association's president for several years, was also a charter member of the National Civic Federation. Under his leadership there had been no conflict between the two business associations' attitudes toward the trade union movement since Search never considered "questions involving the relations between manufacturers and employees" one of the NAM's "proper functions." The Association itself later declared that under Search there had not been "a hint" of an "organized threat against organized labor." [18] But anti-union employers, led by David M. Parry, John Kirby, Jr., and James W. Van Cleave, planned secretly to take control of the NAM in 1902. In a surprise move, Parry won the presidency from Search's candidate, a leather goods manufacturer interested in free hides.[19]

Once Parry, Kirby, and Van Cleave gained control of the NAM its policies changed sharply. Early in 1903, at Parry's urging, the NAM took leadership of the "crusade against unionism" on the theory that organized labor had "exactly the same end and aim as Socialism." The only difference Parry could see was that labor tried to gain this end by "force and arbitrary power," while the Socialists used the ballot.[20] Both in direct opposition to unions on a factory level, and as lobbyists, the NAM counterattacked against the growing trade union movement. In the courts, too, NAM leaders took the initiative. The most threatening action was Van Cleave's Buck's Stove and Range Company suit against the Metal

[18] Robert H. Wiebe, *Businessmen and Reform* (Cambridge, Harvard University Press, 1962), 35, 168–169; Foner, *The Policies and Practice of the A.F.L.*, pp. 36–37.

[19] Parry received only 46 votes of 124 cast in a five man contest. The other four candidates were all foreign trade advocates. Schieren (Search's candidate) endorsed the eight hour day on government contracts, and had corresponded with Gompers on the subject. Wiebe, *Businessmen and Reform*, pp. 26, 169.

[20] Quoted in Foner, *The Policies and Practice of the A.F.L.*, p. 37.

15

Polishers Union and the American Federation of Labor. That action sought to enjoin the unions from continuing a boycott in support of a strike to retain the nine hour day in the stove company.

In opposing these activities of the NAM, Ralph Easley enjoyed emphasizing that the newly formed anti-union employers associations included "none of the great employers of labor representing the basic industries, such as coal, iron and steel, building trades and railroads." [21] Van Cleave was a medium sized stove manufacturer; Parry owned a car factory in Indianapolis; Charles W. Post, president of the NAM's subsidiary, the Citizens Industrial Association, was a cereal manufacturer; and George Pope, who became NAM president in 1913, was a bicycle manufacturer who longed for the labor relations that existed in his childhood when his father had established the business.[22] Of course, it was true that many men associated with the United States Steel Company encouraged the activities of anti-union employers associations, if not the NAM itself. Nevertheless, the NCF had a basic difference in attitude toward the conservative unionists in the AFL. This was demonstrated when Van Cleave initiated the Buck's Stove and Range case. Gompers was defended by Alton B. Parker, a Wall Street lawyer, Presidential candidate, and later president of the NCF, while privately, AFL defense was financed in part by Andrew Carnegie, the NCF's biggest contributor.[23]

The growing attacks on the unions by the NAM and the willingness of the courts to grant injunctions in labor matters, were of genuine concern to the NCF. Combined, they pushed labor toward interest in independent politics after 1905. Many

[21] *NCF Monthly Review*, VI, 4 (June 1904), p. 12.
[22] Wiebe, *Businessmen and Reform*, pp. 25, 27, 29.
[23] Foner, *The Policies and Practice of the A.F.L.*, p. 339: Carnegie to Ralph Easley, New York, February 24, 1908, Box 30, NCF papers.

NCF members saw this as a warning that the loyalty of the workers to the system was weakening. Louis D. Brandeis, an active member of the Massachusetts Civic Federation, commented in 1905 that collective bargaining was essential to the survival of capitalism. "The trade unions also stand," Brandeis understood, "as a strong bulwark against the great wave of socialism." Warning conservative businessmen outside the Federation that "among a free people every excess of capital must in time be repaid by the excessive demands of those who have not the capital," he concluded that "if the capitalists are wise, they will aid us in the effort to prevent injustice." [24] Brandeis' view corresponded almost exactly with that of President Theodore Roosevelt. The "growth of the Socialist party in this country," Roosevelt warned, was "far more ominous than any populist movement in times past." [25]

This did not impel Roosevelt to support unions as such, but it did motivate him to support reform and regulation. By 1909 such men as George W. Perkins of J. P. Morgan and Company and Frank Vanderlip of the National City Bank had joined other business leaders in the NCF who "clearly recognized the public necessity for the choice between trade unionism and state socialism." Espousing trade unionism "as consonant with American institutions" and as an "antidote for the socialistic propaganda," the Federation placed itself squarely against the NAM and its new president, John Kirby, Jr. This, commented *The Survey* (Charity Organization Society journal), was "most significant," because the National Civic Federation numbered among its officers Seth Low, Isaac N. Seligman, President Taft, Secretary of the Treasury Franklin MacVeagh, Elihu Root, Andrew Carnegie,

[24] Quoted in Alpheus T. Mason, *Brandeis: A Free Man's Life* (New York, Viking, 1946), pp. 130, 141, 149.

[25] Theodore Roosevelt to C. F. Gettemy, February 1, 1905, in *The Letters of Theodore Roosevelt*, IV, ed. E. E. Morison (Cambridge, 1951), p. 1113.

August Belmont, and "a score more of equally representative men." [26]

Even so, from 1905 onward NCF activity did not center around direct labor relations. Militant anti-union activity by many businessmen after 1903, stabilization of trade union membership after 1904, and growing labor interest, particularly among the rank and file, in politics and the Socialist party led the NCF to move in new directions and to develop new programs in the years from 1905 to 1908. During this time, the NCF expanded only slightly.

As the open shop campaign of the NAM and the various employers associations gained momentum, welfare work emerged as an important part of NCF thinking. Clearly unable to establish hegemony over the business community on the basis of its trade union policies, Federation leaders turned to welfare as an area of work that would appeal particularly to anti-union employers. By the nature of the work, welfare activity excluded the union members of the Civic Federation; from the beginning it was entirely a businessman's project. This was symbolized by the absence of the union label on Welfare Department stationery—every other NCF department used the "bug"—in order to avoid offending non-union employers while trying to win them to the Federation's views.

The Welfare Department of the Civic Federation was organized in January 1904. At the first meeting some 100 members participated, but the Federation could find only about 50 employers of importance who had developed welfare programs in their factories. After 1905 welfare work increasingly was seen as a substitute for the recognition of unions. As the labor relations role of direct mediator between employers and unions declined in importance within the NCF, welfare work expanded. By 1911 the Welfare Department had

[26] Easley to Bristow, New York, July 17, 1909, Box 46, NCF papers; Graham Taylor, "Industrial Survey of the Month," *The Survey*, XXII (August 7, 1909), 668–669.

500 employer members. In 1914 an NCF survey showed 2,500 employers with welfare programs in operation.[27]

The general approach of the Welfare Department was to promote sympathy and a sense of identification between the employer and his employees by integrating the lives and leisure time of the workers with the functioning of the corporation. This was carried to its fullest development in Southern textile towns, but also in such places as Dayton, Ohio, where John H. Patterson's National Cash Register Company pioneered in such work (and worked closely with the NCF),[28] and in Chicago, under the leadership of Julius Rosenwald of Sears, Roebuck and Company.[29] If welfare work was really to substitute for union membership, it was clear to the employers that it must be conducted so as not to "rob the worker of his self respect." The greatest cause of "employee unrest" was seen to be the workers' lack of control over working conditions, "the lack of opportunity to be heard." At the same time, the employers recognized the paternalism that underlay their programs; this was unavoidable, since the role of the worker in such programs was, at best, "advisory."[30]

Part of the process of integrating the lives of the workers with that of the corporation involved the assumption by corporations of many functions now seen as government responsibilities. These included technical education for workers, kindergarten for their children, low cost housing, recreational

[27] *NCF Monthly Review*, VI, 4 (June 1904), p. 13; *ibid.*, VI, 7 (September 15, 1904); Jensen, "National Civic Federation," pp. 152–154, 159, 162.

[28] Patterson cooperated with the Welfare Department from its inception. In 1912 he sent his regular contribution of $500 to the Department and told Seth Low that he greatly appreciated "the part you have taken in patching up peace between capital and labor." "I trust," he added, "the good work will continue. Nothing can stop it, and I want to thank you, as a manufacturer, for your broad views in the matter." John H. Patterson to Seth Low, Dayton, Ohio, April 29, 1912, Box 49, NCF papers; *NCF Monthly Review*, VI, 7 (September 15, 1904), p. 13.

[29] Jensen, "National Civic Federation," p. 162.

[30] *Ibid.*, pp. 152–153.

facilities and some aspects of public health programs, saving and lending money, insurance, pensions.[31] In addition, companies involved in welfare work were concerned with safety regulations and equipment, in-plant sanitation, bible training, first aid treatment, and even landscaping of company grounds. The welfare activity of Julius Rosenwald's Sears, Roebuck and Company were, perhaps, the most extensive and consciously paternalistic. Rosenwald took "a fatherly interest" in the thousands of young women who worked for him. He rigidly enforced "a cast-iron rule that any man, no matter how important," who attempted to "abuse his position" dismissed himself from the company.

Picnics and other social activities that might encourage familiarity between men and women workers were forbidden, but "elaborate facilities" were provided for "wholesome amusement" and the feeding of employees at low prices. Women and men ate in the same room, at separate tables. Employees were forbidden to enter saloons within eight blocks of the plant. "As transformed by welfare work," writes an historian of the National Civic Federation, the corporation was "no longer merely a private institution organized for the purpose of collecting profits; it was fast becoming a vital social institution, a wholesome center in which a large part of the living of society was becoming concentrated."[32] During the prewar years the NCF played a major role in developing such paternalism and in spreading the word to other corporations. In particular, the United States Steel and International Harvester companies came more and more to take the lead in the field. By the 1920's, in more sophisticated form, paternalistic labor relations undermined union strength and successfully forestalled the organization of new unions.[33]

[31] NCF Monthly Review, VI, 7 (September 15, 1904), p. 13.
[32] Jensen, "National Civic Federation," pp. 162–163.
[33] On International Harvester and U.S. Steel see George W. Perkins, Address to the Tenth Annual Meeting of the National Civic Federation, New York, November 22 and 23, 1909 (New York, 1910), p. 144; "Acci-

Welfare work partially answered the National Civic Federation's need for a program to win support from anti-union employers, but it did not improve the Federation's relations with its labor members or ease their labor leaders' task of justifying their membership in the NCF to the trade union rank and file. As Easley explained in 1904, the Federation and its big business sponsors faced two major opponents: socialism and the "recently formed employers' associations."[34] By socialism, Easley usually meant the Socialist Party, but any form of "class politics" was anathema to the leaders of the Federation. Much of the business support that was given Gompers and the AFL was the result of a widespread agreement in business circles to uphold conservative unionism as against the Socialists and, after 1905, as against the Industrial Workers of the World. Gompers played on this constantly.

However, within the union movement, Gompers and others were often attacked by those opposed to participation in the NCF. At a meeting of the independent, industrial Western Labor Union in 1902, Frank Morrison of the AFL urged the delegates to dissolve and bring their individual unions back into the Federation. In reply, Eugene V. Debs attacked Gompers and John Mitchell for bringing the AFL into the NCF under the pretense that the workingmen had friends among the industrialists. Instead, Debs called upon the delegates to change their name to the American Labor Union, declare in favor of socialism, and begin a nationwide campaign to organize industrial unions. Every one of his proposals was adopted by the convention.[35]

---

dent Relief for Steel Workers," *Review of Reviews*, KLI, 5 (May 1910), p. 533; "Accident Relief of the United States Steel Corporation," *The Survey*, XXIV (April 23, 1910), pp. 136–137; Raynal C. Boling, "Results of Voluntary Relief Plan of the United States Steel Corporation," *Annals AAPSS*, XXXVIII, 1 (July 1911), p. 43; on Dayton see Fred C. Kelly, "Dayton's Uncle Bountiful," *Collier's*, August 1, 1914, p. 8; see also, Wiebe, p. 222.

[34] *NCF Monthly Review*, I, 4 (June 1904), p. 12.

[35] Ray Ginger, *The Bending Cross* (New Brunswick, 1949), pp. 218–219.

Again in 1904, Debs warned that the NCF professed friendship for labor in order to "take it by the hand and guide it into harmless channels." [36] And at the founding convention of the Industrial Workers of the World, the Manifesto adopted stated that the Civic Federation was the industrialist's way to conceal his daggers while hoodwinking those he would rule and exploit.[37] In the conventions of the AFL, Socialists also attacked the NCF. Duncan McDonald, a United Mine Workers delegate and prominent Illinois Socialist, led one fight against the NCF at the 1911 convention of the AFL. McDonald argued that the Civic Federation had been conceived to "chloroform the labor movement into a more submissive mood." This was made clear by the prominence of directors of the United States Steel Corporation, a practitioner of the "vilest and most brutal methods in its treatment of workingmen," in the NCF.[38]

Socialist opposition to the NCF, and Eugene V. Debs' 408,000 votes for President in 1904—a fourfold increase over the Socialist vote of 1900—paralleled the increasingly effective open shop campaign of the NAM under David Parry's leadership. By 1904, the NAM's drive had succeeded in stopping the previously steady growth of the AFL. Just as serious was the Association's antilabor lobbying in Congress and its initiation of antilabor injunctions, usually granted by the courts. Under the impact of the attacks from the right and the growth of the radicals, Gompers and the AFL began moving away from the traditional nonpartisan approach to politics after 1905. In 1906 the AFL drew up a Bill of Grievances to present to Congress and then campaigned against the most antilabor congressmen in the fall election. More important, inspired by the success of the Union Labor Party in San Fran-

[36] *Ibid.*, p. 235.
[37] Reprinted in *Rebel Voices, an I.W.W. Anthology*, ed. Joyce Kornbluh (Ann Arbor, The University of Michigan Press, 1964), pp. 7–8.
[38] Quoted in Marc Karson, *American Labor Unions and Politics, 1900–1918* (Carbondale, Illinois, Southern Illinois Press, 1958), p. 127.

cisco, local and state organizations were instructed to nominate straight labor candidates where regular nominees ignored labor's demands. The result was that six union men were elected to Congress in 1906. Then early in 1908 the Executive Council of the AFL met with farm organization leaders to discuss a farmer-labor alliance, and in the Presidential elections the AFL strongly supported Bryan, after the Democrats endorsed most of the union's program.[39] Socialists hailed the AFL's hesitant entrance into partisan politics. They did so in the hope that it might lead to an independent labor party, such as the English unions had formed in response to a court decision in 1902 that the Amalgamated Society of Railway Engineers was responsible for business losses to the Taff Vale railway during a strike.

Socialist agitation had been continuous since 1902 in the AFL, and in Europe a close relationship between unions and the Socialist Party had always been the rule. The fear that American labor would follow the European example constantly gnawed its way into the consciousness of Civic Federation leaders. Seth Low, who abhorred the idea of "class politics," nevertheless wrote Gompers in 1908 that he could "understand, of course, that the question may occur to men identified with the labor movement whether, under the circumstances, it might not be better to resort to political agitation all along the line, as the English laboring men did after the Taff Vale decision." [40]

The failure of the NCF to win employers to its view of unions in large enough numbers and the simultaneous movement of large numbers of workers toward independent politics paralleled demands of neopopulist groups and municipal reformers for regulation of utilities and other reforms. At the same time, large corporations in many areas of the econ-

---

[39] Jensen, pp. 302–303.
[40] Low to Gompers, February 21, 1908, cited in Jensen, p. 308. Low had become president of the NCF by this time.

omy were themselves beginning to look toward the state and federal governments to stabilize conditions in their industries. Accordingly, between 1905 and 1908 the NCF investigated many areas of social concern, some with care, others casually. Among the areas investigated or looked at were public ownership and operation of public utilities, trust regulation, workmen's compensation, child labor, immigration, government by injunction, and currency reform. Only in the first three of these areas was substantial work done and some agreement reached among the representatives of different groups. The Federation's concern with trust regulation led to a proposal to amend the Sherman Act, written by Seth Low and introduced in the House as the Hepburn bill. The initial thrust came to nothing, but in its outline the Federation's bill was embodied in the Federal Trade Commission Act of 1914. NCF concern with workmen's compensation also led to model legislation and, after an active campaign, to the adoption of many state compensation acts. Both these subjects will be examined in later chapters.

The Commission on Public Ownership of Public Utilities was created by the NCF in October 1905. For the next two years it conducted investigations of public ownership and operation of public utilities under the leadership of Melville E. Ingalls, chairman of the board of directors of the Big Four Railroad. In line with the Federation principle of business-labor-public representation, the Commission's first and second vice chairmen were John Mitchell, president of the United Mine Workers, and John G. Agar, president of the Reform Club of New York. Other members of the Commission's executive committee included Louis D. Brandeis, John R. Commons, bankers Isaac N. Seligman and Frank A. Vanderlip, utilities magnate Samuel Insull, journalist Jacob Riis, reformer Frederick C. Howe, and John P. Frey of the Iron Moulders Union.[41]

[41] *National Civic Federation Review*, II, 6 (Nov. 1, 1905), pp. 1–2.

The stated purpose of the Commission on Public Ownership was to examine the "actual results of public ownership and operation" both in the United States and in Europe. In line with this the Federation raised a special fund of $50,000 and in mid-1906 sent its team of investigators, including Ingalls, Commons, and J. W. Sullivan of the Typographical Union, on a tour of Great Britain and the United States. The next year the Commission published a three-volume report of its findings, which coincided exactly with the views of utilities magnate Samuel Insull, one of the founders of the NCF. Except for the failure to give unqualified endorsement of private ownership (the report took no position on this question, suggesting it be solved in each municipality in the light of local conditions) the report also coincided with the position of the National Electric Light Association. Among the principles put forward were that public utilities are best conducted by legalized, regulated monopoly, that franchise grants to corporations should be for fixed periods and subject to purchase at fair value, that municipalities should have the power to enter the field of municipal ownership upon popular vote, and that utilities should be subject to regulation and examination under a system of uniform records and accounts by an independent administrative agency.

The report of the Commission established a general framework for regulatory laws. The Wisconsin public utilities law, for example, was drawn up on these principles by Commons, working for Charles McCarthy's Legislative Reference Bureau in Wisconsin. It was enacted in the spring of 1907. Similar laws creating public utilities commissions in New York and Massachusetts were also enacted that year. By 1909 many industry people had begun to look favorably on regulation by state commissions and to understand the advantages of taking utilities regulation out of politics. The underlying principles of the regulatory legislation supported responsible private ownership, and the experts appointed to the new commissions were almost invariably conservative in that they did not question the framework of the utilities industry. The result, therefore, was to introduce stability in the industry and to "raise public morality" through the removal of discriminatory rates.[42]

The work of the Federation's Immigrant Department was more publicized than that of the Federation's Public Ownership Commission. But it was less important in the long run both because the business and labor members never reached a common position and because Congress established a Commission to investigate the problem in 1907. Generally, the labor men opposed unrestricted immigration, seeing it as an attack on their wage standards, while businessmen favored unrestricted importation of laborers. As a result, as August Belmont commented at a National Conference on Immigration organized by the NCF in December 1905, the Federation had "no opinions and no policy to advance on the subject." Belmont observed that a change was taking place in the "complexion and character" of immigration which caused many intelligent citizens to argue for restriction. "For years," Belmont explained, "Europe gladly dumped her human refuse in our lap, and we housed, fed and clothed it."

Now, he concluded, "a spirit of what we owe to ourselves has come over us." Samuel Gompers agreed with the substance of Belmont's remarks and argued for restriction as a means of self-preservation. But Andrew Carnegie viewed immigration as a problem not for the United States, but for "the poor, unfortunate countries from which we are draining the best blood." "Taking the cost, the value of a man, a woman or a child in this Republic as low as you put the slave, and that was an average of about $1,000," Carnegie explained, "you are getting 400,000 a year and that means $400,000,000 cash

[42] Forrest McDonald, *Insull* (Chicago, University of Chicago Press, 1962), pp. 120–121; John R. Commons, *Myself* (Madison, Wis., University of Wisconsin Press, 1964), pp. 111–128: Jensen, pp. 173, 203.

26

value." Furthermore, "every man who comes here is a consumer, and ninety percent of all his earnings" went "to employ other labor of some kind." [43]

The National Conference on Immigration sponsored by the NCF was attended by about 500 delegates, including appointees of the governors of states and territories and representatives of business, ecclesiastical, labor, and agricultural organizations. Although it reached no agreement it did authorize the establishment of an NCF Immigration Department, which was organized in March 1906 under the chairmanship of the Chicago banker Franklin MacVeagh. In the next year an elaborate program was laid out for the Department and a good deal of work actually was done. But Gompers and the labor members became increasingly alarmed at what they believed were attempts to help immigrants and therefore to encourage immigration. This attitude and the formation of the United States Immigration Commission in 1907 combined to end the work of the NCF Department, which turned over its findings to the Congressional Commission and dropped all work on the subject.[44]

The other major effort to develop a program of action between 1905 and 1908 dealt with the problem of child labor. Examination of this question began at the NCF's Sixth Annual Meeting in December 1906. Among the participants were representatives of the Southern cotton manufacturers and the coal operators. Both industries had been heavily attacked as among the worst offenders on child labor. At the meeting, these businessmen denied that they encouraged child labor, and insisted that it was a result of shortages of labor in the South and the laziness of the parents of working children. All but the unionists agreed that child labor conditions in the United States were not as bad as they had been painted. The

[43] *National Civic Federation Review*, II, 8 (January–February 1906), pp. 1, 2, 5.
[44] Jensen, "National Civic Federation," pp. 203–206.

Federation's general attitude had earlier been expressed by Easley in a letter to Senator Nelson Aldrich. "The sensational and misleading stuff put out over the country by Socialistic writers has done a great injustice to many fair-minded and humane employers in the South," Easley wrote, thereby injuring the child labor cause, "in which all right-thinking people are deeply interested." Conditions were not perfect, Easley admitted, but in the past fifteen years "great progress has been made." [45]

In this case, the NCF tried to establish a commission that would include representatives from its own ranks, from the NAM, the AFL, the National Child Labor Committee, the main agitator in this field and in Easley's eyes the source of excessive statements, and the General Federation of Women's Clubs. The National Child Labor Committee refused to cooperate, but the NCF went ahead and established a commission in May 1907. As in the case of immigration, however, Congress appropriated money to investigate this field and the Federation disbanded its commission.

Government by injunction and by currency reform were also discussed at the annual dinners, the first in 1906, the second in 1907. Government by injunction was one of the few issues examined by the NCF in which the impetus for action came almost entirely from labor. True, business leaders in the Federation were concerned that "our workmen," as August Belmont put it, were becoming "imbued with the idea that our courts are used by employers for partisan purposes." [46] Yet, however much these men appreciated the importance of restoring "confidence on the part of the rank and file of organized labor in our laws and our courts," they could not agree on legislation limiting the injunction. To the businessmen, this was class legislation in that it would grant "special immunities and privileges before the law not enjoyed by other

[45] Easley to Aldrich, New York, July 20, 1906, Box 25, NCF papers.
[46] Quoted in Jensen, "National Civic Federation," p. 308.

combinations or other classes of the people." In deference to the wishes of the labor members a Commission on Government by Injunction was established, but because of the unwillingness of the Federation's business members to compromise on the matter, no action was ever taken by the commission.[47]

Currency reform was particularly relevant and important to the NCF business members when it came up for discussion in December 1907. The recent panic had convinced all the business speakers of the need for an elastic currency. In addition, there was general support for proposals later to be embodied in the Federal Reserve Act of 1914 for a currency based upon assets, rather than government bonds, and for greater centralization of banking. Victor Morawetz, Chairman of the Executive Board of the Atchison, Topeka and Santa Fe Railroad, argued for the establishment of a central clearing house association to provide "intelligent control over the credit situation through a board of leading bankers under government supervision and control." [48]

General agreement among businessmen present produced a resolution urging that Congress take action on the creation of an elastic currency, but this time it was the nonbusiness members' turn to object. They opposed an elastic currency issued by the banks and argued that the power to expand and contract the currency should be exercised exclusively by the government. An amendment to this effect failed to pass and a compromise was reached. Again, Congress appointed a commission—the National Monetary Commission of 1908—before the Federation could act further on the question.[49]

Discussions within the Federation from 1905 to 1908 rarely produced immediate action, although some agreements were reached and some legislation was passed. The real sig-

[47] *Ibid.*, pp. 211, 309.
[48] *Ibid.*, p. 212.
[49] *Ibid.*, p. 214.

nificance of these early conferences was not in the visible results, but in the changing consciousness of the participants. The business leaders in the NCF were exploring ways in which social questions could be solved wherever possible by extrapolitical means and were coming to understand that these solutions should represent a consensus of business, trade union, and other opinion rather than an external imposition of power. Implicit in the way in which these conferences were organized —in their leadership, financing, and ideological orientation— was a commitment to the strengthening and rationalization of the large corporations.[50]

But Civic Federation leaders knew that this could be done only if the corporations recognized the social responsibilities that went along with domination of the society. The problem was that the size of these corporations, their national scope and power, increasingly focused attention on the federal government, and that this in turn exposed them to the danger of political debate in which different classes might develop their own political parties or factions on a national scale. It was no accident that in Ralph Easley's eyes the Socialists, the followers of Robert M. La Follette and the anti-union businessmen in the NAM were almost coordinate enemies. Each in his own way raised the specter of class politics by publicly exacerbating the conflicts among themselves and between themselves and the large corporations. Easley, on the other hand, argued constantly for informal, which meant private, attempts to reach compromises. In addition to keeping social

[50] Within the NCF the importance of the businessmen was implicit in all internal correspondence. In Easley's correspondence with Seth Low, for example, businessmen, such as George W. Perkins, E. H. Gary, Andrew Carnegie, Cyrus McCormick, Theodore N. Vail (president of American Telephone and Telegraph), or George B. Cortelyou are referred to as the "important members" of the Executive Committee. The labor members are "our friends." See, for example, Easley to Low, New York, March 16, 1911, Box 90, Low Papers, Columbia University.

questions out of the arena of public debate, this approach started with the assumption that problems were essentially technical, that the framework of the political economy need only be rationalized and that "experts" applying their skills in the assumed common interest could best do the job. Whenever possible, NCF leaders sought to keep controversial issues "out of politics," [51] and particularly out of national politics.

Some problems, of course, were national in scope and could be dealt with only through the intervention of the Federal Government. The NCF never shirked consideration of these, as its agitation for an interstate Trade commission proves. But in most areas—workmen's compensation, minimum wages, public utilities regulation, child labor—the emphasis was on state action. One problem here was that reform in one state might tend to drive business enterprise to another where costs were less; in the long run this led many businessmen to accept national legislation which established equal conditions throughout the country. The initial thrust of the NCF, however, was an effort to promote uniform state laws. In the years immediately after Seth Low assumed the presidency of the NCF in 1908 such activity expanded rapidly.

The high point of discussions on uniform legislation came in January 1910 when President Taft addressed the NCF's National Conference on Uniform Legislation, attended by the governors or their representatives of the forty-six states. Taft himself was very much interested in the subject. When Franklin MacVeagh (his Secretary of the Treasury), Ralph Easley, John Hays Hammond (a mining engineer associated with the Guggenheim interests), Samuel Gompers, and John Mitchell called on the President a few months before the conference, he told them that "next to his own work," uniform legislation was "the most important proposition now before the public."

[51] See, for example, Easley to Senator Nelson W. Aldrich, New York, December 24, 1907, Box 25, NCF papers.

31

At the conference, Taft proposed that the governors of the forty-six states come to the White House after the conference to consider the subject further.[52]

In conjunction with this activity, the Civic Federation established state councils of the NCF in twenty-three states in 1910.[53] In many instances the governors of these states called such meetings and presided at their founding conventions. The state councils pressed for uniform legislation thereafter by giving support to laws approved by the Executive Council of the NCF.[54]

In addition to drafting a model workmen's compensation bill, the Federation drew up bills on minimum wages and the regulation of public utilities for the state councils. In 1913 President Low proposed a new Minimum Wage Commission of the NCF. His suggestion received universal support from business and labor members, even though many had no opinion on the question and some were opposed to such legislation. Labor men were divided, but tended to oppose regulatory laws establishing minimum wages, except for women workers. In June 1913 attorney William R. Willcox, Chairman of the New York Public Utilities Commission and of the

[52] Easley to August Belmont, New York, June 11, 1909, Box 35, NCF papers; Easley to John Hays Hammond, New York, October 30, 1909, Box 32, NCF papers.

[53] In connection with setting up the state councils, the NCF greatly expanded its membership in 1909–1910. Most prominent among the new members are presidents of small colleges and universities, such as Buchtel College, Akron, Ohio, Missouri Valley College, Rollins College, Drake University, Alfred University, the University of Montana. Also members of Congress, state legislators, and state judges. Such men as Champ Clark, Miles Poindexter, J. C. Cantrell of Kentucky, Joseph E. Ramsdell of Alabama, and many others joined in 1909. So did Joseph B. Moore, Justice of the Supreme Court of Michigan, Albert W. Gilchrist, Governor of Florida, E. W. Robinson, Speaker of the House of Representatives of Utah, and many others of similar status. In addition, there were many lawyers, farm leaders, and ministers. For letters of acceptance in the NCF in 1909 see Box 46, NCF papers.

[54] Seth Low, Presidential Report, *Eleventh Annual Meeting of the National Civic Federation* (New York, 1911), pp. 1–2.

NCF Welfare Department, recommended an $8.00 minimum wage for women working in New York department stores. Willcox made his suggestion, he said, because "the department store men clearly see that the agitation by trade unions and the Wagner Commission will force a higher wage." That being so, "they would rather have it come at the behest of our Welfare Department than at the demands of the unions or the Commission." But because there was no general agreement within the Federation, Low insisted that Willcox not include a recommendation.[55] Two years later, the NCF was still working on the question, but viewed minimum wages less happily as a result of the early experience under the new minimum wage laws for women in Oregon, Washington, and California.[56]

The work on a public utilities bill was done under the chairmanship of Emerson McMillin, a banker and president and director of several gas, light, and traction companies (including American Light and Traction, Southern Light and Traction, and Consolidated Gas of New Jersey). Underlying McMillin's effort was a belief, expressed by Samuel Insull in 1909, that it was only a matter of time before public clamor would lead to regulation. That being so, Insull preferred to "help shape the right kind of regulation" before "the wrong kind [was] forced upon him." [57] In 1913, Easley was convinced that a model bill could "play a very important part in preventing any serious sentiment from crystallizing in this country for government ownership and operation of public utilities, whether state or interstate." The work of the early NCF

[55] See letters to Low in Box 101, Low papers. The quotation is from William R. Willcox to Low, New York, June 26, 1913, *ibid.*

[56] Low to W. R. Willcox, Bedford Hills, July 2, 1913, *ibid.*; Gertrude Beeks to Herbert Parsons, New York, August 12, 1915, *ibid.* Beeks explained that the problem of inefficient workers got in the way of establishing a uniform minimum wage.

[57] Ralph M. Easley to George W. Perkins, New York, June 9, 1909, Box 38, NCF papers.

33

commission on public utilities, Easley wrote, had begged the question of what is adequate regulation. But it was clear that some form of regulation was needed. "Twenty-five years ago," Easley told Low, "we would have regarded this as a species of socialism," but with the railways submitting completely, even "joyfully in some cases," to regulation, the NCF task of "educating the municipal utilities corporations" was rendered more easy.[58]

McMillin himself recognized that the problem of public utilities regulation was many-sided, and that a model regulatory bill would have to take "all points of view" into account. "Powerful forces are at work," McMillin wrote Low, urging involvement in "new and untried experiments of a most radical nature." Thus in the course of the last dozen years "the conservative brains of the country" had "come to realize the necessity for a change in the manner of conducting public utility enterprises": they had come to see "the public nature and responsibilities of these companies." Yet the new attitudes of the companies had so far not been sufficient. Evidence was "multiplying rapidly of an insistent demand" on the part of "radical and oftentimes unthinking parts of the public" for the "possible overthrow of the system of private ownership of public utilities." The need was for utilities men to rise above their more immediate interests and come to agreement on the basis of their underlying, or long-range interests.[59]

Most of the members of McMillin's commission worked with him and understood this need. George B. Cortelyou of Consolidated Gas of New York, for example, did valuable work. But some, notably Theodore N. Vail, president of American Telephone and Telegraph (AT&T), tried to rewrite the bill from what McMillin called the corporation's point of view. "We cannot," he complained to Low, "accept

[58] Easley to Low, New York, August 1, 1913, Box 101, Low papers.
[59] Emerson McMillin to Seth Low, New York, September 22, 1913, Box 101, Low papers.

the work of interested parties" such as AT&T.[60] Others raised questions about the impact of regulatory agencies on the floating of utilities bonds. Low corresponded at great length with his nephew, William G. Low, Jr., on this point. He was reassured by McMillin that although the commission opposed saying anything about financing in the model bill, it had to because the Massachusetts, Ohio, and Wisconsin acts regulated the financing of utilities. But, as McMillin pointed out, utilities in those states had no more trouble raising money than did those in other states. In fact, they often advertised that the offered securities had been approved by the state utilities commission and were guarded by commission supervision of the finances of these companies. In the end, even Vail was satisfied with McMillin's work, and a model bill was approved in October 1914.[61]

Although the NCF was much more effective under Low's leadership—membership increased from 1,500 in 1907 to over 5,000 in 1912—it was still difficult to reach consensus between the business and labor members and to proceed with dispatch on issues. In the long run, drafting legislation was not the most important aspect of the Federation's work. More important was its educational impact on corporation leaders, especially those who, during the First World War and the New Deal, supported the approaches worked out between 1905 and 1916.

But even in the prewar years there were immediate successes which indicated the power of the Civic Federation when it could proceed in a united manner. The best example is the Newlands Act of July 15, 1913, an amendment to the Erdman Railroad Mediation Act of 1898. The Erdman Act had provided for mediation of railroad labor disputes by the

[60] McMillin to Low, New York, July 8, July 21, September 30, 1913, *ibid*.
[61] See letters from William G. Low to Seth Low and answers in Box 101, Low papers; also McMillin to Low, New York, January 3, 22, 1914, *ibid.*; *New York Evening Post*, November 9, 1914.

chairmen of the Interstate Commerce Commission (ICC) and the commissioner of the Bureau of Labor. In 1913, under an impending threat of a strike of all roads east of Chicago, the mediation process broke down. In March 1913, a joint conference of railroad presidents and the leaders of five railroad Brotherhoods, brought together under NCF auspices, agreed that new procedures were needed. The Federation, under Low's direction, then arranged for what was to become the Newlands Act to be drawn up by Charles P. Neill (former Commissioner of The Bureau of Labor Statistics) and Martin Knapp (former Chairman of the ICC).

The bill was submitted to a committee that included the presidents of the New York Central, Pennsylvania, Union Pacific, Chicago, Burlington and Quincy, Baltimore and Ohio, and Atlanta and West Point railroads; the Chairman of the Board of Directors of the Chesapeake and Ohio Railroad; and the presidents of the brotherhoods of engineers, firemen, trainmen, telegraphers, and the Order of Railway Conductors. After reaching agreement on the bill it was introduced in the Senate on June 10 by Senator Francis G. Newlands. Hearings were held a week later, but a snag developed when Secretary of Labor William B. Wilson insisted that the Board of Mediation be located in the Labor Department. Samuel Rea, president of the Pennsylvania Railroad, objected, and Easley explained to Secretary of Commerce William C. Redfield that that arrangement had been satisfactory when the Commissioner of Labor had been within the Department of Commerce and Labor.

Now that there were separate departments the railroad executives thought that locating the Board in the Labor Department would be prejudicial to their interests. Wilson was adamant on this and a test of wills, and of strength, developed. But in the end, on July 14, 1913, Secretary Wilson wrote to the President that although he was still opposed to a separate Commission of Mediation he would raise no objections because the railroad and labor men unanimously agreed on an independent board. Three days later the Act was passed and signed. Low was appointed one of two impartial arbitrators who settled the dispute.[62] Easley often boasted in later years that this accomplishment demonstrated the power of the Civic Federation when it could reach agreement among its own members. This was true, but the Newlands Act represented a special situation in that all interested parties belonged to the Federation. In the case of workmen's compensation and revision of the Sherman Act, where small businessmen and agrarian interests were also concerned, the Federation proved not to be all-powerful, although in the end it did much to shape legislation in both areas and to secure its passage.

In its first dozen years of existence, then, the National Civic Federation passed through three distinct phases, each roughly corresponding to the period of leadership of its first three presidents. Under Mark Hanna's initial direction the Federation was primarily concerned with mediation and conciliation. During these years Federation members, especially business affiliates, tried to stabilize the relationship between the work force and corporate enterprise. This entailed an insistence that trade unions act responsibly, that they strictly adhere to and enforce contractual agreements, even against the wishes of their members. In effect, what the business

[62] Easley to Charles A. Wickersham (president of the Atlanta and West Point Railroad), New York, March 17, 1913, Box 50, NCF papers; Easley to William B. Wilson, New York, April 3, 1913; Easley to William C. Redfield, New York, June 11, 1913; Seth Low to W. B. Wilson, Bedford Hills, New York, June 28, 1913; Wilson to Low (telegram), June 30, 1913; memo from W. B. Wilson to Woodrow Wilson, July 14, 1913; all in file no. 16/4, Record Group 174, National Archives; Seth Low to Woodrow Wilson, New York, June 7, 1913; Low to Wickersham, New York, June 12, 1913; Easley to Darius Miller (pres., Chicago, Burlington and Quincy Railroad), New York, July 11, 1913; Low to Wilson, New York, October 10, 1913; Treasurer, NCF, to William K. Vanderbilt, New York, Nov. 5, 1913: all Box 50, NCF papers; Easley to Wickersham, Miller, others, New York, June 13, 1913, Box 83, *ibid.*; Easley speech to 21st Annual Meeting, February 14, 1921, Box 187, NCF papers.

leaders asked of the conservative trade unionists was that they become mediating agents between the workers and the corporations, rather than act simply as the representatives of the workers in confrontation with their employers.

In return, NCF leaders sought to gain acceptance of organized labor as a permanent institution in American life and recognition for those labor leaders who would cooperate. Such an approach worked in a limited number of industries where organized labor was relatively strong. By 1904 agreements had been reached in the printing industry, in the building trades, in the brewing industry, in the machine tool industry, in bituminous mining, and on some railroads. In the new mass production industries, however, no agreements of importance were made. The unions were weak, in part because of their retention of craft structure, and businessmen were generally not inclined to see the value of conservative unions over others, except in situations such as Lawrence in 1912.

When the counteroffensive against further organization got under way and trade union membership leveled off, the Civic Federation had to look in new directions to assert leadership. August Belmont's tenure, and his attitude toward the unions, symbolized the turn toward welfare work as an alternative to unionism. The groping toward sponsorship of social reforms acceptable to labor, the middle classes, and the corporations characterized the years from 1905 to 1908.

With the accession of Seth Low to the presidency the Federation entered a new period of aggressive organization and leadership. Actively intervening in the political economy, it sought to anticipate more radical demands of an explicitly class character by sponsoring reforms that represented a consensus of business, trade unions, and other opinion. The Federation also sought further to define the limits of reform, to inhibit the growth of Socialism, and to educate the business community to an awareness and an acceptance of its responsibilities in rationalizing and stabilizing the system of large corporations that had emerged in the preceding period. From 1908 until the United States entered World War I, the NCF played a major role in educating businessmen, professionals, and conservative farm leaders in the principles of modern liberalism. During those years, too, the Federation played an important direct role in the legislative field, both on a state and national level. In the next chapter we will examine the role of the NCF in support of state legislation for workmen's compensation legislation.

CHAPTER TWO

Leadership in Social Reform:

Workmen's Compensation

THE SOCIALLY UNCONTROLLED entrepreneurial initiative that led to America's leap into world predominance as an industrial power in the last third of the nineteenth century was accompanied by a ruthless spirit of competition that left little room for concern about the welfare or working conditions of those at the bottom. Accidents and injury abounded in American industry at the turn of the century, but few seemed to care except the victims and a small circle of "do-good" reformers. When, in 1905, Werner Sombart set out to show that American capitalism was the greediest on earth he used as evidence the relative accident rates on the railways of the United States and Austria. In 1903, according to Sombart, 11,066 workers were injured on American railroads, compared to 172 on Austrian roads. Both by kilometer of road and by millions of passengers carried, many more Americans were killed and wounded on railroads than were their European counterparts.[1] Many popular writers exposed working conditions in the railroad, steel, and packing industries during these years. They revealed that the monthly average of 328 American railroad workers killed during the years from 1888 to 1908 made up only ten percent of an estimated 35,000 killed and 536,000 injured in American industry each year. As the muckraker William Hard reported in "Making Steel and Killing

[1] Werner Sombart, "Study of the Historical Development and Evolution of the American Proletariat," *International Socialist Review*, VI, 3 (September 1905), p. 129.

Men," at the South Chicago plant of the United States Steel Company alone 46 men were killed and an estimated 598 injured in 1906.[2]

Not only were American working conditions worse and accidents more frequent than in European industry, but provisions for the injured worker were virtually nonexistent in the United States, while they were extensive in Europe. Until the end of the first decade of the new century the law in almost every state was based on judicial decisions made in pre-industrial England and the United States. A worker killed or injured at work had recourse to damages only through the courts. Even after expensive and drawn-out litigation, his chances of recovery, or those of his heirs, were slight. The defenses available to the employer were such that only an estimated fifteen percent of the injured employees ever recovered damages, even though 70 percent of industrial accidents were estimated to be the result of the nature of the work or of employer negligence.[3]

There were three common law defenses available to an employer: the fellow servant doctrine, the assumption of risk, and contributory negligence. Under the fellow servant doctrine an injured employee was held responsible for the negligence of other employees, on the theory that he should acquaint himself with the bad habits of his co-workers and exercise a salutary influence upon them. In one case an employee on the night shift at the United States Steel plant in South Chicago plugged an open hearth carelessly. A few minutes later, when the day-shift man had relieved him, the plug blew out and several tons of molten steel engulfed the day

[2] Charles Edward Russell, *Why I Am a Socialist* (New York, George H. Doran, 1910), pp. 52 ff. John M. Gitterman, "The Cruelties of Our Courts," *McClure's Magazine*, XXXV, 2 (June 1910), pp. 151–167. Walter George Smith, "Present Status of Workmen's Compensation Laws," *Annals of the American Association of Political and Social Sciences*, XXXVIII, 1 (November 1911), p. 128; *Everybody's* (November 1907).

[3] Frank W. Lewis, "Employers Liability," *Atlantic Monthly*, CIII (January 1909), p. 60.

man. The night man was eighteen years old. He had worked at his job only one week. The two men had met only once. Yet the court held that the day man had no claim against the company because he and his fellow servant "had ample opportunity to exercise upon each other an influence promotive of care and prudence in the matter of performing their work." [4]

In another case, made famous by Theodore Roosevelt in 1913, a young woman, Sarah Knisley, had her arm torn off by the unprotected gears of a grinding machine on which she was working. The state law provided that the gears should be covered; Miss Knisley had complained to her employer that they were not, and expressed fear about working at the machine in its condition. But the employer warned her to do her job or quit and out of fear of her job she complied. The court held that in so doing she had assumed the risk of the dangerous condition and could not recover damages. Had she not known or complained of the illegal condition she would have had a cause of action; her knowledge made her liable.[5]

In Arizona, a railroad engineer had been forced to work thirty hours straight when his replacement failed to appear. As a result, he fell asleep on the job and was involved in an accident. The law limited straight working hours on railroads to sixteen, and the engineer agreed to continue work only under the threat of discharge. Nevertheless the court held him negligent. He had the free choice of cooperating in a violation of the law or of terminating his employment. His decision to cooperate was held to be contributory negligence.[6]

[4] William Hard, "The Law of the Killed and the Wounded," Everybody's, XIX, 3 (September 1909), pp. 361 ff.

[5] Ibid.; Theodore Roosevelt, "Sarah Knisley's Arm," Collier's, L (January 25, 1913), pp. 8–9; Lewis, "Employers Liability," p. 60.

[6] Hard, "Law of Killed and Wounded," pp. 361 ff. See also Employer's Liability: Common Law and Statutory Fellow Servant Principle in Legislation and Court Decision, Reports of the United States Industrial Commission, Vol. 17 (Washington, 1901), pp. 894–902; "Buying a Man's Arm, by the Corporation Lawyer Who Made the Purchase," American Magazine, 3 (July 1909), pp. 260–262.

As early as 1898, in response to a workman's compensation act passed in Great Britain the year before, the Social Reform Club of New York introduced a bill calling for automatic compensation for injury in case of some industrial accidents.[7] But labor did not generally support the idea of compensation at this time. In New York the Workingmen's Federation argued instead for modification of the traditional common law defenses so that employers would be liable for all injuries where the injured worker himself was not negligent. Such laws modifying the common law defenses were known as employer liability laws and were supported by trade unions generally—by the several railway brotherhoods in 1899, for example. By 1907 agitation for employer liability laws had produced some results in twenty-six states. But most of the liability laws affected only railroads (three states also modified the common law with respect to miners) and most limited the fellow servant doctrine but not the assumption of risk and contributory negligence doctrines.[8]

Labor's opposition to compensation legislation was based in part upon a belief that a weakening of the employer's traditional defenses would produce many court victories and high awards from sympathetic juries.[9] Compensation laws, in contrast, could be expected only to pension off the worker during his period of disablement at something less than his regular wages. In addition, almost all unionists, conservative or socialist, opposed government regulation of working con-

[7] Elizabeth Brandeis, "Labor Legislation," in John R. Commons, *et al.*, *History of the Labor Movement in the United States: 1896–1932*, III (New York, Macmillan, 1935), p. 571; Irwin Yellowitz, *Labor and the Progressive Movement in New York State, 1897–1916* (New York, Cornell University Press, 1965), p. 108.

[8] *Ibid.*; *Employer's Liability*, p. 902; Lindley D. Clark, *The Legal Liability of Employers for Injuries to Their Employees in the United States*, Bulletin of the Bureau of Labor, Number 74 (Washington, D.C., 1908), p. 95.

[9] Yellowitz, *Labor and the Progressive Movement in New York State*, p. 108.

ditions on the theory, often only implicit, that government was controlled by business, either directly or through conservative politicians and judges whose thinking on labor questions was identical to that of leading businessmen. Samuel Gompers, for example, opposed minimum wage and maximum hours legislation for men, and only grudgingly accepted the idea for women; the concept that employers were "the trustees of the property of the world, and hence that they are to be the guardians of the welfare of the employees" made him uneasy. He preferred a voluntary organization of wage workers prepared to advance labor's interests independently.[10]

Even minimum wages for women were opposed by craft unionists at times. Such opposition was based on the fear that state action would weaken labor's prerogatives and "carry with it disintegration of the vital forces of labor." Though, in the face of such state programs, unions might persist in name, "and even grow in membership," the union would be "deprived of its essentials of independence, self-direction and elastic adaptation to the needs of a forceful mass mechanism."[11] Workmen's compensation raised another objection: state provision of guildlike pensions and other welfare benefits would reduce the craftsman's loyalty to the union.

In contrast to labor's opposition to compensation many businessmen, including directors of the largest corporations, had come to favor such legislation. August Belmont told the

[10] Speech at the 16th Annual Meeting of the National Civic Federation, January 1916, typescript in Box 187, NCF papers. Even on the question of minimum wages legislation for women, labor was dubious. In California, in 1915, a minimum wage law was passed over the opposition of organized labor in the state. The National Women's Trade Union League, a pro-union organization of social workers, recommended the establishment of minimum wage boards on which employers, employees, and the public were to be equally represented. In California the wage earning women opposed such legislation, but in 1913 the California Retail Dry Goods Association formally endorsed minimum wages for women. A. J. Porter, Chairman of the Minimum Wage Commission of the National Civic Federation, Minutes of the 16th Annual Meeting, January 17, 1916, Box 187, NCF papers.

[11] Ibid.

National Civic Federation annual meeting in January 1911 that he had been engaged in exhaustive discussions with men from the Otis Elevator, Linen Thread, Coe Brass, United Shoe Machinery, Edison Electric, American Light and Traction, and Ingersoll-Rand companies. They had all approved the principles of compensation legislation. At the same meeting Andrew Carnegie did so too. In part, at least, this support for compensation was the result of fears that the trend toward employer liability laws would accelerate and come to include manufacturers. Such a development would increase uncertainty for business and might substantially raise the cost of liability insurance. As the Civic Federation's expert on compensation warned, "We must make a move toward compensation soon. Otherwise we will continue, with ever-increasing impetus, down the broad way of the employer liability laws, which lead to social destruction." [12]

Arguing from a different point of view, George W. Perkins of the International Harvester and United States Steel corporations had explained another principle that underlay big business support of compensation and other welfare plans in 1909. "Cooperation in business," he said, "is taking and should take the place of ruthless competition." If "this new order of things is better for capital and better for the consumer, then in order to succeed permanently it must demonstrate that it is better for the laborer." Profit sharing, pensions, sick and accident insurance, Perkins emphasized, "must mean cooperation between capital and labor." Perkins then described the International Harvester welfare program. It included a stock purchase plan and a company benefit plan under which the worker paid two percent of his wages in return for two years' pay for accidental death, one year's pay for death by sickness, and half pay for sickness or disability through injury. Seventy-five percent of the workers were said to have joined,

[12] *Eleventh Annual Meeting of the National Civic Federation*, New York, January 12–14, 1911 (New York, 1911), pp. 184, 185, 231.

45

and the company had contributed $50,000. No waiver of the right to sue the company was demanded. In addition, a pension plan provided a minimum of $18.00 per month, and a maximum of $100.00 per month.

The Harvester Company, Perkins explained, "did not do this out of pure philanthropy," but was motivated by "purely business spirit." The idea was "that the plans would so knit [the company's] vast organization together, so stimulate individual initiative," so "strengthen and develop the esprit de corps" that it would enable the company to increase its earnings.[13]

The United States Steel Corporation announced a similar plan for voluntary workmen's compensation in 1910. Modeled on the workmen's compensation laws in Germany and other European countries, the plan provided 35 percent of weekly wages for injured single workers, 50 percent for married workers, and an extra 5 percent for each child over five years of age. Elbert H. Gary carefully explained that these were actually relief payments, not compensation, since an estimated 75 percent of the cases would involve no legal liability on the part of the company. The paternalistic nature of the plan was emphasized in the announcement that the progressive step was not the result "of any demand or suggestion of the employees." [14] One commentator on the United States Steel plan observed that the merit from the manager's standpoint was that it helped keep "intact a non-union working force."

Raynal C. Bolling, assistant general solicitor of the Corporation, in speaking of the Steel plan and workmen's com-

---

[13] George W. Perkins at the *Tenth Annual Meeting of the National Civic Federation*, New York, November 22 and 23, 1909 (New York, 1910), pp. 144–149.

[14] "Accident Relief for Steel Workers," *Review of Reviews*, XLI, 5 (May 1910), p. 533. The Cheney Silk Mills was another major corporation that had instituted a voluntary workmen's compensation plan. See Will Irwin, "The Awakening of the American Business Man," *Century*, LXXXII, 1 (May 1911), p. 118.

pensation laws, went further. He hoped that "the progress of workmen's compensation should be a rebuke and a rebuttal" to those who "assert that the workingmen get nothing except by contest and struggle." [15] In short, company workmen's compensation plans were designed to reduce the need for independent political action by labor, as well as the appeal of unionism in the large corporations.

There were limitations to private welfare and compensation plans, however. Workers often resented the paternalism inherent in them, and only the largest corporations had the resources necessary to their successful operation. Smaller manufacturers agreed with the objectives of such plans, but as the chairman of the Committee on Employer's Liability of the National Association of Manufacturers pointed out, small industrialists could not afford voluntary systems such as the United States Steel Corporation had instituted. Ninety-five percent of the 25,000 employers to whom the NAM sent questionnaires in 1910 favored compensation as a matter of right for industrial accidents; few had the resources to institute such programs privately. The Association was particularly concerned that compensation be assured through insurance and that unlike existing private policies the insurance be efficient. Under existing commercial insurance plans, injured workers usually received less than forty percent of premium payments. The NAM insisted that seventy-five to ninety percent of the premiums go to benefits.[16]

With the agreement of the NAM a general consensus of the business community had been achieved with respect to the need for compensation legislation. As a contemporary journalist commented in 1911, the only remaining opponents

[15] "Accident Relief of the United States Steel Corporation," *The Survey*, XXIV (April 23, 1910), pp. 136–137, Raynal C. Bolling, "Results of Voluntary Relief Plan of the United States Steel Corporation," *Annals*, AAPSS, XXXVIII, 1 (July 1911), p. 43.

[16] F. C. Schwedtman, "Principles of Sound Employer's Liability Legislation," *Annals* of AAPSS, XXXVIII, 1 (July 1911), pp. 202–204.

of this new "scientific system" were "a few old-time manufacturers who can see nothing but next year's dollar." But to the journalist the most important aspect of the new legislation was its contribution to the conservation of labor. "We must realize," he wrote, "that we have broken nearly all our virgin soil, that competition between nations is becoming keener and closer, and that the state which would win must subordinate certain private interests to the interests of the whole body commercial." [17]

By the time the NAM reached this conclusion labor had been induced to change its mind on compensation. In part, this was the result of agitation, starting in 1907, by the American Association for Labor Legislation (AALL), an organization of middle class reformers financed by such men as John D. Rockefeller, Elbert H. Gary, and V. Everitt Macy. But trade unionists had little use for the AALL.[18] Much more important in winning their support was the work of the National Civic Federation, which after 1908 threw its whole weight into the fight for compensation legislation.

The NCF was moved to participate in the campaign for compensation legislation by the desire of Easley, Low, and many of the business members to find some common ground of action with the labor members, who were showing increasing signs of being serious about independent politics. One aspect of labor's new look at politics in the years from 1905 to 1908 particularly bothered businessmen in the Federation, just as it would later alienate many of them from Theodore Roosevelt's Progressive Party. That was a fear that the increasing use of court injunctions against labor would move the AFL to political action designed to limit the independence of the judiciary. "It is a matter of great moment," complained August Belmont at the National Civic Federation's annual

[17] Will Irwin, "The Awakening of the American Business Man," *Century*, LXXXII, 1 (May 1911), pp. 118–121.

[18] Yellowitz, *Labor and the Progressive Movement in New York State*, pp. 72–73, 108.

meeting in 1906, "when our workmen . . . become imbued with the idea that our courts are used by employers for partisan purposes." [19]

Two years later, when Andrew Carnegie contributed to the AFL appeal in the Buck's Stove and Range case, he warned that he was "one member of the National Civic Federation who will very promptly resign if it gives the slightest countenance to attacks on the Supreme Court." "I am as strong a friend of Labor and I think a wiser one than Mr. Gompers," Carnegie continued, "but if we are to fail to preach and practice implicit obedience to the Law as defined by the final tribunals, you can count me out." In a postscript, Carnegie commanded: "I should like to hear whether Mr. Gompers agrees to acquiesce in the decision, whatever it may be." [20]

At the 1906 Annual Meeting of the National Civic Federation it was clear that business and labor could not agree on the role of the courts. The businessmen flatly denied there was "discrimination or inequality, either in the law or its administration as to labor combinations," and attacked labor's opposition to the use of injunctions under the Sherman Act against the unions as "class politics." This reflected a growing anxiety on the part of the business members of the Federation and was part of a process of searching for common ground with labor. What was needed was some course of social action "upon which the non-business members would be willing to follow the lead of the business members." [21]

Since labor's experience with employer liability legislation was unsatisfactory, workmen's compensation emerged as the ideal program for the Civic Federation. The largest corporations were instituting it in their plants; public agitation for relief had created a good political climate; compensation was paternalistic and would probably reduce somewhat the appeal

[19] Quoted in Jensen, "National Civic Federation," p. 308.
[20] Carnegie to Easley, New York, February 24, 1908; February 28, 1908, Box 30, NCF papers.
[21] Jensen, "National Civic Federation," p. 201.

of unionism to workers, yet the unions could be induced to support it. By 1909 the Civic Federation had convinced Gompers and so was able to commit itself fully to the sponsorship of the reform. In so doing it took a large step into its new phase as the leading organization of businessman's reform.[22]

In line with its earlier paternalism, the National Civic Federation had established an Industrial Insurance Commission in 1908, and president Seth Low appointed George W. Perkins of the Steel and Harvester companies as chairman. But the Commission was not very active, and the perspective of the Federation was changing. In 1909, reflecting this change, Low appointed NCF past president August Belmont to head the reorganized Department on Compensation for Industrial Accidents and Their Prevention.[23] From that point on the Federation was at the center of agitation for the workmen's compensation bills. At the annual meeting in 1908 one session was devoted to industrial insurance. Speakers included Louis D. Brandeis, William R. Willcox, a leading banker, Haley Fiske, a vice president of Metropolitan Life Insurance Company, and Major A. E. Piorkowski, of the Krupp Company in Essen, Germany. Lee K. Frankel of the Sage Foundation Fund reminded his audience that the United States was alone among industrial nations in putting the burden of industrial accidents on the workers. "In Germany," he pointed out, "insurance is no longer a business proposition, but a distinct social program." But, in opposition, Frederick L. Hoffman of Prudential Life argued that although "the German government system was specifically devised to do away with Socialism," in fact, "the Socialists never polled as many votes as they do at the present time." [24]

At the next meeting, in 1909, few opposed compensation

[22] *Ibid.*, pp. 167–169.
[23] *Ibid.*, p. 325; Memorandum, n.d., n.p., Box 127, NCF papers.
[24] *Ninth Annual Meeting of the National Civic Federation, New York, December 14–15, 1908* (New York, 1909), pp. 75–77, 120.

laws, only the problem of state versus private insurance remained open: the businessmen generally lined up for private insurance, the trade unionists favored state insurance. Major Piorkowski was present again and spoke on workmen's insurance in Germany; A. H. Gill, a member of Parliament, spoke on workmen's compensation in England. Among the Federation members who spoke, was George M. Gillette of the Minneapolis Steel and Machinery Company (and president of the Minnesota Employers' Association). He commented that "the reactionary" on workmen's compensation was "in such a hopeless minority that he should not be seriously considered." It was clear, Gillette went on, that the existing system was unsatisfactory because it disturbed the relation of employer to employee, bred perjury, failed to prevent or decrease accidents, and was uncertain and wasteful. In his view workmen's compensation was emphatically not "a thin entering wedge for socialism." His thinking was endorsed by most of the speakers, including Louis B. Schram, chairman of the Labor Committee of the United States Brewers Association, and by Major J. G. Pangborn, of the Baltimore and Ohio Railroad, who opined that "with a compensation act friction is reduced to a minimum." [25]

When the Civic Federation began to draw up model compensation bills, and to agitate in state legislatures and among state governors, no state had effective compensation legislation. The federal government had only a weak act passed in 1908 at President Roosevelt's insistence. The few attempts to enact compensation acts before 1909 had either failed, or the limited acts were ruled unconstitutional. In 1907, for example, a commission of the state of Connecticut recommended continuation of the employer liability principle and opposed compensation. But starting in 1909 many states appointed commissions to investigate the feasibility of compensation

[25] *Tenth Annual Meeting of the National Civic Federation, New York, November 22–23, 1909*, pp. 1, 7, 33, 34, 46, 79, 87, 257.

51

acts and to propose specific legislation. Three commissions were appointed in 1909; eight in 1910; twelve in 1911; seven in 1912. All these favored some form of compensation act.[26]

Although there was widespread agreement on the need for compensation, the process of drawing up bills was not smooth. Shortly after Belmont became head of the Federation's compensation department, he appointed a legal committee to draw up a model bill. Chairman of this committee was P. Tecumseh Sherman, a conservative lawyer and former New York Commissioner of Labor. Like most of those engaged in drawing up compensation bills, Sherman looked to Germany and England for guidance. The German system appeared to him to be best, as it was "an intimately interconnected system of compulsory insurance against sickness, accidents, and old age." But Sherman recognized that the paternalistic nature of the German system would raise constitutional problems, as well as hostility from labor. "Eventually," he hoped that "by general recognition of a social necessity, we may work up to some similar system of our own," adapted, of course, to American conditions. Sherman admitted that his proposed bill was "a halfway measure—a mere entering wedge." [27]

Sherman's original draft bill was widely distributed in May 1910. It was sent to the governors and legislators of all states that had appointed commissions to study compensation, and

[26] Elizabeth Brandeis, "Labor Legislation," in John R. Commons (ed.), *History of the Labor Movement in the United States*, III (New York, Macmillan, 1935), p. 571. Several earlier attempts had been made to enact compensation legislation. A bill was introduced in the New York legislature in 1898 (the year after England adopted its first compensation act) but was not passed; Maryland enacted a bill limited to coal miners in 1902, it was declared unconstitutional; Montana adopted a similar bill in 1909, it was also invalidated by the courts. See "State Workmen's Compensation Legislation," *American Labor Legislation Review*, II (1912), p. 565. On the federal act of 1908 see also Launcelot Packer, "The Hazards of Industry," *The Outlook*, XCII (June 5, 1909), pp. 323 ff.

[27] *Eleventh Annual Meeting of the National Civic Federation*, New York, January 12, 13, 14, 1911 (New York, 1911), pp. 173–174, 184.

governors of other states were urged to consider such legislation. But within the Federation and outside, Sherman's draft came under attack. As Sherman admitted to Seth Low, he was "conservative" on workmen's compensation and believed it should be compulsory only in hazardous industries.[28] Raynal C. Bolling, of United States Steel, disagreed. His view was that compensation should be universal and compulsory—that it should include agricultural and domestic workers as well as industrial—so that it could not be condemned as class legislation.[29]

A third view, held by a number of middle class progressives and by Socialists and labor men, favored state insurance against private, and emphasized the need for higher benefits than either Sherman or Bolling proposed. Within the Federation, Hugh V. Mercer was the main opponent of Sherman's draft. Mercer represented Minnesota at a Chicago conference of the National Association of State Commissioners on Compensation in which ten states participated in late 1910. He was chairman of the conference and one of the three-man committee chosen to draw up a model bill. He argued that Sherman's draft was inadequate, and he was supported by George M. Gillette. Stressing the need for uniformity of state laws, a basic concern of the Civic Federation, Gillette suggested that since Mercer's draft would represent the proposals of ten states, the Federation ought not come forward with a different proposal. But Low and Sherman considered Mercer's bill too radical. They insisted on having their own, and even refused to allow Mercer to present his alternative plan as a minority report of Sherman's committee. As Sherman told Easley, "the most conservative and least expensive scheme which is ours may prove the basis of comparative uniformity. At any rate

[28] Sherman to Low, New York, December 29, 1910, Low papers.
[29] Bolling, "Results of Voluntary Relief Plan . . . ," p. 39; Bolling to Gertrude Beeks, New York, February 11, 1911; January 15, 1914, Box 127, NCF papers.

the Civic Federation owes no apologies or explanations for not circulating the most radical and expensive plan of all—Mr. Mercer's." [30]

Sherman's defense of his plan was a tacit admission of the charges leveled against the Civic Federation by Morris Hillquit, Socialist leader, in 1911. Hillquit had described the "game played by the National Civic Federation" as "the shrewdest yet devised by the employers of any country." It took "nothing from capital"; it gave "nothing to labor." But it "does it all with such an appearance of boundless generosity" that "some of the more guileless diplomats in the labor movement are actually overwhelmed by it." Hillquit then quoted the Civic Federation's statement to employers on the need for compensation laws to forestall "legislation which will sweep away all the defenses of the employer." What this really means, Hillquit insisted, was that to ignore the movement for compensation would be to face the "danger that this agitation may give rise to a powerful political labor movement along Socialist lines." But Hillquit had no alternative proposals, and his attack was used by Easley to assert that while the Socialists could offer nothing to labor short of socialism —which even the Socialists admitted was a long way off—the Civic Federation was providing for labor's real and immediate needs.[31]

By December 1910, the Civic Federation was "getting requests from every part of the country by telegram and letter, from governors and legislators" for copies of the bill and other material. In January 1911, Theodore Roosevelt addressed the Eleventh Annual Meeting of the Federation and emphasized

[30] George M. Gillette to August Belmont, Minneapolis, December 5, 1910; Mercer to Easley, Minneapolis, December 13, 1910; P. T. Sherman to Easley, New York, January 17, 1911; Low papers; Raynal C. Bolling to Gertrude Beeks, New York, January 15, 1914, Box 127, NCF papers; Mercer to August Belmont, Minneapolis, December 3, 1910, Box 127, NCF papers.

[31] Morris Hillquit and Ralph M. Easley, *Socialism and the National Civic Federation* (n.p., 1911).

the need for workmen's compensation legislation. In a few years, he said, the Civic Federation's attitude, "while it seemed revolutionary to some very good people of an outworn philosophy," will be "so normal" that people "will be unable to understand how anyone ever took the opposite view." Ten days later, Sherman's bill was approved by the Executive Council of the Civic Federation. Up to that time no state had passed a general compensation act, except New York, where the 1909 compulsory compensation act was declared unconstitutional in March 1911. But during 1911 compensation or accident insurance laws were passed in twelve states.[32]

Although most corporation leaders, and politicians of great prominence, such as Roosevelt and President Taft, had publicly endorsed workmen's compensation,[33] there was a residue of conservative opposition to such "radical" social legislation. This was expressed in the courts, which at that time trailed behind the leaders of the large corporations and those politicians close to them who were developing the new liberal— or progressive—ideology of the welfare state. The issue came to a head in the spring of 1911, when the New York Court of Appeals unanimously held in Ives *v.* South Buffalo Railway Company, that the conservative compensation act of that

[32] Easley to George M. Gillette, New York, December 14, 1910, Low papers; Minutes of the Meeting of the Executive Council of the National Civic Federation, New York, January 23, 1911, Low papers; Robert P. Bass (Governor-elect of New Hampshire) to August Belmont, Peterboro, December 6, 1910; I. V. Barton (Commissioner of Labor of West Virginia) to Launcelot Packer, Wheeling, December 12, 1910; August Belmont to Gertrude Beeks, New York, December 16, 1910; Beeks to Belmont, November 11, 1910, all in Box 127, NCF papers; Ernst Freund, "Constitutional Status of Workmen's Compensation," *American Labor Legislation Review*, II (1912), p. 43; "State Workmen's Compensation Legislation," *ALLR*, II (1912), p. 565; *Eleventh Annual Meeting*, pp. 193–196.

[33] Taft appeared at the National Civic Federation's annual meeting in March 1912 to speak in favor of uniform state legislation. At that time he endorsed the Federation's work for compensation. See Proceedings of the *Twelfth Annual Meeting of the National Civic Federation, Washington, D.C., March 5, 6, 7, 1912* (New York, 1912).

state was unconstitutional. Viewing the act as "plainly revolutionary" judged by common law standards, the court found it to be contrary to the positive limitations against deprivation of property without due process.[34]

This ruling enraged Theodore Roosevelt. Months later he complained to Hiram Johnson that for the past twenty-five years such decisions had served "to absolutely bar the path of social reform," thereby adding "immensely to the strength of the Socialist party."[35] *The Survey,* a progressive magazine with close corporate connections, insisted that the decision would have been different "if a board of broad gauge business men," with "responsibility for vast property interests on their shoulders," had been on the bench when this question was decided. Suppose, *The Survey* mused, J. Pierpont Morgan, Jacob H. Schiff, E. H. Gary, Andrew Carnegie, and James J. Hill were asked to decide whether compensation deprived them of property without due process. "Can anyone doubt what their answer would be. These men control great industrial enterprises. They know the value of the good will of employees. They know the value of public opinion. They know the wastefulness and the wickedness of the existing common law system. . . . They know the danger of such strained interpretations."

These men, *The Survey* concluded, will be "quite as impatient as labor leaders or social reformers at the refusal of the Court of Appeals to pay closer attention to economic facts."[36] This view was confirmed a few months later when Francis Lynde Stetson, lawyer for the International Harvester Company, P. Tecumseh Sherman, and William J. Moran, law

[34] Ives *v.* South Buffalo Railway Co., 201 New York, 271, 285; Freund, "Constitutional Status of Workmen's Compensation," p. 43.

[35] *The Letters of Theodore Roosevelt,* VII, Elting E. Morison, ed. (Cambridge, Harvard University Press, 1951), p. 421, Roosevelt to Hiram Johnson, New York, October 27, 1911.

[36] "Economics, Philosophy and Morals *v.* The Court of Appeals," *The Survey,* XXVI, 2 (April 8, 1911), pp. 78–79.

members of the Civic Federation's compensation commission, criticized the Ives decision in a brief submitted to Congress in behalf of federal compensation legislation.[37]

When Roosevelt announced his candidacy for President in 1912, the Ives decision still irritated him. Speaking at the Ohio Constitutional Convention in Columbus that spring, Roosevelt supported laws permitting the recall of judicial decisions and recommended that the new constitution include such a provision.[38] But the proposal to allow popular review of judicial decisions was too much even for the many businessmen who supported Roosevelt's position on social reform and the trusts. The effect was twofold: Roosevelt lost a good deal of support on this issue, and conservatives rushed to support compensation legislation and to recall the decision of the New York court by more traditional means.

At the January meeting of the New York State legislature an amendment to the state constitution was drawn up to place workmen's compensation legislation outside the reach of the due process clause. The amendment was widely supported as a means to head off the demands of Roosevelt and the Progressive Party for recall of judicial decisions. Urging a vote for the amendment, the *New York Times* told Roosevelt's followers that this was a perfectly "safe, wholesome, proper case of referendum, and in these respects totally different from the revision of judicial decisions advocated by their leader." [39]

In the election, the amendment carried overwhelmingly. *The Nation* hailed this " 'Recall' of the Ives Decision," [40]

[37] "Another Legal Protest Against the New York Court of Appeals Decision," *The Outlook*, DXDVIII (August 12, 1911), p. 807.

[38] George Mowry, *Theodore Roosevelt and the Progressive Movement* (Madison, University of Wisconsin Press, 1946), p. 212; Hoyt Landon Warner, *Progressivism in Ohio, 1897–1917* (Columbus, Ohio State University Press, 1964), pp. 318, 329. The Convention rejected Roosevelt's Proposal.

[39] October 19, 1913.

[40] " 'Recall' of the Ives Decision," *Nation*, DXDVII, 2527 (December 4, 1913).

and it was clear that compensation was no longer a controversial issue. At the Conference of Republicans of the State of New York in 1913, Elihu Root, also an active member of the NCF, spoke in favor of compensation, and the resolution in its favor was carried unanimously. Beyond that, the Conference resolved that "changed and changing social and industrial conditions impose new duties on government." It sympathized "with the humanitarian spirit now abroad in the world," and recognized "that there are other social measures besides workmen's compensation, which have been adopted in other countries and states, which must be seriously considered." The Republican Party, the resolution concluded, must "meet industrial and social demands of modern civilization, so far as they are reasonably consistent with our institutions." [41]

The courts of other states also adopted a more liberal attitude toward compensation, either in reaction to the agitation over the Ives decision or simply as a result of greater sophistication. In Washington, the state compensation act, which was compulsory and unlike the New York law set up a state insurance fund, was upheld as a valid exercise of the police power. The courts of Massachusetts, Ohio, and Wisconsin upheld elective laws in 1912.[42] As Clark B. Firestone, of the Firestone National Bank, Lisbon, Ohio, told the Fourteenth Annual Meeting of the National Civic Federation: "We see things coming our way all over the field. . . . Mr. Dooley has said that if the Constitution does not follow the flag, at least the Supreme Court followed the election returns, and the courts of our country have felt the breath of this new spirit; their later interpretations of the law have modified the rigors of the Common Law fabric of employer's liability which

[41] Minutes of the Conference of Republicans of the State of New York, Waldorf Astoria, New York City, December 5, 1913, p. 34, in Low papers.
[42] Freund, "Constitutional Status of Workmen's Compensation," p. 43.

gave the workman the stone of litigation instead of the bread of prompt and certain compensation." [43]

Widespread agreement on the need for compensation legislation did not end all conflict over the reform. The Civic Federation, businessmen in general, and insurance companies in particular, still clashed with labor and the Socialists over specific bills and over questions of coverage, waiting periods, and state versus commercial insurance. Senator George Sutherland (Republican, Utah), who served as the chairman of the Civic Federation's Committee on Uniform Legislation Upon Workmen's Compensation, was instrumental in helping draw up legislation both for states and for the federal government. A member of the joint Congressional Commission on Workmen's Compensation, Sutherland was also author of a bill that passed the Senate in May 1912. It had the strong support of the Civic Federation, and of the Brotherhood of Locomotive Engineers, the Order of Railway Conductors, and the Brotherhood of Railway Trainmen. But Progressives in the Senate opposed Sutherland's bill, the *New York American* urged House Democrats to vote against it "until the workmen's side of the case has a more considerate hearing," and the Atlanta *Journal of Labor* thought the maximum damages "grossly and grotesquely inadequate." The *New York World* commented wryly that the theory behind the bill appeared to be that the industrial worker should receive compensation for his injuries "corresponding to the soldier's pension for wounds incurred in battle." [44]

A similar debate occurred in 1913 over legislation to replace the bill invalidated by the Ives decision. Three bills were introduced in the New York legislature in the wake of

[43] Fourteenth Annual Meeting minutes, Box 187, NCF papers.

[44] George Sutherland, "Employer's Liability and Workmen's Compensation," *The Independent*, LXXII, 3310 (May 9, 1912), p. 1005; Correspondence in Box 127, NCF papers; "Doubts About the Compensation Bill," *Literary Digest*, XLIV, 20 (May 18, 1912), pp. 1026–1027.

the Ives ruling. One, called the Jackson Bill, was supported by the State Federation of Labor. It provided for exclusive state insurance, for payments of two thirds of weekly wages, with a $15.00 maximum weekly payment and ten years' payment in case of death. The Foley Bill, supported by the administration, provided for commercial or mutual insurance. The McClelland Bill (unofficially favored by the business members of the National Civic Federation) authorized company or state insurance at the option of the employer. Both the McClelland and the Foley bills provided one half of weekly wages, maximum of $10.00 per week. In the hearings on these bills, the Civic Federation took no public position because of the disagreement with its position by the labor members. The State Insurance Department opposed state insurance, and the labor men accused the State Superintendent of Insurance of acting for the insurance companies. Finally, a compromise was agreed upon. The act allowed private insurance companies, as in the Foley and McClelland bills, but provided for payments of two thirds of weekly wages, up to $15.00 per week.[45] The businessmen and their allies in Albany conceded on the amount of money to be given injured workmen, but held out on the principle of private insurance. The business unionists sacrificed the principle of state insurance in return for immediately higher benefits. It was not the last time trade unionists and big business would reach a compromise of this kind.

Socialists continued to criticize many of the bills passed, and insurance companies continued to exert pressure against state insurance—attacking it as "socialistic." The Socialists drew up a model bill for introduction by Party legislators in several states; it provided for state insurance coverage of all industrial, agricultural, domestic, and office workers, and one

[45] Edward T. Devine, "Compensation Bills at Albany," *The Survey*, XIX (February 22, 1913), pp. 722–724; Seth Low to William Low, n.p., *New York Times*, January 18, 26, February 10, 11, 18, 20, 25, 193.

hundred percent of wages for total disability. Their pressure tended to keep rates above fifty percent, but the debate in each state was different and the specific legislation varied widely in details. Despite Socialist and labor criticism, the movement was clearly a success. In 1911 (after the Ives decision invalidated the New York law), no state had an effective compensation law, yet by 1920 every state but six in the South had one, and the federal government had amended the Act of 1908 to include all civil employees.[46] This sweeping achievement was made possible by the concerted activity of the National Civic Federation, with the strong support of its big business affiliates. It represented a growing maturity and sophistication on the part of many large corporation leaders who had come to understand, as Theodore Roosevelt often told them, that social reform was truly conservative.

[46] Paul Kennaday, "Big Business and Workmen's Compensation," *The Survey*, XIX (March 8, 1913), pp. 809–810; Ethelwyn Mills, *Legislative Program of the Socialist Party* (Chicago, Socialist Party, 1914), pp. 50 ff.; Carl Hookstadt, *Comparison of Workmen's Compensation Laws of the United States and Canada up to January 1, 1920* (Washington, D.C., Government Printing Office, 1920), pp. 5–6.

CHAPTER THREE

LEADERSHIP IN REGULATION:

THE FEDERAL TRADE COMMISSION

WHILE THE NATIONAL CIVIC FEDERATION was busy working for compensation laws on the state level it also concerned itself with problems that were national in scope. The most important of these, and the one in which the Federation itself and its leading business members had the greatest and most sustained interest was trust regulation. Indeed, it had been a conference on regulation of the trusts, sponsored by the Chicago Civic Federation in 1899, out of which the NCF grew. From that time until the enactment of the Federal Trade Commission Act in 1914 the question of the status of the new corporations under the Sherman Antitrust Act of 1890 received continuous attention from NCF leaders.

The Federal Trade Commission Act of 1914 is most often thought of as a Wilsonian reform embodying a bias against "big business." In fact, the principles underlying the FTC were enunciated by corporation leaders and their lawyers consistently throughout the Progressive Era in response to a series of legislative and judicial actions stretching over some seventeen years. Most important of these were the Trans-Missouri Freight Association case of 1897, which laid down a narrow interpretation of the Sherman Act; the establishment of the Bureau of Corporations in 1903; the Hepburn Bill of 1908 (an attempt to amend the Sherman Act); and the Standard Oil decision of 1911 which enunciated the Rule of Reason in regard to the trusts. In the course of these developments the National Civic Federation and its business affiliates evolved the legislative principles to be embodied in 1914 in Woodrow Wilson's Federal Trade Commission.

In the years following the enactment of the Sherman Act in 1890 the relation between the large corporations and the federal government was one of uncertainty. The Act was passed before the great wave of consolidations in the years from 1897 to 1904. Superficially and in the popular consciousness of small businessmen and farmers it was a mandate to prevent the spread of trust agreements and corporate consolidations, such as those that had led to the formation of the Standard Oil and American Sugar companies in the late 1870's and 1880's. In fact, the Act had no such effect. Indeed the very years when it was most narrowly enforced—from 1897, when Justice Peckham enunciated the strict majority view in the Trans-Missouri case, to the enunciation of the Rule of Reason by Justice White in the Standard Oil case in 1911—was the period of most rapid consolidation. In eight years from 1897 through 1904, corporations with assets totaling $6,000,000,000 were organized, compared to a total of about $1,000,000,000 in the years between 1879 and 1897. By 1904 the top four percent of American concerns (the great majority of which were corporate in form) produced 57 percent of the total industrial output by value. By any standard of measurement, large corporations had come to dominate the American economy by 1904.[1]

How the judicial history of the Sherman Act accelerated and encouraged the consolidation of industrial enterprises into large corporations, in place of more informal, cartel-like arrangements between relatively small manufacturing concerns is a complex question. The Sherman Act declared illegal "Every contract, combination in the form of trust or other-

[1] Willard L. Thorp, *The Integration of Industrial Operation*, Census Monograph, No. III (Department of Commerce, Bureau of the Census [1924]), pp. 91, 92, 267; Martin L. Sklar, "The Emergence of the Corporate Liberal Order" (unpublished manuscript), pp. 145–146.

wise, or conspiracy, in restraint of trade or commerce" among the states or with foreign nations, and provided punishment for such restraint. It also declared "Every person who shall monopolize, or attempt to monopolize, or combine or conspire with any other person or persons, to monopolize any part" of interstate or foreign commerce to be guilty of a misdemeanor and subject to punishment.[2] The key terms in the judicial interpretation of the law were "restraint of trade," "monopolize," and "attempt to monopolize." In the popular mind these may have had several meanings. Surely to many they meant literally what they said. But in the common law—and in the intention of the drafters of the Act—they had specific meanings developed in English and American law.

These pertain to the nature of trust and cartel agreements, rather than to the size of a particular enterprise. Under common law precedents, agreements among businessmen not to compete or to restrict competition among themselves (either by controlling supply, limiting output, fixing prices, pooling profits, or dividing markets) were legal regardless of size unless they *unduly* or *unreasonably* restrained competition in such a way as to be detrimental to the public interest. Under common law procedure each case was to be settled on its merits in the light of the particular facts. With respect to restraints of trade and monopoly the common law had evolved certain general principles, basic to which was "the well-established distinction . . . between reasonable and unreasonable restraint of trade."[3]

Restraints of trade (restriction or regulation of competi-

---

[2] Act of July 2, 1890, 26 *United States Statutes* 209, 51st Congress, First Session.

[3] Herbert Knox Smith, United States Commissioner of Corporations, memorandum of 1908 quoted in *Hearings Before Subcommittee of the Committee on the Judiciary, United States Senate*, during the 60th, 61st, 62nd Congresses, compiled for consideration of H.R. 15657, 63rd Congress, Second Session, Washington, D.C., 1914, p. 332.

tion) were reasonable under common law doctrine when such restraints were ancillary to legitimate contracts (whether among competitors or noncompetitors) for the purchase, sale or production of goods, services or plant. Contracts or agreements involving direct restraints which undertook to maintain prices at fair levels guaranteeing a fair return on invested capital—that is, those that protected against "ruinous" or "destructive" competition—were also legal. So were those that did not restrict production of goods or raise prices to a point considered dangerous to public interest, and those that did not seek or result in the "artificial" prevention of others from entering into a particular line of business, that is: contracts that left open the possibility of competition.[4]

"Monopolize" and "attempt to monopolize" also had distinct common law meanings which did not hang on the existence of actual monopoly, but on the prevention or attempt to prevent others from entering or competing in a given line of business. A contract to restrict competition in prices, sales, or production that did not close "the channels of trade" was not deemed a monopoly at common law. Nor was it an "attempt to monopolize" if a competitor bought the plant of another in the course of "normal expansion" or in the quest of greater efficiency.[5]

In two respects the Sherman Act did reverse common law procedure: it made restraints of trade a criminal as well as a civil offense (which meant that suits could now be brought by the government); it rendered such restraints liable to private suits for treble damages. But the question remained whether the Sherman Act superseded the common law substantively.

Despite contemporary popular opinion, leading congressional advocates of the Sherman Act clearly saw it only as an

[4] Sklar, "Emergence of the Corporate Liberal Order," p. 88.
[5] *Ibid.*, pp. 91–92.

incorporation into federal law of the common law doctrines with respect to restraint of trade and monopoly. As Hans B. Thorelli observes, Senator Sherman "stated on several occasions that the object of the bill was to make the common law against monopolies and restraint of trade applicable on the federal level. The common law as it had been applied in Britain and in the several states was to be the main guide of the national courts in drawing the line of demarcation between lawful and unlawful combinations." [6] In debate Sherman explained that he accepted the common law doctrine that "all combinations are not void, a proposition which no one doubts." It was only "the unlawful combination tested by the rules of common law and human experience," that was his target, "not the lawful and useful combination." [7] Other senators supported Sherman's view.

But the 1897 decision in the Trans-Missouri case did not distinguish between reasonable and unreasonable restraints of trade. Much to the discomfort of big business, this interpretation of the Sherman Act opened the door to continuing attacks on consolidation. As late as 1911, twenty-one years after the passage of the Sherman Act, neopopulist politicians insisted that the Act meant what it seemed to say on its face. The leading advocate of this view was Robert M. La Follette, who argued that the law forbade "that sort of business that [Theodore] Roosevelt characterized as the business which 'honest men' must do under modern business conditions." La Follette explicitly rejected the common law interpretation of the Act, which, he asserted, "said nothing about *supervising* or *controlling* these combinations 'within reasonable limits.'" Indeed, La Follette contended, had Roosevelt vigorously and sincerely enforced the law when he took office

---

[6] Hans B. Thorelli, *The Federal Antitrust Policy, Origination of an American Tradition* (Baltimore, Johns Hopkins University Press, 1955), p. 183.
[7] *Ibid.*, pp. 181, 184.

(in 1901) he "would have crushed and destroyed the comparatively few trusts which were then in existence." [8]

Roosevelt, of course, accepted the large corporations as the natural culmination of American industrial development, and sought to use the Sherman Act as a means simply of regulating corporate behavior. "Good" trusts, in Roosevelt's terminology, were those which acted in a socially responsible manner; "bad" trusts were those that put their immediate interests above the need for social peace and class harmony. The men under Roosevelt most directly concerned with administering those government agencies responsible for dealing with the corporations—particularly James R. Garfield and Herbert Knox Smith—took the common law view of the Sherman Act. Roosevelt had a somewhat less legalistic approach; he initiated or withheld prosecution under the Act as a means of regulation—that is, he punished what he considered to be irresponsible behavior with suits and rewarded cooperation with the government with informal agreements not to institute action under the law. [9] Some businessmen who agreed that Roosevelt was generally correct in theory, balked at his stance as "a benevolent despot who decides what corporations should be destroyed and what left alone." [10]

Had Roosevelt invoked the Sherman Act against all major corporate formations in the years during which the Harlan majority narrowly interpreted the law, he might, as La Follette claimed, have been able seriously to disrupt the development of the so-called trust. La Follette's attitude was similar to that of the Harlan majority: he desired relentless prosecution of the trusts and a literal interpretation of the Sherman Act. But, because of Roosevelt's attitude, the impact of the Supreme

[8] Robert M. La Follette, *La Follette's Autobiography*, 2nd ed. (Madison, University of Wisconsin Press, 1960), pp. 91, 92, 296.

[9] Robert H. Wiebe, "The House of Morgan and the Executive, 1905–1913," *American Historical Review*, LXV, 1 (October 1959), pp. 49 *Et. Seq.*

[10] Frederick A. Delano to Seth Low, Chicago, March 4, 1913, Box 106, Low papers, Columbia University.

Court's strict interpretation in the Trans-Missouri and subsequent cases was just the opposite of the Court's intention. As Martin J. Sklar has pointed out, Sherman law jurisprudence "in reality contributed to the formation of the great corporate consolidations, as distinguished from cartel-type arrangements among smaller, independent business units." [11] The common law itself had been applied most frequently before the enactment of the Sherman Act against relatively loose-knit business combinations, such as "gentlemen's agreements" and the somewhat more tightly associated "pools." [12] Such suits accelerated the tendency to merge or fuse business enterprises. Tighter forms of combination, of which the trust was one, had the advantage of effecting centralized, single-management units. These mergers were not subject to subsequent disaffection by constituent members, as were the looser, cartel-type associations. Such outright consolidations obviated court intervention through suits filed by recalcitrants.[13] State court decisions, and then the Sherman Act in 1890, led to a shift away from looser forms of fusion and toward a more frequent use of direct fusion through the purchase of the assets of one business by another.[14]

Looser arrangements, such as pools and cartels, assumed the greatest vulnerability in the face of meager federal efforts to prosecute business for restraint of trade under the Sherman Act. The Supreme Court's interpretation of the Sherman Act strengthened this tendency. Thus before 1897, in the Greenhut, *In re Greene*, and E. C. Knight cases, the federal courts sustained the "Whiskey Trust" as a legal combination and ruled that a consolidation in manufacturing by the American Sugar Company was not objectionable per se under the Sher-

---

[11] Sklar, "Emergence of the Corporate Liberal Order," p. 138.

[12] Thorelli, *Federal Antitrust Policy*, p. 143.

[13] *Ibid.* Under the common law, suits against such combinations could be filed only by the contractors against each other, or by directly aggrieved parties. That is, such suits were civil, or private, rather than public.

[14] *Ibid.*, p. 258.

man law. In contrast, in the celebrated Trans-Missouri, Joint Traffic, and Addyston Pipe cases of 1897–1899 (where the strict Harlan interpretation of the Sherman law became established) pools, rather than outright consolidations were involved. The impact on businessmen of Harlan's literal interpretation of the Act, whatever his intention, was to encourage them to seek the relative safety of corporate consolidation.

Rapid consolidation of industrial enterprises into giant corporations and the general public anxiety over this transformation of the American economy led to the establishment by Congress of the United States Industrial Commission in June 1898. In 1900 the Commission proposed as its remedy for the problems created by this process of "industrial combination" the enactment of a federal license or franchise law applying to all corporations or their agents engaged in interstate or foreign commerce. Such legislation would prohibit entrance into interstate trade to all corporations not so licensed, and would give the government authority to refuse or withdraw such license if the applicant or licensee were in violation of federal law. To facilitate the administration of the suggested legislation, the large corporations would be required to publish annual reports stating their assets, liabilities, and profits or losses.[15]

The law establishing the Bureau of Corporations as part of the Department of Commerce and Labor in 1903 fell far short of the Commission's recommendations. The Bureau was empowered only to investigate corporate activities and, with the President's approval, to publish the data. This meant that the Bureau would function primarily as an aid in developing legislation, although it could also be used to restrain dishonest or unethical practices of corporations with the threat of publicity. How the Bureau would actually function, which interests it would serve, and how it would line up on the question

[15] Bureau of Corporations, *Annual Report, 1904*, pp. 47–48; *ibid.*, 1912, p. 14.

of the enforcement of the Sherman Act was apparently initially unclear. The greatest support for the formation of the Bureau came from small and middle-sized business. The expectation that it would serve these interests by checking the "trusts" had led the National Association of Manufacturers to lobby for it in 1903. Small businessmen, especially from the Midwest and South, enthusiastically called upon the Bureau of Corporations to destroy their larger competitors and cheered each move Roosevelt made in the direction of what looked like "trustbusting." [16]

Yet, to their disappointment, the approach of both the Industrial Commission and Bureau of Corporations was fundamentally antagonistic to the literal construction of the Sherman Act enunciated by the Harlan majority of the Supreme Court in 1897–1899. Both agencies assumed the affirmation and regulation of corporate consolidation, rather than its prohibition or breakup. Under the chairmanship of James R. Garfield, the Bureau's first annual report distinguished between "two classes" of "antitrust" legislation—"the one which is aimed at prohibition of monopoly and the restraint of trade, and which is more properly 'antitrust,' and the other, which is aimed at improper rebates, discrimination, and unfair competition, and which has no necessary connection with combinations." The Bureau rejected the first class of legislation as impracticable and unsound (even though it represented the law already in force as a result of the Supreme Court decisions), and recommended its replacement with the second. As interpreted, the Sherman Act was seen as a futile "attempt to stop the operation of strictly economic law by statutory enactment." Not only that, but the attempt to "maintain a state of competition by prohibiting all combination, reasonable or unreasonable," was "wrong in principle." The second class of legislation, however, was seen as "fundamentally correct" in that it was not aimed at the restraint or

[16] Robert H. Wiebe, *Businessmen and Reform*, pp. 44–45.

combination as such, "but at regulating the *methods* of competition." Recognizing the "irresistible tendency toward combination," the Bureau saw the object of such regulation to be that of assuring that "this process shall be attended with as little injustice as may be." Such an approach was "correct in theory." [17] Thus, despite Roosevelt's popular image as a "trustbuster" his policy was that of accommodation to the large corporation system, so long as it operated within the bounds of "natural" development.

"This is an age of combination," Roosevelt told Congress in his Annual Message to Congress in 1905, "and any effort to prevent combination will not only be useless, but in the end vicious, because of the contempt for law which the failure to enforce law inevitably produces." What was needed was "not sweeping prohibition of every arrangement good or bad, which may tend to restrict competition, but such adequate supervision and regulation as will prevent any restriction of competition from being to the detriment of the public." [18] Roosevelt articulated the thoughts of many large corporation leaders in 1905, and of the Bureau of Corporations, but his call for regulatory legislation was not fulfilled until after Woodrow Wilson took office in 1913.

Businessmen and political leaders most committed to regulatory legislation were heavily concentrated in the National Civic Federation. These men, although close to Roosevelt, greatly feared the public clamor for regulation and his use of "trustbusting" as a political issue. It was clear to them that when Roosevelt denounced "bad" trusts his main target was Rockefeller and his Standard Oil Company, rather than the Morgan and other corporations in the Civic Federation. But the obvious political advantage in antitrust rhetoric, and

[17] Bureau of Corporations, *Annual Report, 1904*, pp. 40–41. [Emphasis in original.]

[18] Quoted in Oswald Whitman Knauth, *The Policy of the United States Towards Industrial Monopoly* (New York, Columbia University Studies in History, Economics, and Public Law, Vol. 56, No. 2, 1914), pp. 78–79.

the pressure from small businessmen for more vigorous prosecution of various combinations,[19] made Civic Federation leaders uneasy and desirous of finding ways to change the prevailing law, or at least to quiet popular discontent with the corporations and the demands for more stringent enforcement of the Sherman Act.

In line with Roosevelt's messages to Congress on the subject, the Civic Federation laid plans in 1906 to work up a proposed revision of the Sherman Act that would meet the diverse objections of corporation and labor leaders among its membership. One view of the need to revise the law was expressed at the sixth annual meeting of the Civic Federation in December 1906 by Melville E. Ingalls, chairman of the Big Four Railroad, and of the Federation's newly organized Public Ownership Commission. Ingalls saw the Sherman Act as a "real menace," threatening the very foundations of American business by outlawing all methods of centralization and cooperation essential to its conduct under modern conditions. Ingalls was still smarting over the dissolution of the Joint Traffic Association agreement by the Supreme Court in 1897. "I had the honor to prepare that," Ingalls related, "and it never occurred to me that there was any danger of violating the Sherman Antitrust Law" in so doing. The Court's decision that the agreement was a conspiracy and violated the Sherman Act turned the thirty-two participating railroads into "a sort of Pariah," leaving them without power to agree upon rates and conduct their business "legitimately among themselves."

Nor did Ingalls see the Harlan interpretation of the Sherman Act as harmful solely to railroads. "The same reasoning," he asserted, "applies to other classes of business. Almost everything now is construed to be a trust," despite the fact that a trust was "nothing but a combination of people for doing business more cheaply and largely. It is the evolution of the

---

[19] Wiebe, *Businessmen and Reform*, p. 45.

corporation." The law, he concluded, "should be taken up and amended to suit business conditions." [20]

Heartily seconding Ingalls' and Roosevelt's views, August Belmont, in his presidential address to the Federation, also urged action on amending the antitrust law. This led to the formation of an NCF commission to investigate the situation created by the Sherman Antitrust Law.

The next month Easley told Franklin MacVeagh that the Federation was in the process of appointing a committee to draft a revision of the Sherman Act along the lines proposed by Roosevelt. Easley had exchanged ideas on the subject with Charles G. Dawes, like MacVeagh a Chicago banker, and John S. Miller of the *New York Times*. These original plans called simply for a committee to draft a bill, but with the onset of the panic of 1907 Federation leaders decided that a more public discussion of the problem was needed.

"In view of what has happened in the past two weeks," Easley told Dawes on March 15, 1907, the announcement of a commission "would not be adequate to meet the situation as it exists today." Instead, the Federation decided to call a national conference in Chicago and to invite governors of the various states, commercial, trade, and other organizations to send delegates to "discuss the whole corporation and combination question," as had been done by the Chicago Civic Federation in 1899 in response to the Supreme Court decisions of 1897–1899. Professor Jeremiah W. Jenks of Cornell had visited Easley the day before. As Easley told Dawes, Jenks, who helped organize the 1899 conference, was satisfied that it "had resulted in mollifying the radical sentiment prevailing at that time." Another such conference would very likely serve the same purpose now.[21] The same day, Easley informed E. P.

---

[20] Quoted in Jensen, "National Civic Federation," pp. 270–271.

[21] Easley to Franklin MacVeagh, New York, January 6, 1907, Box 33, NCF papers; Easley to Charles G. Dawes, New York, March 15, 1907, Box 26, *ibid.*

Ripley, president of the Atchison, Topeka and Santa Fe Railroad, that this "new phase of the matter" had been the subject of a conversation at the White House with Secretary of Commerce Oscar S. Straus and Roosevelt. The President, of course, could not be officially known as interested in such a conference, but he thought that "nothing but good can come of it; and, at a time when the public mind is so hysterical, it might have a very calming effect." [22]

The purpose of the Federation's National Conference on Trusts and Combinations, held in Chicago on October 22 to 25, 1907, was, then, twofold. It was motivated by a desire of businessmen to get back to a common law, or evolutionary, concept of regulation, and by an intention to anticipate and divert political agitation against "monopoly." Easley made this clear after the Conference was over and plans had been made to have a commission deliberate prospective legislation. Such a "high class, representative commission studying the question," he wrote Senator Nelson Aldrich, "would not only take the matter out of politics," but would furnish the Attorney General "good grounds" to "slack up a little on its prosecutions." [23]

The Trust Conference in Chicago, October 22 to October 25, 1907, served both the Federation's purposes. It was "broadly representative"—a term the Federation, and Easley and Low in particular, overworked—and it produced a general set of principles, or approaches to the problem of consolidation and combination that helped lead the way back to a common law approach, adjusted to the conditions that existed as a result to the emergence of the large corporations as the dominant form of economic organization. Four hundred

[22] Easley to E. P. Ripley, New York, March 15, 1907, Box 34, *ibid.*
[23] Easley to Aldrich, New York, December 25, 1907, Box 25, *ibid.* See also, Easley to Charles G. Dawes, New York, January 10, 1908, Box 94, *ibid.* In which Easley tells Dawes that Aldrich shares his views and that NCF action "would largely have the effect of taking the trust question out of politics."

and ninety-two delegates comprising 147 delegations appointed by state governors, business associations, labor organizations, and various state and national organizations attended. Businessmen were very much in the majority, but many university professors, government officials, lawyers, labor leaders, and reformers also attended. Nicholas Murray Butler, president of Columbia University and an active member of the NCF, served as Conference chairman. As always, the Federation used the Conference to launch its program with a maximum of publicity and with the appearance of a substantial backing of public opinion.[24] By taking the initiative in sponsoring public debate over solutions to the "trust" problem, the Federation succeeded in winning the support of many reformers whose loyalty was not to the corporations, but to more idealistic goals of society and social responsibility.

The most general conclusion to come from the Conference was neutral enough: it was simply that the time had come to consider revisions in existing legislation (the Sherman Act), and to try new methods. Seventeen years of experience under the Sherman Act *"as interpreted by the courts,"* had led to a "general and just conviction" that new legislation was needed to "render more secure the benefits" already gained and to meet "changed conditions." Several steps were proposed by the Conference committee. First, was the suggestion that railroads be allowed to enter agreements on rates, subject to supervision by the Interstate Commerce Commission, a recommendation of the Commission itself and of President Roosevelt. Second, the committee suggested that the positive accomplishments of the Sherman Act, in "awakening the moral sense of the American people" and in asserting the supremacy of the law over large corporations, had given way to the need for new legislation to "maintain all that the Sherman Act was intended to secure and safeguard interests it was never expected to affect." This was a statement intended to satisfy

[24] Jensen, "National Civic Federation," p. 272.

many interests, particularly the trade unions which were increasingly harassed by injunctions brought under the Sherman Act.

Third, the immediate establishment of a Congressional commission to study the problem of "trust" legislation was proposed. This commission was to be organized along Federation lines—that is, it would represent capital, labor, and the "general public." Its main purpose, expressed in what would later be known as Wilsonian rhetoric, was to explore new methods of regulating corporations so as to "preserve individual initiative, competition, and the *free exercise of a free contract* in all business and industrial relations." The commission would also examine the advisability of a system of federal license or incorporation, a proposal more and more favored by the largest corporations. Current prohibitions on combination should be examined with an eye to relaxing those against business and industrial agreements or combinations "whose objects are in the public interest as distinguished from objects determined to be contrary to the public interest." [25]

The third, and last, recommendation of the Conference committee was that the powers of "examination, inspection, and supervision" of the Bureau of Corporations be expanded by giving the Bureau power to require "complete publicity in the capitalization, accounts, operations, transportation charges paid, and selling prices" of all corporations "whose operations are large enough to have a monopolistic influence." [26] As Easley commented after the Conference, it was, as a whole, "distinctly in favor of the regulation of trusts and combinations, though the details of such regulation presented in the minds of several speakers a wide variety of form."

After the Conference, Federation leaders expected simply to present their recommendations to Congress for the estab-

[25] *Ibid.*, pp. 273–274. [Emphasis added.]
[26] *Ibid.*, pp. 274, 276.

lishment of a federal commission to investigate new "trust" legislation. In January 1908 a delegation of the NCF went to Washington to meet with the President, Cabinet members and Congressional leaders. Much to the Federation's surprise, the congressmen suggested that instead of a commission, the NCF draw up a bill embodying its suggestions. The response was "instantaneous and avid acceptance." [27]

To draw up a bill, Seth Low, the NCF's new president, called together an informal committee that well represented the Federation's scope and ideology. Seven businessmen were included: E. H. Gary, chairman of the board of the United States Steel Corporation, Samuel Mather of Pickands, Mather and Company, Isaac N. Seligman and James Speyer, leading New York bankers, W. A. Clark, president of the United Verde Copper Company, August Belmont, and George W. Perkins.

The lawyers, who did most of the actual work on the bill, were Francis Lynde Stetson, attorney to J. P. Morgan and Company and Victor Morawetz, attorney to the Atchison, Topeka and Santa Fe Railroad. Six labor leaders were included: Samuel Gompers, John Mitchell, Dennis J. Keefe, president of the Longshoremen, James O'Connell, president of the International Association of Machinists, P. H. Morrissey, Grand Master of the Brotherhood of Railway Trainmen, and D. L. Cease, editor of the *Railroad Trainmen's Journal*. The academic community was represented by Nicholas Murray Butler and Jeremiah W. Jenks; the press by Albert Shaw, editor of the *Review of Reviews*, and Talcott Williams of the Philadelphia *Free Press*. Also on the committee were Alton B. Parker and Herbert Knox Smith, Roosevelt's Commissioner of Corporations. Working feverishly, this committee managed to put together a bill by the end of February 1908, and to win Federation approval of it a week or two thereafter. Through-

[27] *Ibid.*, p. 277.

out the process Commissioner of Corporations Herbert K. Smith worked closely with the drafters and approved each section.[28]

The process was one of compromise and negotiation between the various points of view, including even those of the middle-range businessmen in the NAM and the Illinois Manufacturing Association (although in the end these groups opposed the bill). Ralph Easley played a central role in attempting to reconcile these men with the labor leaders. He wrote Gompers that he had met with Charles H. Smith, president of the Illinois Association and with James M. Beck, James Van Cleave's attorney, and assured them that Gompers wanted no special privileges for labor. But Easley was more successful with big businessmen than with small. Later, he told Gompers that he had talked with George Perkins, who was "not at all averse" to exempting labor from the operation of the Sherman Act, "provided it can be done without destroying the whole proposition." At the same time, Easley told Gompers of a meeting with Secretary of War Taft at the White House, at which Taft "said he was perfectly in accord with the idea of taking the railroads and labor unions out from under the operation of the Sherman Act." Taft was also "anxious to have reasonable and fair agreements between industrial organizations." [29]

The bill as finally written was a compromise that was close to Taft's views and unobjectionable to the large corporations and the Morgan men. Reestablishment of the common law doctrine of distinction between reasonable and unreasonable restraints of trade was the key feature of the bill, introduced for the Federation by Representative William P. Hepburn. In addition, the Hepburn bill explicitly returned unions to

[28] *Ibid.*, pp. 279, 280.
[29] Easley to Gompers, New York, February 12, 1908, Box 94; Easley to Gompers, New York, February 25, 1908, Box 31: both NCF papers.

their status under the common law by inserting the word "unreasonable" into the Sherman Act.

Presented as an amendment to the Sherman Act, the bill provided for the voluntary registration of any corporation by submitting a statement of its financial status, contracts and other vital data with the Bureau of Corporations. Once registered, a corporation had the right to file any proposed contract or merger with the Commissioner. If, within thirty days, the Bureau did not declare the contract illegal the corporation involved was exempt from prosecution under the Sherman Act for that contract except if it was in "unreasonable" restraint of trade. Railroads as well as industrial corporations could register under the law, and individuals were given the power to sue corporations for injuries in the federal courts. In effect the Hepburn bill gave the Bureau of Corporations the power to veto many day-to-day operations of business, but, more important, it also provided for much greater certainty in regard to the legality of agreements between corporations because of the implied sanction of business transactions that were not ruled "unreasonable" under the Sherman Act. A contract on which the government had placed its stamp of approval was not likely to be attacked later as an unreasonable restraint of trade.

The Hepburn bill, as has been noted, was drawn in close consultation with Herbert Knox Smith, Commissioner of Corporations, and in constant discussion with President Roosevelt. As Easley informed Edgar A. Bancroft, counsel for International Harvester Company (who had drafted his own bill along the same general line), the President told Easley, Low, Gompers, and Professor Jenks that he would send a special message in support of the bill if necessary. White House consultations were frequent during the month of preparation of the bill.[30]

[30] Easley to Bancroft, New York, February 1, 1908, Box 30; Easley to Gompers, New York, February 25, 1908, Box 31: both NCF papers.

But the opposition from small and middle-sized business was so intense that Roosevelt never did send more than a perfunctory message of support.

During the House hearings on the bill Seth Low testified that 42 governors and 90 commercial, agricultural, and labor organizations had sent delegations to the Federation Conference in 1907, and that the Hepburn bill embodied the substance of their thought on regulation. He argued that the amendment was necessary because so much business then being conducted was in technical violation of the law, and that this created contempt for the law and uncertainty in business circles. "Regulation, not prohibition, should be our watchword in all such matters," Low asserted.

Scores of letters from businessmen and business associations poured into the Committee in opposition to the bill. The National Association of Manufacturers, the American Anti-Boycott Associations, and the Merchants' Association and Board of Trade and Transportation of New York opposed the amendment. Contrary to most interpretations, as Robert H. Wiebe points out, the exemption of the unions from the operation of the Sherman Act was not what medium-sized business groups found most objectionable. Anti-unionism best unified businessmen, so the NAM and the Anti-Boycott Association centered their attack on the proposed relief granted the unions.

But as Wiebe writes, "the crucial issue was the latitude promised to big business." Opponents argued that the right to approve business practices gave the executive autocratic powers over the economy. When Senator Foraker offered a similar bill without the labor provisions, Daniel Davenport of the Anti-Boycott Association stated that he would oppose any measure which tried to separate good big business from bad. In his testimony at the House hearings Davenport reiterated the Harlan interpretation of the Sherman Act, asserting that the insertion of the word "unreasonable" into the Act, as in the Hepburn bill, would absolutely destroy the Act and was clearly unconstitutional.[31] Andrew Carnegie, on the other hand, thought the bill offered "a fair solution of the questions involved," and had "no objection" to "the provision safeguarding the rights of labor."

But as Edgar A. Bancroft complained to Easley, "besides ourselves, I find very little support for the Hepburn Bill." In particular, "small manufacturers and business men" were opposed.[32] These groups, when organized and aroused, carried considerable influence in the Republican party and were probably the cause of Roosevelt's failure to support the bill as vigorously as he had promised Low and Easley. Low observed that the Federation had hoped to submit a bill "which would command a large support, not only from employers, but also from organized labor." Yet the bill "commanded no large measure of support from either." Writing to Roosevelt, Low said that he thought "the large interests, such as Judge Gary represents, are still loyally behind our bill. The objection comes from the mercantile element, as distinguished from the corporation element." But apparently there was even some opposition from the less sophisticated corporate leaders. Writing to Smith, George Perkins lamented that "If the opponents to Governmental supervision could only know how intelligently and how fairly you have worked for the very highest and best interests of American corporations, I am sure they would abandon their present attitude." Smith thanked Perkins for his remarks. "It is disappointing, of course," Smith wrote, "and especially disappointing where the opposition is due to lack of comprehension. I think, however, in time we shall be able to work out the matter on substantially the lines we have

[31] *Hearings on House Bill 19745 Before Subcommittee No. 3 of the Committee on the Judiciary,* 60th Congress, 1st Session (Washington, D.C., 1908), pp. 10–12; Wiebe, *Businessmen and Reform,* p. 81; *Hearings on House Bill 19745,* p. 166; Jensen, pp. 287–288.

[32] Andrew Carnegie to Ralph M. Easley, New York, March 24, 1908, Box 95; Bancroft to Easley, Chicago, April 11, 1908, Box 30: both NCF papers.

laid down." [33] Essentially, Smith was correct. Although the principles embodied in the Hepburn bill were not yet politically feasible, they were to form the basis of future court decisions and legislation.

The defeat of the Federation's bill did not end its concern with the regulation of corporations, but it did lead to a somewhat different approach and a search for a formula that would be more generally acceptable. As early as 1908 both Andrew Carnegie and Melville E. Ingalls had suggested to the Civic Federation an alternative that was to succeed—the idea of an interstate trade commission, modeled on the Interstate Commerce Commission and the British Board of Trade. As Carnegie put it, an "Interstate Commission" with "the power to judge combinations and contracts proposed" was needed. This had "been found all sufficient in other countries and will be so with us. We must have our industrial as we have a Judicial Supreme Court." [34] Ingalls also called for a commission with "the power to turn the limelight on" the corporations, as under the Board of Trade Act in Great Britain. "That great industrial country," he argued, "has found a way to control those corporations without bringing their managers into court." [35]

In 1909, having lost the first legislative round, the Civic Federation appointed a new committee, headed by President Low, to draft further proposals. Concrete suggestions did not come forth until after the Supreme Court's decision in the Standard Oil case in May 1911. That decision changed the framework in which the discussion of regulation took place, since it overruled the strict interpretation of the Sherman Act adopted by the Court in 1897 and enunciated the "rule of

[33] Jensen, "National Civic Federation," p. 288; Seth Low to Theodore Roosevelt, New York, April 11, 1908; Perkins to Herbert Knox Smith, New York, April 18, 1908; Smith to Perkins, Washington, D.C., April 20, 1908, Files of the Bureau of Corporations, RG 122, National Archives.

[34] Carnegie to Easley, New York, March 24, 1908, Box 95, NCF papers.

[35] Quoted in Jensen, "National Civic Federation," p. 289.

reason." Under Justice White's new majority view, the Sherman Act was held simply to apply common law standards to the terms monopolize and restraint of trade. As White put it, "in determining what is meant by restraint of trade we must have regard to the common law and common law usages of the time when the Sherman Act was passed." [36]

This decision was extremely important. Taft, who agreed all along with the Civic Federation's attempts to amend the Sherman Act (as a federal judge back in 1898 Taft had disagreed with the Supreme Court's strict interpretation of the Act), saw it as eliminating the need for further legislative action, except of an advisory nature. Not only did he praise the Standard Oil and American Tobacco decisions as prescribing a standard of business practices "not difficult for honest and intelligent business men to follow," but he now began to use prosecutions under the Act as a means of regulation. In the last year and a half of his term, Taft instituted two thirds of the 89 cases brought under the Sherman Act during his administration.[37]

The dominant business interests, however, were not at all happy with Taft's legalistic approach to the problem. Their prior experience with the Supreme Court had not been satisfactory, and in any case litigation was too uncertain and too lengthy. Uncertainty was inevitable during the entire course of a prosecution under the Sherman Act, and the judicial procedure from indictment to trial and through the appeals could take several years. To a lawyer like Taft such a process seemed natural; to businessmen it was intolerable. Political relations between Taft and Roosevelt had been previously strained by the Pinchot-Ballinger controversy, but with Taft's initiation of prosecution of the United States Steel Corporation the final break occurred. While Taft increasingly relied on litigation, his Attorney General, George W. Wickersham, began

[36] Quoted in the *New York Commercial*, May 31, 1911.
[37] Sklar, "Emergence of the Corporate Liberal Order," pp. 222–224.

to emphasize the excellence of the Sherman Act and to oppose legislation to specify and prohibit particular unfair practices.[38] To men like George W. Perkins, Elbert H. Gary,
Cyrus McCormick, and Frederick A. Delano, such a development was inexcusable. Roosevelt articulated their views in his
attack on Taft in November 1911, in which he defended his
detente with United States Steel in 1905–1907 and again
called for regulation by an executive agency.

Roosevelt's approach was supported widely in big business
circles. Frederick Delano argued before the Toledo Transportation Club that an interstate trade commission with "exactly
the authority which the Interstate Commerce Commission
has over the railroads" was needed. "The Commission does
not make rates," he observed, "but it has a right to say that
they are too high or to fix a maximum, and the right to say
that they are discriminatory, which obviously gives them the
right to say that they are too low." [39] A few months earlier,
at hearings of the Stanley Committee of the House to investigate United States Steel, Gary told the astonished Democratic majority that he believed in enforced publicity and government control "even as to prices." "I would," he added, "be
very glad if we knew exactly where we stand, if we could be
freed from danger, trouble, and criticism by the public." What
he sought was some means to go "to a responsible governmental authority, and say to them, 'Here are our facts and figures
. . . now you tell us what we have the right to do and what
prices we have the right to charge.'" The Democratic majority, representing the consciousness of the small producer,
viewed Gary's proposals as "semisocialistic." [40]

The same day that Gary testified, Cyrus McCormick

[38] *Ibid.*, p. 224.
[39] "Questions of the Hour," F. A. Delano, Toledo, November 24, 1911,
copy in Low papers, Box 123.
[40] Quoted in Gabriel Kolko, *The Triumph of Conservatism* (New York,
Free Press, Macmillan, 1963), p. 174.

dropped into the Civic Federation office in New York and urged its committee to draw up legislation. McCormick told Easley that he agreed with Roosevelt's position entirely and that he would be glad to have the government fix the price of the products of the International Harvester Company. As Easley reported to Seth Low, "All this is certainly going along pretty rapidly." [41]

The new ferment over the meaning of the Sherman Act, and the continuing uncertainty of threatened litigation, led George Perkins and Low to agree that the country was "now ripe for a solution of this question." [42] Even Senator La Follette now saw a need for an interstate trade commission to control the trusts. Otherwise, he commented in his speech to the Periodical Publishers Association in February 1912, control of the corporations will be left in the hands of the federal courts, "acting as a commission." La Follette proposed a commission empowered to enforce "specific prohibitions against well-known practices that constitute unreasonable restraints of trade," such as price cutting in particular localities for the purpose of destroying competition, and other forms of direct discrimination against retailers. [43]

These proposals were acceptable to the large corporations; some had been made by Roosevelt's Attorney General Philander Knox as early as 1903. [44]

La Follette also suggested that the burden of proof that a particular contract in restraint of trade was reasonable be placed on the "trust" involved, and he opposed government price fixing of manufactured goods on the ground that price setting "assumes that we are dealing with a necessary monopoly," whereas the commercial monopolies (as opposed to

[41] Easley to Low, New York, June 2, 1911, Box 146, Low papers.
[42] Easley to Low, New York, September 15, 1911, Box 146, Low papers.
[43] *La Follette's Autobiography*, p. 336.
[44] Knauth, *The Policy of the United States Towards Industrial Monopoly*, pp. 75–76.

railroads and public utilities) were "based on unfair and discriminatory practices." [45] These latter proposals were contrary to the views of large corporation leaders, but price fixing was not an important issue, and the question of the burden of proof could easily be dropped in the process of legislative jockeying. The point was that the Standard Oil decision brought even the arch neopopulist La Follette to favor administrative regulation, so long sought by the Civic Federation.

Actually, even while the Supreme Court was preparing its decision in the Standard Oil case, Senator Francis G. Newlands, a Nevada Democrat, was consulting with Herbert Knox Smith and Perkins about a bill to create an interstate trade commission. Newlands was himself a member of the National Civic Federation and worked closely with Easley and Low. Early in July, Easley spent a morning with him discussing his trade commission bill and the possibilities of a bill for federal licensing of corporations.[46] But Newlands' bill was not a Federation bill, although it corresponded closely to the Federation's general objectives. It eliminated the Bureau of Corporations, substituted a commission and required all corporations in interstate trade with annual receipts of over five million dollars to file organizational and financial data with the commission. Even Newlands saw his proposal as tentative. Its value was in raising the issue publicly and in the hearings that gave a forum to businessmen. Perkins used the occasion of the hearings to urge upon Seth Low that his committee on combinations and regulation produce some resolutions, or, better, a bill of its own. He saw previous meetings of the Federation on the "trust" question, although "pertinent and valuable," as educational undertakings that were "ahead of the times for real action." By late 1911, however,

[45] *La Follette's Autobiography*, p. 336.
[46] Easley to Low, New York, July 10, 1911, Box 146, Low papers.

the passage of some form of trade commission act seemed assured.[47]

Seeing the time ready for action, the Federation rapidly undertook to develop a proposed bill. Support from business leaders and corporations indicated that there was a general understanding that the "rule of reason" decision had set the stage for amending the Sherman Act. It was now clear that under that law bigness per se was no longer an issue, nor was combination or consolidation. Since, in the absence of legislative definition, it was now up to the courts to decide what constituted unreasonable restraints of trade, it was inevitable that small producers would attempt to draw such legislative definitions. Corporation leaders therefore rushed to apply the principle enunciated by Samuel Insull in 1909: when it is only a matter of time before regulation shall be brought about, it is better to "help shape the right kind of regulation than to have the wrong kind forced upon" you.[48] Following this maxim, Elbert H. Gary, acting in his capacity as president of the American Iron and Steel Institute, assigned its counsel to work with the Federation in drawing up a bill and to assist it "in every possible way."[49]

The Federation moved on two fronts in the fall of 1911: it sent a questionnaire on the desirability of a commission to some thirty thousand businessmen, and it began to draw up a model bill. In November, at the Newlands hearings, Low testified that preliminary returns indicated that American businessmen favored federal incorporation by almost four to one, that they favored a federal licensing law by nearly two to one, and that they favored an interstate trade commission "with powers not unlike those now enjoyed by the Interstate

[47] Kolko, *Triumph of Conservatism*, p. 175; Easley to Low, New York, September 15, 1911, Box 146, Low papers.
[48] Easley to George W. Perkins, New York, June 9, 1909, Box 38, NCF papers.
[49] Easley to Low, New York, September 23, 1911, Box 146, Low papers.

Commerce Commission" by almost three to one.[50] On the legislative proposals, the Federation set up a committee that met for a year and then appointed a subcommittee consisting of Seth Low, Jeremiah W. Jenks, Professor John B. Clark, and Talcott Williams to prepare specific legislation. The product of these discussions was a bill that won Federation approval and was finally printed (and marked "confidential") on December 16, 1913. That bill was then sent to Senator Newlands, to Representative Henry D. Clayton, to newly elected President Wilson's Commissioner of Corporations, Joseph E. Davies, and to the President himself.[51] The Federation's timing coincided almost exactly with the actions of Newlands, Clayton, and the President with respect to legislation leading to the Federal Trade Commission Act.

According to Senator Newlands' report on the history of the Commission legislation, he and Representative Clayton (as chairman of the Interstate Commerce Committee of the Senate and of the Judiciary Committee of the House) met with the President in December 1913 to frame tentative measures to submit to their respective committees. The next month, on January 20, 1914, Wilson spoke of the need to define what was legal in business practice and what was not, that is, to remove the "uncertainty" under which business was suffering. At that time he publicly called for a commission. A day or two later Clayton and Newlands introduced identical bills in the House and the Senate.[52]

There were, of course, many bills for a trade commission in both the Senate and the House by 1914. La Follette had introduced his own bill in 1911 and Senator Albert B. Cummins had introduced one in 1912 after consultation with

[50] Kolko, *Triumph of Conservatism*, p. 176.

[51] Low to Newlands and Clayton, both New York, December 13, 1913, Box 50; Easley to Davies, New York, January 15, 1914, Box 51; Low to Woodrow Wilson, New York, January 13, 1914, Box 51: all NCF papers.

[52] *Senate Report No. 597*, 63rd Congress, Second Session, June 13, 1914 (Federal Trade Commission). Copy in Box 105, Low papers.

Perkins and correspondence with Easley.[53] But Newlands' bill was similar to Low's draft and differed from the final Federal Trade Commission (FTC) Act in the same manner—both Low's and Newlands' drafts included a federal licensing provision for the conduct of interstate business. Low's bill was almost a model for the final legislation in every other respect. In Low's draft the Bureau of Corporations was to be dissolved and absorbed into the trade commission. That commission was to have the power to investigate corporation practices and to require annual reports of corporation activities. It was to regulate corporation practices under the principles of the Supreme Court's rule of reason, that is, in accordance with common law precedents. The FTC Act included these same provisions. In Low's draft the Commission was to have seven members with no more than four from one party. In the FTC Act the Commission consisted of five members with no more than three from one party.

The actual process of negotiation on the Federal Trade Commission Act between January 1914, when the first draft was introduced by Newlands and Clayton, and September 26, when the Act was signed by Wilson, was complex. George Rublee, an attorney who had been active in Roosevelt's Progressive Party was closely involved in discussions with Wilson, as were Charles McCarthy of the Wisconsin Legislative Reference Bureau and Louis D. Brandeis.[54] But the details of the legislative process in these months was of no great significance. The ideas embodied in the Federal Trade Commission Act represented a triumph of the agitation and education done by the NCF over the previous seven years. As Talcott Williams commented to the Federation's Executive Council in 1916, "nothing could have been more chaotic than the opinions of the country in regard to trusts" in 1907. Indeed, at that time

[53] Albert B. Cummins to Easley, Washington, D.C., September 5, 1911, Box 146, Low papers; Kolko, *Triumph of Conservatism*, p. 178.

[54] Kolko, *Triumph of Conservatism*, pp. 264–265.

"the people believed that they should be abolished and liqui-
dated." Of course, Williams added, "everyone is familiar with"
the platform adopted by the Civic Federation, and "when one
reads the bills now on the statute books one will see the profound effect which we had on the action of Congress." [55]

Jeremiah W. Jenks was much more specific in reviewing
the Federation's role in his report of the Department of Regulation of Industrial Corporations at the 17th Annual Meeting
of the Federation in January 1917. The panic of 1907, Jenks
began, brought to the fore interest in "the industrial corporations and the part that they play in our business system."
President Roosevelt, who had been "one of the strongest advocates of rigid supervision and control of the great corporations while at the same time believing that mere size and
power of a corporation ought not to be condemned," consulted
closely with president Low in preparation of the Hepburn bill.
"The bill had the full approval of the President," Jenks reminded his audience, "and in fact had been shaped in part in
accordance with his suggestions, although leading lawyers and
officials of corporations and labor men and special students
of the question had all cooperated" in preparing it. The substance of the bill, Jenks continued, was that "in the interpretation of the Sherman Act the 'rule of reason' should apply,"
and further, that the powers of the Bureau of Corporations
should be extended "so as to give it substantially the powers
now exercised by the Federal Trade Commission."

The decisions of the Supreme Court in the Standard Oil
and Tobacco cases in 1911, Jenks explained, "went far toward
clarifying the law by declaring that the rule of reason should
apply in the application of the law to specific cases." But this
created a more urgent need "for an administrative body that
should be in a position to make clear in certain cases of corporations the legal propriety of certain lines of business ac-

[55] "Proceedings of the Meeting of the Executive Council of the NCF,"
October 23, 1916, p. 13, Box 189, NCF papers.

tivity," and to "secure information of such a nature as to further general public interests." This need had been met by the Federal Trade Commission, which was in a position to "indicate clearly what are considered 'unfair methods of competition' in commerce, to investigate thoroughly foreign trade combinations, to prescribe certain uniform methods of report which determines likewise methods of accounting," and which had also "certain quasi-judicial powers in making recommendation to the Attorney General for the readjustment of any corporation found to be violating the antitrust acts." The Federal Trade Commission, Jenks added happily, "has apparently been carrying on its work with the purpose of securing the confidence of well intentioned business men, members of the great corporations as well as others." [56] In short, for Jenks as for most of the business members of the NCF, the judicial, legislative, and administrative history of the FTC had been on the whole satisfactory. After years of uncertainty and contest, both with the smaller businessmen in the NAM and with the insurgent progressives, the large corporations achieved the stability they sought, at the hands of Woodrow Wilson. In a second speech to the Federation meeting, Jenks affirmed the general feeling of relief among leaders of the large corporations and their understanding that the FTC was helpful to the corporations in every way.

[56] J. W. Jenks, "Report of the Department of Regulation of Industrial Corporations, 17th Annual Meeting," Departmental Reports folder, Box 187, NCF papers; Minutes of the meeting of the NCF, New York, January 22, 1917, Box 188, *ibid.*

CHAPTER FOUR

The Small Businessman as Big Businessman: The City Commission and Manager Movements

On a national scale big businessmen tended to be the leaders for reform and regulation, while the smaller manufacturers and commercial men often took a narrower, or more immediately interest-conscious, view. In the movement for an interstate trade commission, later embodied in the Federal Trade Commission, and in the agitation for workmen's compensation, as we have seen, the executives of leading financial institutions and of large corporations (especially those associated with the National Civic Federation), assumed the initiative. The National Association of Manufacturers, which represented small manufacturers and was suspicious of financiers, dragged its feet until its membership was gradually converted to support for, or acquiescence in, the new reforms. But on a municipal level the small businessman sometimes displayed a broader vision. He was in his own domain and tended, on this scale, to assume attitudes of social responsibility. As participants in local chambers of commerce and boards of trade, local businessmen could identify the future of their cities with that of their own business interests. To rationalize and make more attractive a particular city meant more business for its local entrepreneurs. The centralization of power, or the removal of decision making from "politics," favored businessmen over workingmen or white collar employees. In no area of political or social reform did small businessmen more clearly demonstrate the force of this logic than in the movements for city commission and manager governments.

The idea later embodied in commission and council manager government was enunciated as early as 1896 by Dayton, Ohio, industrial pioneer, John H. Patterson. In a speech at the Dayton centennial, the founder and president of the National Cash Register Company argued that "a city is a great business enterprise whose stockholders are the people." If Patterson had his way, "municipal affairs would be placed on a strict business basis" and directed "not by partisans, either Republican or Democratic, but by men who are skilled in business management and social science." [1] It was not until five years after Patterson spoke that the first commission government came into being, and it was a dozen years before the movement took root and began rapidly to spread. At first, the commission idea was only one plan in what a leading civic reformer described in 1903 as a "hopeless diversity" of remedies for the inefficiency and poor service of American city governments.[2] Yet so well did this "most far reaching progressive proposal for institutional change" [3] fulfill the requirements of business that it was quickly adopted by hundreds of boards of trade and chambers of commerce. Today commission and council manager governments are the prevailing forms of municipal organization, in use in almost half of all American cities.

Of course, the drive for municipal reform at the turn of the century did not come from businessmen alone. Graft, corruption, and the misery of slum life had been given wide publicity by reformers and journalists, and by single taxers and

[1] Quoted in Landrum C. Bolling, "Dayton, Ohio," in Frederick C. Mosher, et al., *City Manager Government in Seven Cities* (Chicago, Public Administration Service, 1940), p. 266.

[2] Clinton R. Woodruff, "An American Municipal Program," *Political Science Quarterly*, XVIII (March 1903), p. 48.

[3] Arthur S. Link, *American Epoch: The History of the United States since the 1890's* (New York, Alfred A. Knopf, 1958), p. 85.

socialists. Muckrakers Jacob Riis, Lincoln Steffens, B. O. Flower, and others had exposed the "Shame of the Cities"; successful reform movements had been led by mayors Tom Johnson of Cleveland and Samuel (Golden Rule) Jones of Toledo, and by many other men less well known. The business community did not support this variety of reform, tinged as it was with radical social theories. Indeed, many early reformers concluded that business interests strongly supported the old system of corruption. In 1906 the Cleveland reformer, Frederick C. Howe, wrote that it was "privilege of an industrial rather than a personal sort that has given birth to the boss." Howe had entered political life "with the conviction that our evils were traceable to personal causes"—to the "foreign voter" and to the indifference of the "best" citizens. But experience forced him to a new belief: democracy had failed "by virtue of the privileged interests which have taken possession of our institutions for their own enrichment." From a belief in a "businessman's government" he, like Lincoln Steffens and journalist-reformer Brand Whitlock, had come to believe in a "people's government." [4] Even so conservative a man as William J. Gaynor, mayor of New York City, commented in 1910 that the true corrupters were the "so-called 'leading' citizens" who "get a million dollars out of the city dishonestly while the 'boss' gets a thousand." [5]

As Howe understood, businessmen opposed social reformers such as Jones and Johnson because their administrations disrupted the working relationships between business and the local political machine without providing a suitable and dependable alternative—and also because Jones and Johnson in-

[4] Frederick C. Howe, *The City, The Hope of Democracy* (New York, Charles Scribner's Sons, 1906), quoted in *Arena*, XXV (May 1906), pp. 512–513; see also Lincoln Steffens, *Autobiography* (New York, Harcourt Brace, 1931), pp. 430–435, 572–574.

[5] William J. Gaynor, "The Problem of Efficient City Government," *Century*, LXXX (September 1910), p. 666.

creased the political power of labor and radicals.[6] Aversion to graft, alone, was not enough to move businessmen to sponsor reform. Though costly, business had accepted and lived with graft for many years. What converted these men into civic reformers was the increased importance of the public functions of the twentieth-century city. Streets had to be paved for newly developed motor vehicles; harbors had to be deepened and wharves improved for big, new freighters. In addition, electric lighting systems, street railways, sewage disposal plants, water supplies, and fire departments had to be installed or drastically improved to meet the needs of inhabitants, human and commercial, of hundreds of rapidly growing industrial centers.

Municipal services had always been expensive, but as they increased in magnitude and number, costs tended to grow more and more burdensome. In city after city, business circles came to realize that something had to be done. Boston in 1909 was described as "another city whose businessmen have awakened to a new sense of their civic responsibilities" because "the debt of the city was increasing by leaps and bounds, apparently out of all proportion to the improvements for which it was incurred." At the same time the "extraordinary expenses" of municipal services in Chicago moved the Commercial Club of that city to work out a "general scheme of public improvements," known as the "Plan of Chicago." [7] In

[6] Frederick C. Howe, *Confessions of a Reformer* (New York, Charles Scribner's Sons, 1925), pp. 98 ff. Neither Jones nor Johnson, both of whom were single taxers, succeeded in building a permanent political base. This instability was typical of reform administrations in those years; it was rare that one lasted two terms or more. See, for example, Bird S. Coler, "Mistakes of Professional Reformers," *Independent*, LIII (June 20, 1901), pp. 1405–1407; Joseph D. Miller, "The Futilities of Reformers," *Arena*, XXVI (November 1901), pp. 481–489; E. R. L. Gould, "Civic Reform and Social Progress," *International Monthly*, III (March 1901), pp. 344–358.

[7] Arthur H. Grant, "The Conning Tower," *American City* (October 1909), p. 68; Walter B. Snow, "The Cost of Inefficiency in Municipal Work," *ibid.*, pp. 77–82. Charles H. Wacker, "The Plan of Chicago," *ibid.*, p. 50.

the search for alternatives, the commission and manager plans emerged as most promising. They offered stability; they were less expensive; they were devoid of commitment to radical social theories; and they assured businessmen of a more direct and central role in municipal affairs.

The first commission government emerged from the backwash of the great tidal wave that virtually destroyed Galveston, Texas, in 1900. Left in ruins, with a government unable to cope with the situation, the city was on the edge of bankruptcy. In the emergency, the old, corrupt aldermanic system was abandoned and an organization of local businessmen, the Deepwater Committee, took control. This group, which had been formed earlier to promote harbor improvements, looked on Galveston "not as a city, but [as] a great ruined business." Setting out to establish a new government capable of quick, efficient action in rebuilding a modern city and port, these businessmen evolved a plan for government that closely followed the most efficient form of organization known to them: the business corporation.[8] The theory of the commission plan echoed John H. Patterson's view. It was that "a municipality is largely a business corporation," and, as such, that it should seek "to apply business methods to public service." The voters were seen as stockholders, and the commissioners as corresponding to the board of directors of "an ordinary business corporation."[9]

As adopted, the Galveston plan provided for a five man commission vested with the combined powers of mayor and board of aldermen. Each commissioner headed a city department and functioned as legislator and administrator. The Commission, because it handled all city business, could act

[8] George K. Turner, "Galveston: A Business Corporation," *McClure's*, XXVII (October 1906), p. 612.

[9] Carl Doheney, "Commission Government and Democracy," *American City*, II (February 1910), p. 77.

promptly and efficiently, and the relative prominence and broad powers given each commissioner "assured" the attraction of "good" men to office. In short, it was a plan to make government more businesslike and to attract businessmen to government.

Commission government spread rapidly through Texas: first to Houston in 1903, then by 1907 to Dallas, Dennison, Fort Worth, El Paso, Greenville, and Sherman. In 1907 Des Moines, Iowa, enacted a commission charter, and to the accompaniment of nationwide publicity the "Texas Idea" was renamed for its Northern imitator. By 1913 over 300 cities from coast to coast had adopted the "Des Moines Plan."

Yet even while commission government was winning quick and widespread acceptance, serious structural weaknesses appeared. The election of popular but incompetent administrators, men who played politics better than they ran city departments, revealed the disadvantages of combining executive and legislative functions in the commissioners. Individual commissioners often attempted to consolidate their positions by securing excessive appropriations in order either to strengthen their own departments or simply to reward their supporters with city jobs. Since the commissions as a whole fixed both appropriations and policy, the consent of the other commissioners was necessary, and a system of favor-trading often developed in the commissions, side by side with interdepartmental rivalries. In many cases "five separate governments" tended to develop around the five commissioners.[10]

To overcome these weaknesses, municipal reform leader H. S. Gilbertson drew up a "commission-manager" plan in 1910, and the board of trade of Lockport, New York, spon-

[10] H. S. Gilbertson, "Some Serious Weaknesses of the Commission Plan," *American City*, IX (September 1913), pp. 236–237; Charles M. Fasset, "The Weakness of Commission Government," *National Municipal Review*, IX (October 1920), pp. 642–647.

sored it as its proposed new city charter.[11] The Lockport proposal, as Gilbertson's plan was called, separated the legislative and executive functions by retaining an elected commission to legislate for the city, while providing for an appointed manager to assume all executive functions. Under this plan executive ability was no longer a prerequisite for successful commissioners. At the same time the day-to-day management of city affairs was removed from more direct political pressures by the creation of an independent office for the manager, who was hired on a contractual basis to carry out the policies set by the commission.

Under the Lockport proposal departmental appointments, as well as the expenditure of city funds, were, for the most part, placed in the manager's hands. Despite the efforts of the Lockport board of trade, the manager charter was defeated in the New York legislature in 1911, and once again the South took the lead when Sumter, South Carolina, secured a "commission-manager" charter the same year. But, as with the original commission plan, the manager movement received national impetus only after a Northern city, Dayton, Ohio, adopted the plan in 1913. Thereafter, the "Dayton Plan" spread rapidly, and in six years more than 130 cities had put through manager charters.[12]

[11] Staunton, Virginia, had appointed a manager in 1908, but because of charter limitations the Staunton experiment did not include commission government and was not conceived as a refinement of that plan. See Henry Oyen, "A City with a General Manager," *World's Work*, XXIII (December 1911), p. 223.

[12] Richard S. Childs, "The Lockport Proposal," *American City*, IV (June 1911), pp. 285–287; F. D. Silvernail, "The Lockport Proposal," *Annals of the American Academy of Political and Social Science*, XXXVIII (November 1911), pp. 884–887; City Managers' Association, *Fifth Yearbook* (New York, 1919), p. 161; Harold A. Stone, Don K. Price, and Katherine H. Stone, *City Manager Government in the United States* (Chicago, Public Administration Service, 1940), pp. 10–11; Don K. Price, "The Promotion of the City Manager Plan," *Public Opinion Quarterly*, V (Winter 1941), pp. 563–578.

The Small Businessman as Big Businessman

The initiative for commission and manager government came consistently from chambers of commerce and other organized business groups; they were the decisive element, in coalition with civic reformers, which made the movement a sweeping success. We have seen that the businessmen's Deepwater Committee originated the commission plan in Galveston, and that the Board of Trade sponsored the manager plan in Lockport. Similarly, in Des Moines, the Commercial Club led the commission movement after a local lawyer, James G. Berryhill, had discovered "a city government approaching the ideal" on a business trip to Galveston in 1905. Berryhill, exulting over the idea that the commission managed Galveston "as a board of directors manages a bank," returned home a champion of the new reform.

After securing its adoption in Des Moines he turned his attention to Pennsylvania, where the plan won approval of the Pittsburgh chamber of commerce in 1909. In turn, the Pittsburgh businessmen organized a convention of representatives of commercial bodies of all the second- and third-class cities of Pennsylvania, which met at Williamsport in 1910. After hearing Berryhill describe the advantages of Commission government, the delegates—bankers, merchants, and manufacturers who stood in the first rank of Pennsylvania businessmen—voted unanimously to support legislation to permit the adoption of commission charters. They also pledged to press a campaign of education for the new form of civic government and went home to do battle with their local political machines. In June 1913, their efforts bore fruit when an act passed the Pennsylvania legislature *requiring* all cities of the third class to adopt commission charters.[13]

[13] "The Originator of the Des Moines Plan," *Hampton's Magazine* (February 1911), pp. 248–249; Benjamin F. Shambaugh, "Commission Government in Iowa: The Des Moines Plan," *Annals*, XXXVIII (November 1911), pp. 698–718; A. M. Fuller, "Commission Government of all Third-Class

In individual cities, too, business leaders pushed through commission charters. In Dallas, Texas, a "prominent banker" headed a "citizens committee" that drafted a charter enacted by the state legislature in 1907. In Columbia, South Carolina, the local chamber of commerce recommended a commission charter in 1912. And in Charlotte, North Carolina, the chamber of commerce led the movement for commission government in 1917.[14]

The manager movement, like the commission, also was led by chambers of commerce and boards of trade. The first manager charter in Sumter, South Carolina, for example, was promoted by the local chamber. Dayton was a model of business sponsorship. There the chamber of commerce set up a committee of five members, headed by John H. Patterson. He set up a Bureau of Municipal Research, which, in turn, "plunged into an aggressive campaign of public education."

Meanwhile, the chamber "began to suspect that its open sponsorship of a new charter might seem an evil omen to many of the ordinary workingclass voters." Accordingly, it ceased its official participation, and the original committee was increased, first to fifteen, and finally to one hundred. The new citizens' committee then hired the former secretary of the Detroit Board of Commerce, who built a broad coalition in support of the reform. Despite these efforts the opposition to the new charter on the part of the Democratic and Socialist parties appeared to doom the manager plan in Dayton, until,

Cities of Pennsylvania," *American City*, IX (August 1913), pp. 123–124; League of Cities of Third Class of Pennsylvania," *Proceedings of the Annual Convention* (1910), p. 126; *Board of Trade and Engineering Journal* (Scranton, Pennsylvania), VI (November 1910), pp. 7–8.

[14] Stone, Price, and Stone, *City Manager Government in Dallas* (Chicago, Public Administration Service, 1939), p. 9; Stone, *et al.*, *City Manager Government in Janesville (Wisconsin)* (Chicago, P.A.S., 1939), p. 6; Christie Benet, "A Campaign for a Commission Form of Government," *American City*, III (December 1910), pp. 276–278; Stone, *et al.*, *City Manager Government in Charlotte* (Chicago, P.A.S., 1939), p. 4.

as in Galveston, an act of God intervened in behalf of the businessmen. A short time before the charter election, Dayton suffered a devastating flood; when the mayor proved unable to cope with the problems it created, John H. Patterson took charge of the city. Patterson used his factory, fortunately located on high ground, as a rescue headquarters; quickly manufactured many makeshift boats; housed and fed flood victims; and as the waters receded stood out as hero and leader.[15] In the election, the manager charter carried easily.

After Dayton installed its new manager, chambers of commerce rapidly extended their activity in behalf of the plan. In Glen Falls, New York, the local chamber conducted a canvass for a manager charter. In Jackson, Michigan, the chamber proposed a "commission-manager system," which carried despite opposition from working class wards. In Kalamazoo, the newly organized chamber of commerce listed manager government as the second point on its program. In Defiance, Ohio, the chamber sponsored a high school oratorical contest on city government: the winner spoke on "One Man Management of Cities." In St. Augustine, Florida, the chamber prepared a manager charter and secured its adoption. In Benton Harbor, Michigan, the manager charter was twice rejected at the polls; undaunted, the local chamber of commerce pressed again for its acceptance.

Commission and manager government had become the favorite of local business—because the new municipal governments met their most obvious needs.[16] From the be-

[15] "The City Manager Adopted by Sumter, South Carolina," *American City*, VII (July 1912), p. 38; Fred W. Francher, "Two Epoch-Making Campaigns in Dayton, Ohio," *ibid.*, IX (July 1913), pp. 47–49; Isaac F. Marcosson, "Business Managing a City," *Collier's*, January 3, 1914, pp. 5–6; Landrum C. Bolling, "Dayton, Ohio," pp. 268 ff.

[16] *American City*, XII (May, June 1915), pp. 416, 515; XIII (July, August, November 1914), pp. 44, 136–137, 421; Stone, *et al.*, *City Manager Government in Jackson (Michigan)* (Chicago, P.A.S., 1939), p. 8.

ginning the new form of government permitted substantial increases in the services provided by the city, at little or no extra cost, and often at considerable savings. In Galveston, for example, the commission found the city bankrupt in 1901. By 1906 it had brought the value of the city's paper to above par. In these years the entire city had been rebuilt, a giant seawall erected, the grade of most of the city raised, and the harbor improved by the addition of many new deepwater wharves: all at an annual saving of $220,000, one third of the old budget. In Houston, too, after five years of commission government, the tax rate had been reduced 30¢ per $100, while the cost of city water had been reduced from 50¢ to 15¢ per 1,000 gallons. During this period the commission expended $1,865,757 for improvements, all out of current revenue. In Des Moines, after one year the commission showed a saving of $184,000 over the old system of "graft and extravagance." During this year new public buildings were built, the civic center was landscaped, and the river banks were walled. Similarly, in Leavenworth, Kansas, a saving of $26,000 was anticipated in the first year of the commission, despite the expense of better services.[17]

Manager cities followed the same pattern. In the three years from 1908 to 1911, Staunton, Virginia, was "lifted from mud to asphalt" and placed on a sound financial basis, with no increase in expenditures. The new manager paved streets at ten times the former pace, improved the water system, and installed modern lighting; in the process he increased the value of the city's paper by almost one hundred percent. In Austin, Texas, similar improvements were made. In Dayton, under

[17] Turner, "Galveston," pp. 610–620; William O. Scroggs, Commission Government in the South," AAP&SS *Annals*, XXXVIII (November 1911), pp. 682–687; H. J. Haskell, "The Texas Idea: 'City Government by a Board of Directors,'" *The Outlook*, LXXXV (April 3, 1907), pp. 839–843; *American City*, II (April 1910), p. 190; "The Des Moines Plan of City Government," *World's Work*, XVIII (May 1909), p. 11533.

the manager, the tax rate was increased slightly, but improvements were achieved in all areas of municipal activity.[18]

In addition to the money saved and the indirect benefits to business in the form of improved facilities and services, some commission and manager governments directly subsidized their local entrepreneurs. When, for example, the Oakland, California, commission floated a bond issue of $2,500,-000 for harbor improvements it also imposed a tax of 2½¢ per $1,000 for municipal advertising and the entertainment of visitors. And in Amarillo, Texas, the commission-manager government imposed a direct tax of two mills to maintain the local chamber of commerce.[19]

The argument that commission and manager charters would assure the election of "good" (i.e., business) men to office usually proved valid. The first commission in Galveston comprised five businessmen—"a veteran wholesale merchant," a "promising young . . . banker," "an active partner in a prosperous wholesale house," "a successful real estate dealer," and the secretary-treasurer of a livestock concern—all "good, clean, representative men." In Austin, Mayor A. P. Wooldrige, himself a prominent banker, headed a "businessman's government" that stayed in office for ten years. In Janesville, businessmen were in the leadership under both the commission and manager charters. In Dayton, John H. Patterson and the chamber of commerce put up a hand-picked slate that won easily. In Springfield, Ohio, five experienced businessmen made up the commission, while in Jackson, Michigan, most of the councilmen from 1914 to 1919 were business executives,

[18] Oyen, "A City with a General Manager," pp. 221, 228; Burton J. Hendrick, "Taking the American City out of Politics," *Harper's*, CXXXVII (June 1918), pp. 106–113; Bolling, "Dayton, Ohio," pp. 276–277; Stone, *et al.*, *City Manager Government in Austin* (Chicago, P.A.S., 1939), pp. 5 ff.

[19] *American City*, V (October 1911), p. 225; Fulton, New York, Chamber of Commerce, Commission Manager Form of Government, August 19, 1915 (New York Public Library, New York), p. 1.

bankers or merchants, and the mayor during these years was also president of the chamber of commerce. In Illinois, too, the new commissions generally included several active businessmen, some of whom had not previously been active in politics.[20]

Even in cities where businessmen did not constitute a majority of its members, the commission remained strongly under their influence. In Des Moines, for example, the city council frequently met with the advisory board of the Commercial Club to consult on matters of public importance. In Omaha, the Commercial Club organized an advisory committee with the intention of meeting regularly with the seven-man commission, so that the commissioners might "profit by the advice of men who know." The logical culmination of this development occurred in Beaufort, South Carolina, where the offices of city manager and secretary of the board of trade were combined, with the city government and the local businessmen each paying one half the manager's salary. Commission and manager governments did, indeed, encourage businessmen to play a more direct role in municipal affairs.[21]

This being so, most businessmen were well satisfied with the operation of the new form of municipal government. In 1915, in an effort to decide whether or not to sponsor a commission-manager charter in its city, the chamber of commerce of Fulton, New York, sent a confidential inquiry to bankers and other leading businessmen in cities that had adopted the manager plan. Replies were received from thirty-two cities.

[20] Turner, "Galveston," p. 613; Stone, et al., *City Manager Government in Austin*, p. 5, *City Manager Government in Janesville* (*Wisconsin*), pp. 4–6; Francher, "Two Epoch-Making Campaigns in Dayton," pp. 47–49; Fulton Chamber of Commerce, Commission Manager Form of Government, p. 15; Stone, et al., *City Manager Government in Jackson* (*Michigan*), p. 15; John A. Fairlie, "Commission Government in Illinois Cities," AAP&SS *Annals*, XXXVIII (November 1911), p. 755.

[21] Ray F. Wierick, "The Development of Des Moines," *American City*, IV (May 1911), p. 203; VII (November 1912), pp. 567–568; X (April 1914), p. 381.

In twenty-eight, business leaders found the manager system highly satisfactory; in three they were disappointed; in one city they were divided.

Many reported substantial savings in the operation of their city government, while almost all boasted of increased services with no extra cost. Bank presidents and cashiers were almost unanimous in their praise of manager government. The assistant cashier of the River National Bank in Springfield, Ohio, wrote that "the business class of our citizens are very well satisfied." A bank president from Sherman, Texas, reported that "those who pay taxes are generally satisfied with the new system." The cashier of the Union Bank in Jackson, Michigan, wrote, "Its effect on business is favorable." From Montrose, Colorado, Charles A. Black replied, "I am one of the largest property owners and taxpayers here. . . . I find that our present city manager government is far superior and more satisfactory all around." Finally, the city manager of Manistee, Michigan, advised: "You cannot make any mistake in adopting this business form of government." [22]

Reformers in organizations of the genteel, such as the National Municipal League, often praised commission and manager government in traditional terms—for its simplicity, its concentration of responsibility, its intelligibility to the average voter.[23] But the main burden of defense of the new reform fell on business organizations, and they carried on the debate in business parlance. At the various conventions of state leagues of municipalities and at meetings of commercial bodies both critics and champions addressed themselves to the merits (or demerits) of businesslike government. At the 1910 convention of the League of Cities of the Third Class of Pennsylvania, for example, the delegates were told that "the

---

[22] Fulton Chamber of Commerce, Commission Manager Form of Government, pp. 1–16.

[23] See, for example, William B. Munro, "Ten Years of Commission Government," *National Municipal Review*, I (October 1912), pp. 567–568; also Childs, "The Lockport Proposal," pp. 285–287.

controlling idea" of commission government was the creation of a governing body which would conform as nearly as possible "to the organization of a great business corporation"; conventions of the League of Virginia Municipalities in 1909 and 1911 heard similar arguments. At the later meeting, E. A. Sherman, who described himself as "a practical businessman . . . and nothing else," told the delegates they should adopt the commission in order to attract new business concerns to their Southern cities—thus placing himself squarely in the mainstream of the concern of the new Southern progressives.[24]

The evolution of the commission into the council-manager plan only refined the argument. Defenders of the modification explained that it simply brought municipal government more closely into correspondence with corporate organization. The first manager charter, adopted in Sumter, South Carolina, was described as the "concentration of the administrative organization under the control of a single appointive manager in exactly the same way as a private business corporation." Similarly, in Dayton, the procedure of looking for a manager followed "precisely that of a large corporation looking for an executive head." In Cleveland a local newspaper urged that city "to adopt the modern method of managing a city like a stock company." [25]

The opponents of the new plans attacked the concept of the city-as-business. At the 1913 meeting of the League of Kansas Municipalities, the visiting secretary of the Iowa League argued that "a city is more than a business corpora-

[24] Joshua C. Taylor, "Causes and Effect of Commission Government," League of Cities of the Third Class of Pennsylvania, *Proceedings of the Annual Convention, 1910*, p. 117; League of Virginia Municipalities, *Sixth Annual Convention Report*, pp. 77–89. See, also, *Fourth Annual Convention Report*.

[25] "The City Manager Plan Adopted by Sumter, S.C.," p. 38; Hendrick, "Taking the American City out of Politics," p. 110; *Literary Digest*, LIV (February 17, 1917), p. 99.

tion," and that, while business principles should control financial actions, this was not the primary function of municipal government. "Good health," he concluded, "is more important than a low tax rate." [26] The same year the Washington League of Municipalities convention heard Spokane's commissioner of public safety complain of the tendency to run municipal government from a "cold-blooded business standpoint." Municipal government, the commissioner observed, "is more than a mere organization for business." [27]

Other opponents, particularly political machines in Northern cities, Socialists, and trade unionists, had more specific grievances. Their fears and opposition came from a belief that the commission and manager charters would, by design or not, eliminate workers or their representatives from active participation in the process of government.

The Socialist Party, which between 1910 and 1919 elected various municipal officers in over 300 cities, led in opposing many features of commission and manager plans. Three major features of the plans bore the brunt of Socialist criticism: the elimination of ward representation, which meant the end of minority representation; the extreme concentration of power in the hands of the commission, which meant quick decisions and little time to mobilize opposition; and the "fallacy" of the nonpartisan ballot, which meant the elimination of three-way contests for office and an emphasis on personality, rather than party.

One report of a Connecticut Socialist found that commission government was the product of the " 'merchant and capitalist class,' " and that commission-governed cities afforded a fine medium for " 'capitalists to advertise their business.' " In Pocatello, Idaho, the Socialist party took the lead in defeating a commission government charter, arguing that it was an

[26] League of Kansas Municipalities, *Proceedings*, 1913, p. 25.
[27] Washington League of Municipalities, *Proceedings*, 1913, p. 176.

" 'autocratic and exclusive form of city government.' " In Manitowoc, Wisconsin, where a Socialist was mayor, the party opposed a proposal for commission government and defeated the new charter by a vote of 298 to 1,049. In Hamilton, Ohio, a few days after the United States entered the First World War, the Socialists defeated an attempt to form a manager government. In Dayton, the Socialists became the main source of opposition to the manager charter, although the United Trades and Labor Council also opposed the new reform. There, the Socialists, Democrats, and Prohibitionists issued a pamphlet entitled *Dayton's Commission Manager Plan: Why Big Manufacturers, Bond Holders, and Public Franchise Grabbers Favor It, and Workingmen and Common People Oppose.*[28]

The elimination of patronage undoubtedly moved political machines in many cities to oppose commission government, but the opposition of the Socialists and labor, neither of which had much patronage to lose, cannot be so easily dismissed. Several features of the electoral process in commission and manager cities did favor business groups against labor and its political allies. The first of these was simple limitation of the right to vote. In Galveston, the original plan provided for the appointment of all five commissioners. The state legislature modified this to provide for the election of two of the five, but it took a court decision decreeing appointive government unconstitutional to make the Galveston commission fully elective. In Houston, the second commission city, a poll tax of $2.50 limited democracy by eliminating 7,500 "irresponsible" voters in a potential electorate of 12,000. And in New-

[28] William C. Seyler, "The Rise and Decline of the Socialist Party in the United States" (unpublished Ph.D. thesis, Duke University, 1952), pp. 237–238; *American City*, XII (June 1915), pp. 509–510; *Wisconsin Comrade*, I (June 1914), p. 1; Howard White, "Hamilton, Ohio," in Frederick C. Mosher, *et al.*, *City Manager Government in Seven Cities*, p. 183. Bolling, "Dayton, Ohio," p. 269.

port, Rhode Island, there was a similar restriction of the right to vote.[29] Overt limitation of suffrage, however, was out of keeping with the prevailing spirit of these years. Thus, when James G. Berryhill—himself a Progressive—introduced the plan in Des Moines, he added the initiative, the referendum, and the recall, as well as the nonpartisan ballot. These features became characteristic of commission and manager charters.[30]

Nevertheless, the heart of the plan, that of electing only a few men on a citywide vote, made election of minority or labor candidates more difficult and less likely. Before the widespread adoption of commission and manager government it was common for workingmen to enter politics and serve as aldermen, or even mayor. Socialists elected teamsters, machinists, cigar makers, railroad conductors and trainmen, tinners, carpenters, miners, and other workers to the mayoralty of dozens of cities and towns in these years.[31] But once the commission plan was in effect this became rare. Workingclass aldermen were hard hit because the resources needed to conduct a citywide campaign were much greater than those needed for a ward election, and because minorities—political, racial, or national—were usually concentrated in specific wards. In Dayton, for example, the Socialists received twenty-five percent of the vote in the election immediately preceding the adoption of the manager reform, electing two ward councilmen and three assessors. In 1913, after the manager charter was adopted, they received thirty-five percent of the vote and elected no one to the commission. In 1917 the party again

[29] Childs, "The Lockport Proposal," p. 285; Haskell, "The Texas Idea," p. 842; "Three Great Experiments," *Independent*, LXIV (June 18, 1908), pp. 1409–1410. Newport imposed a $134 property restriction on the right to vote.

[30] "The Originator of the Des Moines Plan," pp. 248–250. Berryhill had agitated for state regulation of railroads, when he was a state legislator in the late 1880's.

[31] See James Weinstein, *The Decline of Socialism in America, 1912–1925* (New York, Monthly Review Press, 1967), pp. 42–44.

increased its vote, this time to forty-four percent; again they elected no candidate.[32]

The nonpartisan ballot, a feature of most commission-manager plans and widely heralded as a great advance in democracy, also tended to operate against minority groups. Socialists claimed that the nonpartisan ballot gave great advantage to men of wealth and prominence, and that it gave a "terrific advantage" to the commercial press—although in fact, the Socialist Party often maintained its strength better in nonpartisan elections than did the major parties which depended heavily on patronage to hold together their organizations. To some degree, however, the nonpartisan ballot did handicap the workingclass candidates—most of whom were known only in their own neighborhoods and were without access to the press or adequate campaign funds. Theirs was a double task: to present themselves and their principles to the public. The nonpartisan ballot was a boon to the well-known man, and the well-known man, more often than not, was a leading merchant, manufacturer, or the lawyer of one or the other.[33] In addition, the combination of administrative and executive functions in the commission plan meant that the city could function smoothly only when experienced business executives were chosen to run it. The people of Wichita, Kansas, learned this when a former street laborer was elected to the commission. Being a street laborer, wrote reformer H. S.

[32] Seyler, "Rise and Decline of the Socialist Party," p. 237; *Dayton News*, November 7, 1917.

[33] Seyler, "Rise and Decline of the Socialist Party," p. 239. Socialists did not always oppose commission government. Home rule was the decisive test for them. In North Dakota, where a system of preferential voting was in effect, the Socialists were quite pleased with the commission plan. See William E. Walling (ed.), *Socialism of Today* (New York, Henry Holt, 1916), pp. 549 ff. In Birmingham, Alabama, Arlie Barber, a Socialist who campaigned as a party member, was elected to the commission on a nonpartisan ballot in 1915 but was defeated for re-election in 1917 after he had opposed the United States intervention in the war, and conscription. *Cleveland Citizen*, December 4, 1915; *Birmingham Age-Herald*, April 10, October 5, 9, 1917.

Gilbertson, was "an honest calling," and workers did have a right to representation. But, he asked, does this give "a man quite the preparation for managing one of the departments of a city?" [34]

Although the manager plan eliminated the problem of electing incompetent administrators, it strengthened the already strong tendency to regard the city as a "stock company." The method of electing the commission or council remained the same, and the manager, chosen by the commission or council, proved most often to be a man of limited social outlook, one who tended to think purely in business or, more narrowly, engineering terms. The reduction of expenditures made by the manager, while of great benefit to the taxpaying citizens, was often made at labor's expense. In Staunton, Virginia, for example, the new manager saved money by paying formerly full-time city employees only for those hours actually worked.[35]

The managers were usually proficient at increasing the efficiency of a fire department or reducing the cost of street paving, but social and political problems were often outside their range of interest. In 1918 Richard S. Childs (under whose direction H. S. Gilbertson had drawn up the Lockport Manager charter) suggested to the City Managers' Association, "Some day we shall have managers here who have achieved national reputation, not by . . . running their cities for a freakishly low expense per capita, but managers who have successfully led their commissions into great new enterprises of service." The advice was met with hostility. The managers, Leonard D. White notes, told Childs "directly that theorists were not welcome at the meetings of the Association." [36] Civil engineering, not social engineering, interested the manager; economy, not service, was his basic principle.

[34] Gilbertson, "Some Serious Weaknesses of the Commission Plan," p. 237.
[35] Oyen, "A City with a General Manager," p. 220.
[36] Leonard D. White, *The City Manager* (Chicago, 1927), p. 149.

Because of his training, the manager tended to share the corporate concept of the city: All elements of the community must be harmonized, but in the interest of the major stockholders. He identified with the growing tendency among Progressives to remove as many areas of social and economic decision making as possible from the realm of politics. An extreme statement of this view appeared in the magazine *Engineering and Contracting:* ". . . our entire system of 'representative government,' in which representation comes solely through elections, is an uneconomic system, and is destined shortly to be changed." [37]

There were many, besides the Socialists, who thought commission government had already changed the system of representation and had guaranteed business rule. Most of these men did not oppose the new plans *in toto,* but only wished to assure that the commissions reflect the makeup of the entire community. To this end, they proposed proportional representation in the elections to the commission, and revived the Proportional Representation League to lead the fight.

The League, which had been in existence since the early 1890's, had lain dormant for many years. In 1914, a year after Dayton installed its first city manager, the *Proportional Representation Review* renewed publication, and that year and the next many new members joined the League's council. Active in the rejuvenated League were Progressives like John R. Commons, William S. U'Ren, Charles A. Beard, and Ben B. Lindsey. The genteel reformers were represented by Charles W. Eliot, Albert Shaw, Charles Francis Adams, and DeLancy Verplanck, and the Socialists by Carl D. Thompson and Charles P. Steinmetz. Despite the activity of the League, however, proportional representation made little headway. In

[37] Quoted in *Literary Digest,* LIV (February 17, 1917), p. 399.

the eight years from 1914 to 1922 only five cities adopted this reform.[38]

In Dayton, where opposition to the unrepresentative council developed rapidly after the adoption of the manager charter, proportional representation failed because business groups opposed a reform which they believed could benefit only Socialists and Negroes.[39]

Nor was the fear of the Dayton businessmen without basis. In Kalamazoo, in the first proportional representation election in 1918, Truxton Talbot, a "radical Socialist," was elected to the commission. Thereafter, the inclination of Kalamazoo's "really representative" commission to do something "more directly of benefit to the people than cleaning the streets and lighting them" disturbed the business interests of the city, or so the manager claimed.[40] What happened in Kalamazoo must have confirmed the fears of many chambers of commerce and thereby strengthened their opposition to modifications of commission or manager charters. At any rate, the proportional representation movement had no more success than did Socialist and trade union attacks on the commission plans.

Business leaders did not intend to share with other classes in their cities any more than was necessary. They were willing to make concessions on program, however, particularly since many of the programs supported or demanded by reformers and workingmen made for greater efficiency and lessened class antagonisms. This led them, perhaps unknowingly in some instances, in the direction of municipal ownership, of increased planning, and, especially where the competition from radicals was keen, even toward social reform. In Dayton, for

[38] *Proportional Representation Review*, s.3 (October 1914–January 1922). The cities were Ashtabula, Ohio, 1915; Kalamazoo, Michigan, 1918; Sacramento, California, 1921; West Hartford, Connecticut, 1921; and Cleveland, Ohio, 1921.
[39] White, *City Manager*, pp. 77–78.
[40] *Proportional Representation Review*, s.3 (January 1920), p. 9.

example, after five years of manager government, municipal garbage collection had been instituted, a municipal asphalt plant built, new sewers (based on the projected needs of 1950) constructed, parks improved, new bridges erected, and a Department of Public Welfare established. The Welfare Department instituted milk inspection, free legal aid, a municipal employment agency, a municipal lodging house, medical examinations for school children, free vaccination, playgrounds, play festivals, and other social services, all on the theory that "happy workers are more efficient." [41]

The achievements in Dayton followed closely the ideology of John H. Patterson, a pioneer in the field of enlightened paternalism, as well as Dayton's leading citizen. Patterson, in consultation with the National Civic Federation, established a welfare organization of the National Cash Register Company to further the health and education of his employees, and to improve their working conditions. In addition, he built a schoolhouse on the factory grounds, which were landscaped as an "industrial garden." His motives as much "materialistic" as "humanitarian," Patterson boasted that he made the improvement because "it pays." Often a ruthless employer, he demanded and received maximum efficiency from his workers. His paternalism applied also to Dayton. For example, he created a vast park of several hundred acres and made it "as public as if it belonged to the city," but he retained the title to it. [42]

Dayton's attitude toward the functions of city government had much in common with other commission and manager cities. In Houston, for instance, there were no outstanding personalities like Patterson, no radical opposition, and the

[41] Hendrick, "Taking the American City out of Politics," pp. 111–113; the quotation is from Marcosson, "Business Managing a City," p. 24.
[42] Harry A. Toulmin, Jr., "John Henry Patterson," *Dictionary of American Biography*, XIV, pp. 304–305; Fred C. Kelly, "Dayton's Uncle Bountiful," *Collier's*, August 1, 1914, p. 8; *Encyclopedia of American Biography*, XXVII, p. 18.

poll tax restricted the electorate to a minority of the adult males. Yet the commission took over operation of the water works (and saved the city $400 per month), and at the same time the Health commissioner set up a city pharmacy and surgical room for the city poor in which he saved $100 to $150 per month by filling prescriptions and treating patients in the municipally owned clinic.[43]

All commissions aimed to reduce costs and increase services, and, since these were their first principles, most followed a policy of municipal planning and municipal ownership of some, if not all, utilities. To a large degree, therefore, the programs of the various business groups which led the commission and manager movements had points in common with those of many social reformers, and even with those of the Socialists.[44]

Fundamental differences between business groups and the genteel reformers, on the one hand, and Socialists, labor, and some of the more radical social reformers, on the other, did exist both in regard to what class should administer these programs and what the ultimate purpose of the programs should be. But the similarity of many immediate goals often debilitated the political opposition and helped assure the adoption of the commission and manager charters. Developed and led by business groups, the movement fulfilled the requirements of progressivism by rationalizing city government and institutionalizing the methods and values of the corporations that had come to dominate American economic life. The end result of the movements was to place city government firmly in the hands of the business class. And, interestingly, at what is normally considered the end of the Progressive Era, 1917, the manager movement spurted ahead at its highest rate of growth. This occurred in the five years from 1918 to 1923,

[43] Haskell, "The Texas Idea," pp. 840–841.
[44] See, for example, Raymond Moley, "Representation in Dayton and Ashtabula," *National Municipal Review*, VI (January 1918), pp. 28–29.

when 153 cities adopted manager charters, as compared to 87 in the five years before 1918, and 84 in the five years after 1923.[45]

During the First World War, chambers of commerce and boards of trade greatly intensified their antiradical and anti-labor activities, and in hundreds of small cities and towns Socialist locals were destroyed by the superpatriotic business groups. Just as the war would serve to institutionalize corporation-controlled regulatory agencies on a national level—as we will see—so on a local level the business organizations were able rapidly to press forward their political domination of American municipalities.

[45] Stone, *et al., City Manager Government in the United States* (Chicago, Public Administration Service, 1940), p. 30.

CHAPTER FIVE

SOCIALISM AND ITS ALTERNATIVE

ON A STATE AND NATIONAL level, as we have seen, the National Civic Federation concerned itself with specific reform legislation, while on a municipal level groups of local business leaders organized for reform of city government. In addition, the NCF and business leaders in and out of the Federation were concerned with general political and ideological problems. Central to these until after World War I was the problem of socialism, which, from its inception the NCF had understood to be the only serious ideological alternative to its politics of social responsibility. True, Easley and others railed against the "anarchism" of the small businessmen in the NAM and other "irresponsible" trade associations, but this was only because the laissez faire views of these men hindered the work of the NCF in winning the loyalty of workers and middle class groups to the emerging corporate system. Socialism, however, was the ideology with which the NCF had to compete *within* the union movement and among reformers.

As Ralph Easley commented time and time again, the worker with a Socialist philosophy "consistently and conscientiously oppose[d] anything that makes for peace," because the Socialist wanted "to help usher in at the earliest possible opportunity the revolution that he believes must be brought about before we can get back and begin afresh." [1] The NCF,

[1] Easley to Edward Kellog Baird, Esq., New York, April 18, 1913, Box 82, NCF papers. This view of the Socialists was expressed continuously by Easley from the inception of the NCF until the War.

of course, saw no need to "begin afresh." Seeking to win the firm loyalty of the workers to the corporations and the system as it existed, NCF leaders constantly identified the large corporations with an idealized social reality. Their attempts to convince individual entrepreneurs of the value of such an identification, and to win them to programs that would move other classes of people to accept their assertions as true lay at the center of NCF activity. As Marcus A. Hanna told the Executive Committee of the Federation in 1903, "success is not for today," but "for the future." "A movement like this, contributing to the advantage of all classes," had "a higher motive and better objects than the mere gaining of a point or points to a controversy. Looking into the future, this movement means the elevation of the laboring class to a higher plane." [2]

Hanna was not overly concerned with the danger that the Civic Federation would be bettered by Socialism. During his tenure as president, the Federation did little more than bait the Socialists for acting as allies of the Parryites within the National Association of Manufacturers in their hostility to interclass harmony. Hanna's lack of concern was natural; the Socialist Party was not formally organized until after the formation of the NCF, and showed no great strength between 1900 and 1904. Furthermore, with half the AFL membership being Irish Catholics, Hanna was convinced that the Church, along with the American school system, stood as a sufficient bulwark against Socialism.[3]

Eugene V. Debs' fourfold increase in votes in 1904, along with the increasing interest in independent politics shown by organized labor, created renewed interest in Socialism among NCF members and friends. Both Louis D. Brandeis and

[2] *NCF Monthly Review*, VI, 2 (June 1903), p. 7.
[3] See, for example, *ibid.*, I, 8 (October 15, 1904), p. 9; *ibid.*, I, 9 (November 15, 1904), p. 5; *ibid.*, VI, 4 (June 1904), p. 7.

Theodore Roosevelt were concerned by the growth of Socialism in 1905.[4] After that year the Industrial Economics Department, under the chairmanship of Nicholas Murray Butler, stressed the growth and "danger" of the Party in its meetings and its appeals for funds. Easley also discussed "the menace of Socialism as evidenced by its growth in the colleges, churches, newspapers" with such men as Hart Lyman, editor of the *New York Tribune*, H. H. Vreeland, president of the National Street Railway Association (whose son was a member of the Intercollegiate Socialist Society at Yale), and with Theodore Roosevelt, and President Taft.[5]

The spread of the Intercollegiate Socialist Society and other groups that he viewed as fronts for the Party particularly concerned Easley. When the National Association for the Advancement of Colored People was organized in 1909, for example, he wrote President Taft that "this movement has been exploited by the East Side papers for the past three months as a scheme to further Socialist propaganda. Two-thirds of the names on the list I saw were avowed Socialists. Their theory is, that there are 10,000,000 citizens who are being deprived of their constitutional liberties in this free land, and who would be willing to join any party or movement to stand for their rights." [6] Even so, the rapid expansion of NCF activity after 1908 and the failure of the Socialists to increase their vote between 1904 and 1908 (Debs polled 408,000 in

[4] See Chapter One, p. 17, above.

[5] Nicholas Murray Butler to Dear Sir (form letter), New York, July 1, 1908, Box 46, NCF papers; Easley to Vreeland, September 3, 1908, *ibid.*; Easley to Roosevelt, New York, February 17, 1909, Box 38, *ibid.*

[6] Easley to Taft, New York, June 1, 1909, Box 47, *ibid.* In 1919, during the race riots, Easley was again concerned with the Negro question. His solution to the threat that Negro "Bolshevists" (by which he meant Socialists), such as A. Philip Randolph and Chandler Owen, would "get hold of the negroes" was to organize an NCF Division on the Negro. For this he sought a Negro as head. "The way to fraternize," Easley wrote, "is to fraternize." Easley to Mrs. F. L. Ames, New York, June 9, 1919, Box 56, *ibid.*

1904 and 420,000 in 1908) softened the attitude of most Federation leaders and reduced the need for specific anti-Socialist activity.

But by 1911 the rapid growth of the Socialist Party and the increasing disaffection of the labor members with the NCF had led to a change in Federation attitudes. In 1910 Victor Berger became the first party member elected to Congress and the Socialists captured the mayoralty of Milwaukee. In 1911 Socialists elected mayors in 73 municipalities throughout the United States, along with some 1,200 lesser officials in 340 cities and towns. Articles in popular magazines about "The Rising Tide of Socialism" became commonplace and party membership increased in spurts. Within the unions Socialist activity against the Civic Federation spread rapidly in 1911 and 1912.

A major casualty of these attacks was John Mitchell, who since 1908 had headed the NCF's Trade Agreements Department at a salary of $8,000 per year. Early in 1911 Mitchell was forced to resign from the Federation after the United Mine Workers convention adopted a resolution making NCF membership an automatic cause of expulsion from the union. The next year, president William Huber of the carpenters union was forced to withdraw, and Ralph Easley complained that the Federation "had this spirit to contend with through the labor movement in the crafts where the Socialists are strong." The loss of Huber had been expected "for the last two years," Easley confided, as the Socialists "practically control that organization." [7] In the 1911 convention of the AFL three resolutions condemning membership in the NCF were introduced. The vote on the question was lost by the radicals 11,815 to 4,924 after Gompers and other top AFL leaders

[7] John Mitchell to Seth Low, n.p., February 15, 1911, Box 104, folder 502, NCF papers; Easley to Walter Weyl, New York, September 28, 1912, Box 49, NCF papers.

spoke against it. But there, too, Socialist strength was rising.[8]

That same year Gompers' Cigarmakers Union elected several of his longtime Socialist opponents to international office, and a few months later the International Association of Machinists voted James O'Connell, first vice president of the AFL and member of the Executive Committee of NCF, out of office. His successor was William H. Johnston, a leading Socialist. The next year, 1912, the Socialist leader of Pennsylvania, James H. Maurer won election as president of that state's Federation of Labor. Following that, John H. Walker, a Socialist UMW leader, was elected president of the Illinois Federation of Labor.[9]

Even among some of the top old-line AFL leadership dissatisfaction with the NCF was growing. James Duncan, head of the Granite Cutters Association, an AFL vice president, and lifelong Republican, announced his intention to resign from the Executive Committee of the Federation in early 1913. "Blame without cause is laid [by the NCF] on unions for so-called limitation of output," Duncan complained, "while not one word of criticism is applied (unless by the labor group) to trusts and corporations like the coal mine owners for instance, for limiting output by preventing men from working little over two hundred days a year." The labor men had reduced strikes wherever employers agreed to reasonable adjustments without them, Duncan continued, "but what have the other groups of the Executive Committee done in that direction?" Few of the businessmen represented industries which recognize organized labor at all, Duncan pointed out, "and still fewer sign trade agreements although it contains a method for as nearly eliminating strikes as in our time is advisable." The absence of any evidence that employers

[8] Karson, *American Labor Unions and Politics, 1900–1918*, pp. 125–128.
[9] *Ibid.*, p. 130; James H. Maurer, *It Can Be Done* (New York, Rand School, 1938), pp. 109–110; *Quincy* (Illinois) *Labor News*, October 25, 1913.

connected with the Civic Federation were pro-union gave Duncan reason to quit the Executive Board.[10]

Another member of the NCF Executive Committee, John F. Tobin of the Boot and Shoe Workers, made what John Golden of the Textile Workers called "quite a Socialist speech" in 1912, during the course of which he went out of his way to announce that he had voted the Socialist Party ticket for twenty-two years, though not a party member.[11]

Easley had always been highly sensitive to signs of Socialist strength or growth; by 1912 many others, both within the Federation and outside, had come to share his concern. The Catholic Church in particular began a major counterattack within the trade union movement through the Militia of Christ. The Militia had been organized by a committee of AFL leaders and Father Peter E. Dietz, an anti-Socialist priest who had led a secession from the 1909 convention of the Ohio State Federation of Labor when the Socialist delegates carried a motion for independent political action.

Dietz' Militia was not the first anti-Socialist organization in the labor movement; the Central Society and several others preceded it.

Like these other organizations, the Militia's purpose was "to cultivate the aspirations of the workers to better their conditions through organization in conservative trade unions." [12] Unlike the others, the Militia included an imposing array of Catholic trade union leaders on its directorate, even

[10] James Duncan to Easley, Quincy, Mass., February 11, 1913, Box 50, NCF papers. Easley's reply, on the whole, avoided answering Duncan's charges. Instead, he blamed the problem in the mines on "the importation of immigrants which flood the labor market and cause overproduction" and the need to shut down part of each year. Easley refused to accept Duncan's resignation, and traveled to Quincy to see him about it in June 1913. Easley to Duncan, New York, February 20, 1913, ibid.; Duncan to Easley, June 3, 1913, ibid.; Easley to Duncan, June 6, 1913, ibid.

[11] Golden to Easley, Fall River, April 24, 1912, Box 49, ibid.

[12] Foner, The Policies and Practices of the A.F.L., pp. 119–120.

though in its first year of existence Dietz complained that they did "little beyond lending their names." But in 1912, the Militia began to enjoy active support from the Church and from Catholic trade unionists. With Gompers' aid, the Militia furnished weekly newsletters to 300 labor papers and sponsored hundreds of meetings and conferences at which its representatives spoke.[13] In 1912, too, the militant anti-Socialist Catholics began publishing *Common Cause,* a magazine devoted to the destruction of Socialist influence among workers.

Within the Civic Federation Easley pushed for new action parallel to that of the Catholics. After talking to John Hays Hammond, August Belmont, Gompers, John Mitchell, Charles R. Miller (editor of the *New York Times*) and "our Catholic friends," Easley helped set up a joint conference between representatives of the Industrial Economics Department of the Federation and *Common Cause.* On May 29, 1912, some fifty people attended the meeting to consider "the menace of Socialism to our institutions" and to establish a plan to combat it.[14] Out of that meeting and others, the Federation revitalized its Industrial Economics Department, set up a special $50,000 fund, and embarked on an Industrial Survey to test the validity of Socialist theories about American capitalism.

Once the Civic Federation decided to conduct a major campaign against the further spread of Socialism it moved rapidly to gain the widest sponsorship for its activity. Significantly, the Federation did not concentrate on opposing so-

[13] *Ibid.,* p. 121. David Goldstein, *Autobiography of a Campaigner for Christ* (Boston, Astor Station, 1936), pp. 116, 135–143; Karson, *American Labor Unions and Politics, 1900–1918,* Chapter 9.

[14] N.s. to Seth Low, July 23, 1912, Box 104, Low papers; Marguerite Green, *The National Civic Federation and the American Labor Movement, 1900–1925* (Washington, D.C., Catholic University of America Press, 1956), pp. 182–183.

cialism in the unions; the "militant" part of the work was left to *Common Cause* and the Militia of Christ.[15] Instead, the Federation concentrated on what it rightly considered to be the opinionmakers of the day, seeking to produce and distribute an alternative ideology to socialism. Everett W. Burdett, general counsel of the National Electric Light Association and a director of Edison Electric of Boston, expressed one aspect of this approach to Easley. Commenting on the "enormous importance of the socialistic movement," Burdett noted "the startling fact" that socialism was "being nurtured not only by the outcast and revolutionist, but by those charged with the education of youth." What was needed was a campaign of education on the part of the Federation.[16]

To carry on this campaign the Federation initiated a grandiose Survey of Social, Civic, and Economic Progress, under the general chairmanship of William D. Baldwin, president of the Otis Elevator Company. The National Industrial Survey, as it came to be known, was conducted under the immediate supervision of Talcott Williams, a professor of journalism at Columbia University. His Committee on Plan and Scope included Jeremiah W. Jenks, of Cornell, Columbia economist Edwin R. A. Seligman, Charles R. Miller of the *New York Times*, Charles P. Neill, Samuel Gompers, Frank Trumbull of the Chesapeake and Ohio Railroad, George B. Cortelyou and George W. Perkins. The committee recognized that "a new period of industrial development of our nation began with the formation of the trusts" in the late 1880's. This development, along with the massive immigration from Southern and Southeastern Europe, had "brought profound shiftings in the distribution of wealth, the relations between employer and employed and the circumstances in which peo-

[15] *Ibid.*, p. 183.
[16] Everett W. Burdett to Easley, Boston, March 22, 1913, Box 82, NCF papers.

ple with large and small incomes" lived. The expenditure of the rich was "more visible," and the "standards and desires among people of moderate income and in the wage earning class" had risen, "emphasizing a disparity in the enjoyment of life and opportunities."

The resulting discontent had been aggravated by the immigrants, who swelled "the ranks of those prompt to put the worst construction on the motives of the more fortunate." Before condemning the system, the committee intended to "find out where we stand." But, instead of attempting to ascertain what the level of technology and the extent of industrialization had made historically possible, it sought to discover whether "we have gone forward, or gone backward, or are merely marking time." [17]

The committee put into question some of the criticisms of capitalism made by the Socialists, testing it against the corporations' assumption "that the force and initiative of individual enterprise, restrained or instructed, where need be, by state control or by organized public opinion, make most surely for progress and general welfare." "Is wealth being concentrated in fewer hands? Has the organization of the large corporations resulted in a great withdrawal of wealth from the people or a more general distribution of wealth? Has it resulted in the reduction of small establishments? Are the small business men thrown into the class of propertyless wage-workers?"

In addition, it asked if the farmer was holding his own in private ownership or lapsing into tenancy, if child labor, factory regulation, and other reforms had really benefited workers, or if they had merely been a " 'sop thrown by the capitalists to the toilers to blind them to their real conditions of wage slavery.' " Further, the committee asked whether the

[17] "A National Industrial Survey," press release, October 13, 1913, Box 82, NCF papers.

spending of millions of dollars by the Carnegie, Rockefeller, and Sage Foundations had been justified by the results, or whether philanthropy should be undertaken by the State. It then inquired as to the "practical value" in the municipal and industrial reform work "undertaken by hundreds of Boards of Trade, Chambers of Commerce, etc." [18]

Finally, the committee revealed its conclusion before beginning the survey. At the last election, it noted, "one million votes were cast in favor of an economic program calling for a revolutionary transformation of society." Does this program "point the way to progress?" it asked. The survey and report would help "us" to "see the need to face the evils yet to be fought" but at the same time to "take fresh heart from the good fights won." [19]

The survey, in other words, was not intended as an investigation into the validity of the Marxian critique of capitalism. Indeed, it so misstated Socialist views that it could not have done that if that were the purpose. Instead, it sought to discover how more effectively to combat the renewed growth of socialism even in the face of the beginnings of reform. Despite this bias, however, the attempt was important in the support it won from business and other leaders, and in the approach it devised to the problem of growing socialist influence.

The special fifty thousand dollar fund for the Industrial survey was raised by Ogden L. Mills, a leading New York Republican and a director of several corporations, including the Atchison, Topeka and Santa Fe Railroad and Lackawanna Steel, Willard Straight of J. P. Morgan and Company, and John T. Pratt. Among the larger contributors were William K. Vanderbilt, Theodore N. Vail of American Telephone and Telegraph and Colonel Robert M. Thompson, a financier and

[18] *Ibid.*
[19] *Ibid.*

126

chairman of the Board of Directors of International Nickel. Each gave $5,000.[20]

Support came from well beyond the business community. Jane Addams, for example, was "very much interested in the plan" and accepted sponsorship of the Survey. "The prospectus," she wrote, was "exceedingly well done and quite stirs one to be of assistance in the undertaking." [21]

Over 400 persons were listed as sponsors of the Survey. By 1914, twenty-five subcommittees were at work on different aspects of the program and were receiving assistance from hundreds of professors, newspaper editors, and trade unionists. Among the sponsors were Arthur Capper, Henry Ford, Cardinal Gibbons, Henry Pratt Judson (president of the University of Chicago), Frank B. Kellogg, Judge Ben B. Lindsey, Cyrus McCormick, Alton B. Parker, Roscoe Pound, Ogden M. Reid (of the *New York Tribune*), E. P. Ripley (president of the Atchison, Topeka and Santa Fe Railroad), Elihu Root, Edward A. Ross (sociologist), Henry L. Stimson, Senator George Sutherland, William H. Taft, Oswald G. Villard, Henry C. Wallace, Frank P. Walsh, John Wanamaker, Booker T. Washington, Walter E. Weyl (of the *New Republic*), Benjamin Ide Wheeler (president of the University of California), and William Allen White.[22]

The approach of the Industrial Economics Department to the problem of socialism in the United States was two-sided. Officially—and ideologically—a soft line was taken, one which was designed to woo away from the Socialist Party those

[20] Easley to Andrew Carnegie, New York, March 31, 1914, Box 51, NCF papers. Carnegie had pledged $2,500 and Easley wrote to ask that it be doubled, since he feared that no one would give more than Carnegie as a matter of protocol.

[21] Jane Addams to Seth Low, Chicago, October 15, 1913, Box 82, NCF papers.

[22] List of members of the Advisory Council of the Industrial Economics Department, May 1914, corrected to June 20, 1915. List of 404 names. Box 82, NCF papers. Easley to Carnegie, New York, March 31, 1914, Box 51, *ibid.*

who shared its morality and social goals, but were not firmly committed to underlying socialist theories of capitalism and antagonistic class interest. Unofficially, NCF leaders worked closely with those who were prepared to do what was necessary to destroy socialist influence, especially in the mass media and in educational institutions. The soft approach was reflected in a privately circulated memorandum concerning the policy to be pursued by the Industrial Economics Department of the NCF. "In view of the rapid spread in the United States of socialistic doctrines," and of the "persistent and able propaganda for those doctrines now being carried on," the memorandum began, "it is important that there should be a carefully planned and wisely directed effort to instruct public opinion as to the real meaning of socialism," and of the need to combat it "if our American political system and its underlying economic institutions are to be preserved."

But recognizing the need "not to give unjust offense" or to create "a false impression of partisanship," the proposed education of public opinion "must be very skillfully and tactfully carried on." Such a campaign "should not violently attack socialism and anarchism as such," for these doctrines were "held and preached by many persons who are quite sincere" and who were "held in high regard by the public." The campaign should be "patient and persuasive" in defense of three fundamental institutions under attack: "(1) individual liberty; (2) private property; and (3) inviolability of contract."

Public education was to be conducted along three paths. The first was to furnish newspapers, particularly weekly and monthly journals that reached large numbers of readers of special classes—such as religious weeklies, labor journals, journals of education, philanthropy, and mutual benefit organizations—with well-written articles on socialism and "expounding and defending the foundations of our existing industrial order in a similar spirit." The second was to provide "tactful and well instructed" speakers to go before women's clubs, teachers and farmers institutes, lodge and Chautauqua meetings to combat socialism. The third was to encourage the preparation, publication, and circulation of attractive popular books on the subject. The need for good judgment and persuasiveness were stressed, because the Federation understood that "Socialism has the great sentimental advantage of being based upon a desire to benefit all human beings," and that "in opposing socialism this same sentimental advantage must be claimed and held for the anti-socialist view."

Finally, the oft-repeated touchstone of the new liberalism: "It is important that a distinction should be made between proposals and direct undertakings which are socialistic and anarchistic in principle," and those which socialists "would naturally favor," but which were "not necessarily in conflict with the underlying principles of the existing industrial order." [23]

The harder side of NCF antisocialist activity went on in private. This was largely informal. One aspect occurred in 1915, when the University of Pennsylvania fired Scott Nearing, an instructor of economics and a Socialist. In a letter to John C. Bell, a trustee of the University, Easley confided that he was getting up some material on Nearing, and that he would send it along to Bell. "If some of your friends will go through Nearing's writings," Easley suggested, "they will find plenty of reasons why he should have been kicked out of the university long before this." [24] Another was the campaign that F. G. R. Gordon—a former Socialist and now an "industrial expert" who worked closely with Easley—conducted against *Metropolitan Magazine* because of its support for Socialism. Gordon's attack was twofold. He wrote to Harry Payne Whitney, a principal owner of the magazine, and to Theodore Roosevelt

[23] Memorandum concerning the policy to be pursued by the Department of Industrial Economics of the National Civic Federation [1914], Box 84, NCF papers.
[24] Easley to Bell, New York, July 2, 1915, Box 52, NCF papers.

129

suggesting they use their influence to get antisocialist views in its columns, and he wrote to the advertisers in *Metropolitan* telling them of *Metropolitan's* editorial policy and suggesting that they not support a magazine whose policies would, if enforced, lead to the confiscation of the advertiser's property.[25] In some cases Gordon was successful. Bartlett Arkell, president of the Beech-Nut Packing Company, for example, replied that he would bring the matter up with the board of directors of the Company and would "study much more carefully the editorial policy of the *Metropolitan Magazine* in the future." [26]

The overall impact of the Federation's attack on Socialism is difficult to assess. The Survey was partially completed, but never published because labor member Warren S. Stone of the Brotherhood of Locomotive Engineers objected to it as a whitewash of the NCF and its limited program.[27] And after 1916, preparedness and then actual participation in the war created different problems, and the opportunity for the federal and state governments to assume much of the burden that the NCF had at first carried more or less alone.

This is not to say that there was not earlier a widespread consciousness among political leaders of the need to use the government as a primary means of incorporating other social classes than business into the system, and even as a direct ideological opponent of socialism. We will see that in 1912 all three parties understood the need for reform as a means to

[25] F. G. R. Gordon to Harry Payne Whitney, Haverhill, Mass., April 1, 1915, Box 82, NCF papers; Gordon to Theodore Roosevelt, Haverhill, April 20, 1915, *ibid.*; Gordon to Hudson Motor Company and many others, various April dates, *ibid.*

[26] Bartlett Arkell to Gordon, Canajoharie, New York, April 29, 1915, *ibid.* Some advertisers were less susceptible to Gordon's pressure. The first vice president of the Chalmers Motor Company, for example, replied that the magazine's editorial policy did "not interest us particularly as we think they have a right to run their magazine in their own way. We do not think any advertiser has the right to dictate to a magazine anything in connection with their editorial policy." L. Olwell to Gordon, Detroit, April 30, 1915, *ibid.*

[27] Green, *The NCF and the American Labor Movement*, p. 188.

combat socialism. The need to do this and to use the state to rationalize and stabilize the market economy was understood by the Socialists, or by some of them, as well. In August 1912, for example, Robert Rives LaMonte, a leftwing Socialist from Connecticut, wrote that no matter whether the Republicans or the Democrats won the election "we shall get more workmen's compensation acts, more and more restriction upon child labor, more and more regulation of women in industry." LaMonte even predicted that woman suffrage, old age pensions, and attempts by government to reduce unemployment would be among the reforms forthcoming. He saw this as a result of two things: the need to increase the efficiency of workers, and the need to reduce agitation for socialism. "Very soon," LaMonte wrote, "there will cease to be any real opposition to reforms aimed at preserving [workers'] health and efficiency." "Old age pensions and insurance against sickness, accident and unemployment are cheaper, are better business than jails, poor houses, asylums, hospitals" to care for the "unemployable."

Capitalists, LaMonte continued, were "even learning that too widespread joblessness and a wage too far below a decent subsistence level leads to agitations that threaten the whole fabric of capitalism." As a result of social work and other forms of investigation, the rich had come to know more about the poor than ever before, LaMonte asserted, "and this increased knowledge begets increased sympathy." This added another dimension to reform. "Altogether apart from self-interest," the rich "want to help the poor. And this kindly desire is a factor in all modern social legislation." But the rich were so placed that they could "afford to help the poor only when by doing so they help themselves still more."

The conclusion was clear to LaMonte: reforms were the business of progressives. Socialists must make only "impossible demands"—demands that pointed up the limitations of the reformers and the basic inhumanity of the system they bolstered. Socialist demands must not be of the rationalizing variety, but must embody a vision of socialism and raise the question of control over fundamental decisions. As the editors of the *International Socialist Review* put it, the "next step" would be for the businessman to discover "that he can carry on certain portions of the productive process more efficiently through *his* government than through private corporations." "Some muddleheads," the *Review* mused, "think that will be Socialism, but the capitalist knows better." The right of "wage-workers to organize and to control" the productive process was the true "issue that must be fought out between the two great opposing classes." [28]

In the end, the role of government—municipal, state, and federal—was more important than the NCF in combating socialism. Yet many Socialists identified the need for reform and social responsibility with government intervention in a manner that tended to overlook who ultimately controlled the government at various levels. In this respect many of the conservative trade unionists were more astute in understanding the role of the State in relation to the large corporations. In his debate with Morris Hillquit of the Socialist Party during the hearings of the Commission on Industrial Relations in 1914, Samuel Gompers insisted that he was "very suspicious of the activities of governmental agencies." Hillquit baited Gompers for his opposition to minimum wage legislation, but

[28] Robert Rives LaMonte, "You and Your Vote," *International Socialist Review*, XIII, 2 (August 1912), p. 116; "Editorial," *ibid.*, XIII, 6 (December 1912), p. 495. Another dimension of LaMonte's argument was that the speed of reform would depend on the size of the Socialist vote. This reasoning received support in 1916 in a letter to Frank P. Walsh, Chairman of the Commission on Industrial Relations. The writer told Walsh he was a Wilson man, but was "tempted almost against my better judgement to come out for Benson" (the Socialist candidate). "I'm tired of shin plasters and make-shifts. . . . Of course, I am not a Socialist, but they are the only people who are speaking out their full minds, and one has to be a radical to accomplish even a little bit of what we hope for." Pat F. Cook to Walsh, St. Louis, November 6, 1916, Box 13, Walsh papers, New York Public Library.

a trade union member of the Commission rescued Gompers by asking whether he had observed "that the insistence, the quiet insistence, behind the scenes for the enactment of legislation placing in a government board the power to fix these conditions was always traceable to the larger interests that employ men?"

Gompers replied that it was. There was "an underground process constantly at work to devise ways and means ostensibly and superficially well-sounding, like a sugarcoated pill is well tasting," to "fix the status of workmen, to tie them to their labor" so that the "right of the freedom of action shall be first impaired and then denied." Yet, Gompers charged, the leaders of the Socialist Party "would very gladly establish that in the wholesale. They do not understand the struggle for freedom." [29]

This was not entirely true of the Socialist Party at the time, but Gompers' criticism did apply to certain tendencies within the movement that became dominant in American Socialism and Communism in the 1920's and 1930's. During Wilson's New Freedom, despite all his reforms and the work of his Commission on Industrial Relations, Socialism did not become irrelevant and the party did not decline substantially.[30] Indeed, in 1915 and 1916 the issue of preparedness and war revealed the extent to which socialist concepts had permeated the consciousness of workers and farmers. By 1916 Civic Federation leaders took a new look at the role of education as a matter of concern to the State, rather than simply to the NCF.

Many prominent men perceived the relation of political attitudes to that of public education not only in the sense in which the Federation had traditionally used the term, but also as it related directly to indoctrinating children in the public

[29] United States Commission on Industrial Relations, *Final Report and Testimony* (Washington, D.C., 1916), II, pp. 1499–1500, 1544.
[30] See Weinstein, *Decline of Socialism in America*, Chapters II, III.

school system. In 1916, at the NCF Annual Meeting, Senator Wadsworth of New York argued for compulsory military training. In doing so he revealed the developing consciousness of the role of the public school among Federation members. "Nearly every state of this union compels its children to go to school," Wadsworth noted. Asking why we have compulsory education, Wadsworth answered that it was "to protect the nation against destruction from forces operating within. It is to train the boy and the girl to be good citizens, to protect against ignorance and dissipation." Military training for all, Wadsworth argued, was necessary to counteract the "danger internally in this country" that "these people of ours shall be divided into classes." That tendency "is going on today," but Wadsworth hoped for "a system under which the son of a man who works for his living at two dollars a day shall serve his country . . . alongside of the man whose father does not work for a living, so that they will know each other better."

"A part of this agitation—if I may use that term—for preparedness," Wadsworth continued, "involves inevitably this consideration, that our people shall be prepared mentally as well as in a purely military sense. We must let our young men know that they owe some responsibility to this country." [31]

The Governor of Pennsylvania concurred with Wadsworth's views. He told Ralph Easley that "back of all this preparedness doctrine there should be a reorganization of our whole educational policy," to assure "an educated citizenry, trained in the real American doctrines and holding substantially the same fundamental ideals of government organization for the protection of our industries and of our working people." [32] It remained for Seth Low's successor as president of the Civic Federation, V. Everitt Macy, to state the issue most clearly. The approaching involvement of the United States in

[31] Minutes of the 16th Annual Meeting, Box 187, NCF papers.
[32] Martin G. Brumbaugh to Easley, Harrisburg, January 9, 1917, Box 187, NCF papers.

the First World War raised the question of loyalty and patriotism, particularly among youth. It was not, Macy asserted, "beside the mark to call attention to the nearly thirty million minors marching steadily toward full citizenship" and ask "at what stage of their journey we should lend assistance to the work of quickening . . . the sense of responsibility and partnership in the business of maintaining and perfecting the splendid social, industrial, and commercial structure which has been reared under the American flag." Unfortunately, Macy noted, the need was urgent. Among American youth there was a widespread "indifference toward, and aloofness from, individual responsibility for the successful maintenance and upbuilding of the industrial and commercial structure which is the indispensable shelter of us all."

Macy wished to "vitalize and visualize the wonderful story" of "our industrial, commercial, and financial structure in such a way as to make every child feel that he is to be a responsible builder" of a society that "secures to him the rights and privileges of joint control," but "imposes on him also the liabilities and limitations of ownership." "The possible cumulative influence of this movement in obliterating class lines, in developing the sense of citizenship in industry and in steadying and directing efforts for needed adjustments in industrial relations, cannot be calculated." "Thus far," Macy concluded, "the Chambers of Commerce and the manufacturers, cooperating with the Boards of Education in a few large cities are the chief sponsors for the project of making industrial architecture . . . a vital part of the public school curricula." [33]

Macy's deep concern over the spread of socialist ideas among the workers and farmers was widely shared by business and political leaders in early 1917. George W. Perkins even came to look upon Billy Sunday's fundamentalist evangelism as a helpful antidote to political radicalism. At first, Perkins

[33] Presidential address, 17th Annual Meeting, January 22, 1917, Speeches folder, Box 187, NCF papers.

told the Reverend Dr. W. S. Rainsford he, too, had been shocked by Sunday's preaching. But the more he talked "with men of real parts" who had "been connected with it," the more he had come to feel that Sunday was "performing in his way and in his place a very real service."

What the country sadly needed, Perkins told Rainsford, was "a religious revival and reawakening," and "anybody who will come anywhere near doing the job should," in Perkins' judgment, be encouraged. "Our religious spirit is flabby, our spirit of patriotism has well nigh oozed out," Perkins complained. "We need a most thorough reawakening religiously, patriotically, morally. I have felt for some time that the church was not measuring up to the present day necessities." [34]

The same spirit animated John Hays Hammond, when he asked the 17th Annual Meeting of NCF, in January: "Is our country worth defending?" It seemed incredible to him that such a question could be taken seriously, but he insisted that he was "raising no imaginary issue in telling you that men who do challenge that proposition directly or by implication are today having a marked influence in the shaping of public thought here in the United States." Hammond had become convinced that the activity of pacifists and socialists was "far more deadly than anything" that spies or enemy aliens could do. "The subtle undermining of the spirit of patriotism" was accomplished by the "unbridled propaganda" of radical preachers, radical college professors, Socialists, and others "viciously denouncing all proposals to prepare our nation for defending itself against threatened attacks from without or within." Hammond complained that "neither workingmen nor farmers—the two great groups upon which our national life depends"—were taking "any part or interest in the efforts of the security or defense leagues or other movements for national preparedness." No matter how the war ends, he added,

[34] Perkins to W. S. Rainsford, n.p., January 6, 1917, Box 28, Perkins papers.

"we shall have the task of overcoming this doctrine, incessantly preached in every corner of the land, that we have nothing worth defending because our institutions have brought no real gain to humanity, that in fact the worker is as hopeless under one government as another and will remain so until he overthrows them all and takes possession of the wealth of the world for himself." [35]

In fact, as Socialist activity in the next year would soon demonstrate, Hammond exaggerated but slightly. Despite the NCF's activity in opposition to socialism, its strength had remained fairly constant from 1912 to 1917—although, for many reasons, among them the reforms made during the Wilson administration, there had been a small decline. But the war seemed to confirm Socialist criticisms of American society in the minds of hundreds of thousands, if not millions, of workers and farmers. Despite heavy attacks on the Party after American entrance into the war in April 1917, Socialists substantially increased their vote in 1917 and again in 1918 in those areas where their organization had not been suppressed.[36] After the war, for reasons that cannot briefly be summarized, the Socialist Party broke up and the movement declined, but this had little to do with NCF activity except to the degree that it was a result of frontal attacks on Socialists and their press for being traitorous during the war.

Yet the failure of Federation attempts to destroy the Socialist movement should not becloud the importance of the NCF activity. The approach to organized labor and to social reform developed by Federation leaders over the years did set very definite limits on the potential of revolutionary politics as long as the economy could continue to expand. The extent to which the Federation had succeeded in educating businessmen to the need for longterm responsibility and to an under-

[35] Speeches, 17th Annual Meeting of the National Civic Federation, Box 187, NCF papers.
[36] See James Weinstein, *Decline*, Chapter III.

standing of the value of co-optation of potential revolutionaries among workers, farmers, and in the middle classes was first clearly demonstrated in the wartime policies of the Wilson Administration. After a period of stabilization and consolidation in the 1920's, the full impact of Federation teaching became apparent once again in the New Deal. There were other factors, especially the character of the dominant socialist groups, that further limited the possibilities for the building of a socialist-conscious popular movement in the 1930's; but as in the 1910's, the sophistication and ability of those in power to move to the left in the face of real, imminent, or anticipated threats from the radicals circumscribed the space within which revolutionaries could act. In its confrontation of the problem of socialism, the Federation had helped develop a basic aspect of politics in the United States in the twentieth century.

CHAPTER SIX

The Politics of Social Reform: 1912
and the Progressive Party

THE POLITICS OF 1912 was dominated by the two great questions of the Progressive Era: the relation of the federal government to the large corporations, and the challenge from Socialism to the emerging corporate system for the loyalty of workers and farmers. The debate on these issues was complicated by the entrance of Theodore Roosevelt into the race for the presidency as an independent candidate, particularly since there was a large element of personal hostility between Roosevelt and Taft. But Roosevelt's displacement of La Follette as the candidate of the Progressives, and the subsequent formation of the Progressive Party served ultimately only to highlight the two major issues, and facilitated their resolution in a manner most satisfactory to the more sophisticated corporation and financial leaders. In the middle of 1911 a serious threat to big business hegemony in the major political parties appeared to be shaping up; by the summer of 1912 that challenge had been dissipated. La Follette had been pushed aside by Roosevelt; the Progressive Party had shifted the focus of debate onto the problem of trust regulation; Wilson, despite the rhetorical device of the New Freedom, had made it plain that he favored and would protect the "natural" developments of the business world. Although Eugene V. Debs achieved his highest vote in 1912—some 900,000 votes, or six percent of the total—Wilson's victory signaled the beginning of a period of consolidation and sta-

139

bilization of the new liberal state. Before the events of 1912 the course of American politics appeared uncertain. After 1912, despite instability in specific areas, the general direction of the dominant politics was clear to those who could see through the rhetoric.

The movement within the Republican Party that eventually led to Roosevelt's entrance into the presidential contest and to the formation of the Progressive Party in 1912 began early in Taft's tenure. The first issue was the tariff; the opposition was by La Follette and some Midwestern allies in the Senate. Pledged to a revision of tariff duties, Taft called a special session of Congress to reduce the existing Dingley Tariff rates as soon as he took office in 1909. In the House, the Payne bill lowered rates, although not enough to satisfy La Follette; but in the Senate Nelson W. Aldrich revised most rates, especially those on manufactured goods, sharply upward.

In addition to the high rates, Aldrich substituted a tax oñ corporate income for the personal income tax provision in the House bill. This particularly enraged La Follette, who pointed out that large corporations with no substantial competition from unincorporated manufacturers would simply pass the tax on to the consumer. In addition to the consumer, only small corporations in immediate competition with unincorporated enterprises would suffer. The income tax, on the other hand, would have affected only persons with very large incomes, such as Rockefeller and Morgan.[1]

In response to Aldrich's revisions, a group of senators, including La Follette, Jonathan Dolliver and Albert Cummins of Iowa, Joseph L. Bristow of Kansas, Albert Beveridge of Indiana, and Moses Clapp of Minnesota, agreed to oppose the tariff in a bloc. "It was," La Follette wrote later, "the fight on the Payne-Aldrich tariff bill which brought us all

[1] "Who Pays the Tax?", *La Follette's Weekly Magazine*, I, 27 (July 10, 1909), 3; "The Roll Call," *ibid.*, p. 5.

together." [2] La Follette's argument against the tariff, as on railroad rate regulation, was an expression of the best of contemporary antimonopoly analyses, but it also revealed the limitations of neopopulist theory inherent in the failure to examine the underlying nature of an economy that had come to maturity with the emergence of the large corporation. La Follette argued, for example, that America was "ruled by a closely related group of interests, which have fastened monopoly upon the people by means of legislation. They form an economic oligarchy. They run and ramify into every congressional district. They send their friends and their stockholders to Congress to do their will. They form a class as sympathetic as any board of directors and they control the tools of democracy as readily as they ever controlled the tools of the countries of Europe." [3]

La Follette's description of who controlled the federal government was as near to reality as any man in public life has come. But it was not legislation that had "fastened monopoly upon the people" of the United States; the large corporations had grown out of the very free competition to which La Follette longed to return. As a self-proclaimed spokesman for independent bankers, businessmen, and small producers,[4] he consistently opposed the dominant Eastern financial groups, the large corporations, and the railroads, but his opposition was necessarily a patchwork of defenses against particular evils because he never attempted a general criticism of the underlying tendencies of the political economy. Control of the state by the corporations was a result of their need to rationalize and stabilize the system that had grown out of laissez faire. La Follette's failure to come to grips with this led him into an inconsistent pragmatism.

[2] *La Follette's Autobiography*, p. 187.
[3] "The Meaning of Cannonism," *La Follette's Weekly Magazine*, II, 5 (February 5, 1910), p. 3.
[4] See, for example, *La Follette's Autobiography*, pp. 200–201.

He had, for example, supported the McKinley tariff in 1890, arguing that while the high duties would protect American wage standards, free competition between domestic manufacturers would keep prices down. Nineteen years later, with the intervening emergence of the large corporations, the tariff had become "one form" of special privilege, enabling monopoly to charge high prices. In 1909 La Follette argued that a low tariff was needed in order to permit competition from European industry. Competition was still the goal, but now it was pursued overseas—a position, incidentally, that implicitly accepted the large corporation (or "monopoly") at home if only it were brought to heel by international price competition (a view La Follette repudiated in other contexts).[5] But the greater efficiency and higher labor productivity of basic American manufacturing (based as they were on the newest technological developments) were already leading large corporations to an appreciation of free trade as an instrument of penetration into foreign markets. It was true that particular Eastern manufacturing interests favored high duties on their own goods, and, of course, that they preferred a corporation tax to an income tax, but it was not true that the tariff remained a source of "law-made monopolies," as La Follette charged.[6]

The fight on the tariff produced a bloc of Middle Western congressmen opposed to Taft, but the initial group around La Follette had not been large enough to produce an explicit move to deny Taft renomination in 1912. For that, additional forces were needed. They were forthcoming as a result of the Pinchot-Ballinger controversy over the disposition of some Alaskan coal lands.

The Pinchot-Ballinger controversy centered around Gifford Pinchot and James R. Garfield on one side, and Richard A.

[5] *Ibid.*, pp. 46–47; "What Makes High Prices," *La Follette's Weekly Magazine*, II, 6 (February 12, 1910), p. 4.
[6] *Ibid.*

Ballinger and the President on the other. Pinchot and Garfield were both close personal friends of Roosevelt. During his administrations they had been instrumental in developing programs of cooperation with the "good" large corporations. Pinchot, as head of the Bureau of Forestry, had developed a program of sustained yield planting that won the approval of the Northern Pacific Railroad, Weyerhauser Timber, King Lumber, and other corporations, although opposed by the "preservationists" who would have left the forests intact.[7] Garfield, as Commissioner of the Bureau of Corporations during Roosevelt's first term and as Secretary of the Interior during his second, had always enjoyed cordial relations with Morgan men, particularly with Francis Lynde Stetson, a Morgan lawyer. It was Garfield who, in 1905, had arranged a personal conference between Elbert H. Gary of the United States Steel Corporation and President Roosevelt at which arrangements were made for the informal cooperation of the corporation and the government. "The function of the Bureau of Corporations," Garfield decided, was "not to enforce the anti-trust laws," but to obtain the "hearty cooperation" of business and industrial interests in order to obviate the necessity of "extreme remedial legislation" (such as might be advocated by La Follette) that would be disastrous not only to "abnormal" or "bad" corporations, but also to "good" ones.[8]

The Pinchot-Ballinger controversy arose over the disposition of the "Cunningham" claims, held by a group of Seattle men, to about fifteen percent of the Bering River coal fields in Alaska, part of the national domain. Richard A. Ballinger, a former mayor of Seattle and a friend of some of the claimants, served as Commissioner of the General Land Office in

[7] Kolko, *Triumph of Conservatism*, p. 111; Samuel P. Hays, *Conservation and the Gospel of Efficiency* (Cambridge, Harvard University Press, 1959), pp. 1–2, 127.

[8] Kolko, *Triumph of Conservatism*, pp. 72, 75–76; Robert H. Wiebe, "The House of Morgan and the Executive, 1905–1913," *American Historical Review*, LXV, 1 (October 1959), pp. 51–52.

1907 under Secretary of the Interior Garfield. At that time, Ballinger had clear-listed the claims, but Garfield had reversed his action when an investigation indicated that the claimants intended to sell a major interest in the coal lands to a Morgan-Guggenheim syndicate. When Taft succeeded to the presidency he did not reappoint Garfield, as Garfield and Pinchot expected, but replaced him with Ballinger. Soon afterward, the new Secretary of the Interior removed the investigator into the Cunningham claims (Louis R. Glavis) and ordered an immediate hearing with the apparent intention of settling the matter by granting the claims. Glavis then appealed to Pinchot who, objecting to the improper manner in which the Morgan interests had acted and resenting Ballinger's role in the matter, arranged an interview for the investigator with Taft. The President upheld Ballinger and ordered Glavis discharged.[9]

Taft did not mention Pinchot's role when he fired Glavis because of the close public identification of Roosevelt and Pinchot, but Pinchot chose to press the matter and forced Taft to dismiss him. In part he may have been motivated by career considerations, since Taft had closed all the avenues to political advancement that had been open when Roosevelt held office. But there seems no question that he believed Ballinger to have acted improperly in collusion with the Morgan-Guggenheim interests. A year after Pinchot was dismissed, his younger brother Amos wrote that if the Cunningham claims were "not cancelled now by the President the Guggenheims will ultimately get them, and as they are the key to the Alaskan situation they will certainly be an important factor in developing a great and oppressive coal monopoly." [10]

Whatever their motives, the dismissal of Pinchot brought a number of young Roosevelt men into the opposition to Taft.

[9] For a summary of the Pinchot-Ballinger controversy see George E. Mowry, *The Era of Theodore Roosevelt* (New York, Harper and Brothers, 1958), pp. 250–254.

[10] Amos Pinchot to Gilson Gardner, n.p., January 23, 1911, Box 9, Amos R. E. Pinchot papers, Library of Congress.

These included Pinchot's brother Amos, James R. Garfield, Gilson Gardner (Washington correspondent for the Scripps newspapers) and E. A. Van Valkenberg of the *Philadelphia North American*. With the possible exception of Amos Pinchot, whose radicalism was similar to La Follette's, none of these men shared the Senator's views on the corporations. Yet, as La Follette commented later, the "peculiarly close relation of these men to Roosevelt and their active cooperation was a source of special encouragement" to the Progressives in Congress.[11] The neopopulists around La Follette would soon learn that the new recruits were ideologically closer to Taft, Roosevelt, and the National Civic Federation than they were to their temporary allies, that their opposition to Taft was essentially personal, more a product of the President's political clumsiness than of a difference in principle. Nevertheless, with the addition of Pinchot and his friends the anti-Taft forces were sufficient to permit public opposition within the Republican Party. In January 1911 the National Progressive Republican League was formally organized at La Follette's Washington residence for that purpose.

Although Roosevelt's young friends were active in the leadership of the new Progressive League, and he himself looked with increasing disfavor upon his successor, Roosevelt refused to identify with the League, or to endorse La Follette's actions. At the time the League was formed, and in the following months, Roosevelt maintained public silence, while telling his friends that he thought it impossible to defeat Taft for the nomination. He preferred Taft's renomination and defeat by a Democrat to pushing for the nomination of an "ultraradical." This seemed the best path to the recapture of the party by Roosevelt-style Progressives.[12] La Follette, on the

[11] *La Follette's Autobiography*, p. 217.
[12] Mowry, *Theodore Roosevelt and the Progressive Movement*, p. 176; *La Follette's Autobiography*, p. 215; Gifford Pinchot to Amos Pinchot, Washington, D.C., Box 9, Amos Pinchot papers.

other hand, pushed the League to name someone to oppose Taft within the party. As Amos Pinchot told his brother, La Follette was "anxious to take immediate steps looking to the nomination of a proper Republican candidate for President." [13]

By May 1911, having secured promises of adequate money from Charles R. Crane, of the Crane plumbing supply company, the Pinchots and one or two others, the Progressive League was ready to launch La Follette's candidacy.[14] Apparently, in order to secure the loyalty of the Roosevelt men, La Follette suggested to Gifford Pinchot that he run as vice presidential candidate. Gilson Gardner and others were hopeful that an early declaration of La Follette's entrance into the race would "develop a real chance to elect him." Pinchot was "not so clear," but since Roosevelt was not available, viewed that course as "obviously the one thing to do." [15] On June 17 the La Follette candidacy was announced.

In Wisconsin and in the specific battles in the Senate La Follette had been, and continued to be, a champion of the small producer against the domination of American society by the large corporations. As Senator Joseph L. Bristow told Ralph Easley when Easley complained about La Follette's attacks on the National Civic Federation because it was "supported by rich men," La Follette's opposition was a result of his belief that NCF harmonized differences with labor "in the interests of the large owners of corporate property," and "not from the view of the welfare of the general public." [16] The statement of the National Progressive Republican League

[13] Amos Pinchot to Gifford Pinchot, n.p., March 21, 1911; A. P. to William Kent, n.p., March 19, 1911, Box 9, Amos Pinchot papers.

[14] Mowry, *op. cit.*, (n. 12, *supra.*) p. 173; *La Follette's Autobiography*, p. 224. Amos Pinchot, Rudolph Spreckels, and Alfred Baker became La Follette's finance committee. Pinchot contributed $10,000. John Hanna to Amos Pinchot, Washington, D.C., July 15, 1911, Box 9, Amos Pinchot papers.

[15] Gifford Pinchot to Amos Pinchot, Washington, D.C., May 17, 1911, Box 9, Amos Pinchot papers.

[16] Easley to Joseph L. Bristow, New York, July 17, 1909; Bristow to Easley, Washington, D.C., July 21, 1909, Box 46, NCF papers.

claimed that it was organized "solely for the promotion of popular government"; its program was for direct election of United States Senators, direct primary elections, a presidential preference primary, the popular legislative initiative, and a corrupt practices act. A reader of *La Follette's Weekly Magazine* would know that La Follette and his friends conceived of this program as an attack on such interests as the Steel Trust and the Hill railroads,[17] but there was nothing inherent in the specific demands to challenge these interests in general.

Because the League's program, and La Follette himself, spoke of purging politics of special privilege and substituting for it "the general welfare of the whole people," [18] it was possible for many men, especially those like Amos Pinchot and William Allen White, to see the differences between La Follette and Roosevelt as simply those of style, rather than principle. Unlike his brother, Amos Pinchot believed La Follette was the best instrument for putting American politics "on a different level." [19] But that was an aim vague enough to be identified with Roosevelt as well.

Throughout his career La Follette was plagued by a contradiction between the radical implications in his attacks on the large corporations and the inherent conservatism of his ideology. This would be true in 1917, when he opposed American participation in World War I, and again in 1924 when he opposed the Farmer-Labor party but ran as an independent candidate for the presidency.[20] In 1911 the great popular response to his candidacy led directly to his defeat and his re-

[17] Statement of the National Progressive Republican League, in Box 9, Amos Pinchot papers; see, for example, Lewis R. Larson, "The Saturday Lunch Club of Minneapolis," *La Follette's Weekly Magazine*, I, 30 (July 31, 1909), p. 5.

[18] Statement of NPRL.

[19] Amos Pinchot to Norman H. Hapgood, n.p., August 4, 1911, Box 9, Amos Pinchot papers.

[20] On the latter point see James Weinstein, *Decline*, Chapter VIII.

147

placement by Roosevelt. To many men who opposed Taft—and who identified with Roosevelt's politics—a weak La Follette candidacy was tolerable; the stronger La Follette became the less bearable he was.

Ironically, it was Taft who turned Roosevelt's originally personal opposition to him into a campaign to defend the detente system with the Morgan men and vigorously to assert the need for federal supervision and regulation of the large corporations through an interstate trade commission. After the Rule of Reason decision in the Standard Oil Case and as La Follette's strength increased, Taft's action ran more and more directly counter to Roosevelt's policies. By October 1911 he had initiated an antitrust suit against United States Steel and had become committed to action against the International Harvester Company. What was worse, both to Roosevelt personally and to George W. Perkins, Elbert H. Gary, and other Morgan men, was that Taft chose to make what Attorney General George W. Wickersham described as "an open declaration of war" on Roosevelt by placing the acquisition of the Tennessee Coal and Iron Company in 1907 at the center of the complaint against the Steel corporation.

Administration leaders understood that Roosevelt's reputation as a reformer was particularly vulnerable on this point, since he had explicitly approved the merger during the 1907 panic; what they did not anticipate was the effect an attack on Roosevelt's policies would have on the leaders of the corporations involved in the National Civic Federation. As Taft began implicitly attacking Roosevelt—before the announcement of the Steel corporation prosecution—Ralph Easley and Seth Low expressed their private concern. To Low, Easley wrote that in a recent speech at Waterloo, Iowa, Taft had taken a stand squarely "in favor of competition and anti-combination of any character whatever," and also took "a wallop at all of our people who do not agree with him. If he were not President," Easley concluded, "I would say that he did not know what he was talking about." To this Low could only sigh: "Certainly the President is not making it easier to deal with the problem." [21] As Gabriel Kolko has observed, by the end of 1911, Taft had not only managed to alienate the Midwestern insurgents, but many of the party's key business supporters as well.[22]

Taft's indictment of the United States Steel Corporation was the turning point in La Follette's fortunes; it brought Roosevelt into open opposition and convinced many Morgan associates that the President's reliance on litigation under the Sherman Act had to be publicly opposed. Roosevelt's response was an article published in *The Outlook* on "The Trusts, the People, and the Square Deal," which, "like a stroke of summer lightning" brought the possibility of his candidacy again before the country.[23] Reiterating his belief that only those corporations guilty of unfair practices toward competitors and of procuring unfair advantages from railroads should be prosecuted under the Sherman Act, Roosevelt reasoned that "business cannot be successfully conducted in accordance with the practices and theories of sixty years ago" unless we abolish "all the modern conditions of our civilization." The effort to prohibit all combinations, good or bad, was "bound to fail, and ought to fail." The problem was not how to strangle the new giant corporations, but how to regulate them so that their activity was consistent with the public interest. Along this line, Roosevelt urged the creation of an interstate trade commission and provision for federal incorporation of concerns in interstate commerce. He also defended his approval of the merger of Tennessee Coal and Iron and United States Steel.[24]

Roosevelt was quickly commended for his answer to Taft

[21] Easley to Low, New York, September 29, 1911; Low to Easley, Bedford Hills, September 30, 1911, Box 146, Low papers.
[22] Kolko, *Triumph of Conservatism*, p. 192; Mowry, *T.R./Progressive Movement*, pp. 184–189.
[23] Mowry, *T.R. and the Progressive Movement*, p. 192.
[24] Theodore Roosevelt, "The Trusts, the People, and the Square Deal," *The Outlook*, XCIX (November 18, 1911), pp. 649–656.

by Andrew Carnegie, Elbert H. Gary, Frank A. Vanderlip of the National City Bank, Grenville M. Dodge, and other business leaders. One businessman wrote that his article had made a great impression in Wall Street circles.[25] His position was, of course, exactly in line with that of the Civic Federation and of the business leaders who were closest to it. Such men were prepared now to oppose Taft, but not to support La Follette. As Easley wrote Low, it was important to "hit such stuff as La Follette is talking about as well as the Socialists." [26]

Within the National Progressive Republican League, the key man in pushing Roosevelt was James R. Garfield. Immediately after the indictment of the Steel corporation was announced, Garfield wrote Amos Pinchot that the action was "another example of destructive litigation, unless the government has some facts of which I am ignorant. This is where the Progressive leaders in Congress have a splendid opportunity to formulate and make public the constructive legislation." Garfield believed that the NCF bill (the Hepburn Bill) which, he said, "we introduced during the closing days of our administration" (1908) was the "right foundation upon which to build." [27] A few weeks later (before Roosevelt's *Outlook* article appeared), Garfield wrote to Amos and Gifford Pinchot that the fight in Ohio must be for unpledged delegates—that is anti-Taft but not committed to La Follette—and again, that meetings showed that anti-Taft sentiment was strong, but that Ohio leaders found La Follette unacceptable.[28]

Even before Roosevelt's candidacy had become a public possibility, La Follette had suffered from an inability to convince businessmen that he was in fact a conservative. The at-

[25] Mowry, *T.R. and the Progressive Movement*, p. 192.
[26] Easley to Low, New York, July 31, 1912, Box 146, Low papers.
[27] James R. Garfield to Amos Pinchot, n.p., October 27, 1911, Container 118, James R. Garfield papers, Library of Congress.
[28] Garfield to Gifford Pinchot, n.p., November 16, 23, 1911, *ibid.*; Garfield to Amos Pinchot, Cleveland, September 28, 1911, Box 10, Amos Pinchot papers.

titude expressed by Easley that La Follette and the Socialists were twin evils made fund raising extremely difficult and led to the need for clarification on the part of La Follette supporters.

La Follette's finance committee consisted of Amos Pinchot, Alfred L. Baker, and Rudolph Spreckels. None of them raised any significant amount of money, and were it not for Charles Crane (who contributed $5,000 per month) even the office expenses could not have been met. Pinchot, in particular, complained of the impossibility of raising money in New York. In a vain attempt to solicit funds, Pinchot wrote John R. Drexel that "people should learn that La Follette is not a wild man, but a sane and constructive statesman, who wants to aid business by constructive legislation and has no desire to destroy it." [29] These and other attempts to raise money for La Follette's campaign annoyed *The Nation*, which first simply reported the Senator's attempts to woo Wall Street as a misunderstood man and the greatest friend of business, and then attacked his attempts to minimize his radicalism and pose as a true conservative. This was no good, *The Nation* declared. La Follette was too irresponsible. His "wild and whirring words" uttered about "the men of his imagination who wickedly bring on needless financial panics" disqualified him from serious consideration.[30]

La Follette's response was to point to the tranquil and prosperous state of affairs in Wisconsin as a result of his work. His supporters in Wisconsin went further. The Milwaukee *Journal*, a La Follette paper, defended him against charges of socialism by insisting that the "Tory press" could not distinguish between sound liberalism and socialism. "They make

[29] Pinchot to Walter L. Houser, n.p., October 30, 1911; Medill McCormick to Gifford Pinchot, Chicago, November 13, 1911; Pinchot to John R. Drexel, New York, October 30, 1911, Box 10, Amos Pinchot papers.

[30] "The Wooing of Wall Street," *Nation*, XCIII, 2422 (November 30, 1911), p. 5; "Placatory Radicals," *Nation*, XCIV, 2428 (January 4, 1912), p. 7.

the common and very stupid mistake of pronouncing social-istic all men and measures that are not to their way of think-ing," the *Journal* complained. But in so doing the Tories "fight socialism blindly, all the time standing for abuses and conditions that make for its growth, while the Progressives fight it intelligently and seek to remedy the abuses and conditions upon which it thrives." [31] The argument was, of course, an old one and one which sophisticated business leaders understood and accepted. The problem was that these men saw it as valid only for those who supported the new industrial system. They saw only two real alternatives, a society dominated by the large corporations or socialism; but La Follette attacked the corporations in the name of nineteenth century competitive capitalism. Moving back to that earlier day was impossible; anyone who took seriously the rhetoric of trustbusting could not be considered safe.

Many business leaders naturally turned to Roosevelt rather than La Follette once they concluded that Taft should be defeated. Those who had been active in the National Civic Federation's attempts to clarify the legal status of the large corporations—that is, to amend the Sherman Act with the establishment of an interstate commerce commission—had not been part of the Pinchot-Garfield revolt. George Perkins had sided with Taft in the Pinchot-Ballinger controversy and only entered Progressive ranks after the indictment of United States Steel and Roosevelt's emergence as a potential candidate. [32]

Perkins, of course, had also been concerned with other questions that underlay progressivism and that would be central to the Progressive Party. In November 1910 he had written Judson Harmon, the governor of Ohio, about the "very large increase in the Socialistic vote everywhere." For a couple of years, he added, it had been "growing and growing on me

[31] Quoted in "Senator La Follette as a Candidate," *The Outlook*, C (January 20, 1912), p. 122.
[32] Kolko, *Triumph of Conservatism*, p. 192.

that we are rapidly approaching a crisis in this country on the question of the relation between capital and labor and business and the state." Having "given a good deal more of my time to these questions than my business problems warranted," he was "deeply impressed with the fact that some businessmen, who have had the right sort of experience," ought to take a hand in the solution of the question. "To my mind," he continued, "we have unquestionably entered a period of regulation and control of at least certain forms of business by the state." This was "all right and as it should be," but could not be done successfully by men without business experience. "On the other hand," he believed that with the "proper sort of cooperation between our statesmen and our businessmen," the next eight or ten years could be used "to lay the foundation for a commercial development that would put the United States to the front both at home and abroad and keep her there." Personally, Perkins assured Harmon, he would rather have a hand in that undertaking than do anything else he saw in sight.[33]

The next month, Perkins resigned his partnership in J. P. Morgan and Company to devote himself to general corporate work and public activity. "When a man approaches fifty," he wrote a friend, he must face the question of "whether to try to make some more money which he cannot spend or take with him, or perform some service that will be of benefit to the world at large." With a fortune of $5,500,000 in securities, Perkins chose the latter path.[34] Another friend, congratulating Perkins on the move, guessed Perkins' motives: "To build and endow colleges is commendable," he wrote. "To erect and maintain libraries is also commendable, and such donors deserve great credit, but when you have added to man's

[33] Perkins to Judson Harmon, n.p., November 14, 1910, Box 21, Perkins papers.
[34] Perkins to John C. Greenway, n.p., December 19, 1910, *ibid.*; John Arthur Garraty, *Right Hand Man* (New York, Harper & Brothers, 1960), p. 238.

productive power, when you have increased man's efficiency," whether by "increased loyalty, increased knowledge or increased enthusiasm, you have created something." [35]

Long a heavy financial supporter of Taft and the Republican Party, Perkins broke with them slowly. In late 1910 he had written Morgan that Taft was the logical choice for 1912, and as late as November 25, 1911, after the United States Steel suit had been inaugurated and Roosevelt's reply had been published, Perkins met with Taft in an attempt to come to terms with him.[36] Then, along with Frank Munsey (a magazine publisher and director of United States Steel), Dan Hanna, son of the late Mark Hanna, and others, Perkins got behind the rapidly booming candidacy of Roosevelt. Quickly taking charge of raising funds, Perkins donated and collected over $600,000 for the preconvention campaign.[37]

The decisive swing to Roosevelt occurred in Ohio, home of Garfield and Hanna. There La Follette's speaking tour in late December brought forth unexpectedly large and friendly audiences, but also was a harbinger of his elimination from the race. By the time La Follette entered Ohio, Dan Hanna's *Toledo Blade* and *Cleveland Leader* had been booming Roosevelt's as yet unannounced candidacy for a month. Hanna's views on the trust question had always been close to Roosevelt's, but his support may also have been the result of a lawsuit brought against him under a federal antirebate law by Attorney General Wickersham. In any case, Dan Hanna not only supported Roosevelt with his own newspapers, but when Charles A. Otis' *Cleveland News* would not support the Colonel, Hanna purchased that paper too.[38]

[35] F. L. Campbell to George W. Perkins, Omaha, December 13, 1910, Box 21, Perkins papers.
[36] Kolko, *Triumph of Conservatism*, p. 192; Garraty, *Right Hand Man*, p. 253.
[37] Kolko, *Triumph of Conservatism*, p. 193.
[38] Hoyt Landon Warner, *Progressivism in Ohio, 1897–1917* (Columbus, Ohio State University Press, 1964), pp. 357–358, 377, n. 7.

At the New Year's Day (1912) convention of the Ohio Progressive Republican League, La Follette was still the overwhelming choice of the members. Roosevelt had already told Garfield and Gifford Pinchot to work for his nomination, but shied from a public announcement. The Roosevelt forces therefore fought to keep the door open for him by insisting that the League endorse no one. A resolution opposing Taft and pledging support to a Progressive was prepared by Garfield and Pinchot; after winning the support of La Follette's manager in Ohio, it was adopted. Throughout the country, politicians and the press understood this as a silent bid for Roosevelt. The boom was on.

On January 9, Daniel Willard of the Baltimore and Ohio Railroad decided that of the leading Progressives Roosevelt was the safest. Frank Munsey, writing to Roosevelt, explained what safety meant. The United States, he wrote, must move from excessive democracy toward a more "parental guardianship of the people," who needed "the sustaining and guiding hand of the State." As Munsey saw it, it was "the work of the state to think for the people and plan for the people— to teach them how to do, what to do, and to sustain them in the doing." [39] In his view, Roosevelt was best suited to advance these concepts.

La Follette also understood that Roosevelt was "safe" from the point of view of big business. In part that was why he opposed Roosevelt even after it was clear that his own campaign could not get the financial support it needed or even retain the loyalty of many of the original organizers of the National Progressive Republican League. Personal rivalry played its role—La Follette wished to be the leader of the Progressive movement, even though he seems to have known full well that he could not win the presidential nomination from Taft—but his personal ambition was inextricably intertwined with his ideology. La Follette insisted that "a halfway

[39] Mowry, *Theodore Roosevelt and the Progressive Movement*, p. 212.

measure never fairly tests the principle and may utterly discredit it," that such a measure was "certain to weaken, disappoint and dissipate public interest." [40]

As William Allen White keenly observed in 1911, La Follette won by losing; he saw politics as an educational task in which compromise was defeat.[41] In contrast, as La Follette charged, Roosevelt "acted upon the maxim that half a loaf is better than no bread." [42] But there was more than a difference in style involved. Roosevelt saw the great corporations not only as a natural and inevitable development, but also as the source of American prosperity and power. Only the evil actions of the more socially irresponsible corporations concerned him. "If," Roosevelt warned, the people insisted "in a spirit of sullen envy," upon "pulling down those who have profited most in the years of fatness, they will bury themselves in the crash of the common disaster." [43] The problem was not to destroy the new system, but to control its excesses and spread its benefits. The very essence of such a political program was compromise and accommodation by all parties. Thus what appeared to La Follette to be the result of Roosevelt's personal weaknesses—a striving for popularity and an avoidance of discord among his supporters—was in fact the core of his social philosophy.

Yet neither Roosevelt nor his supporters could publicly attack La Follette on an ideological level: his antitrust rhetoric was too widely popular. From late November 1911, Roosevelt's boom was under way and La Follette's organization was in a state of collapse. Yet La Follette's greatest public triumphs occurred in Ohio at the end of December and at Carnegie Hall in New York on January 22, 1912. Since

[40] Quoted in Gabriel Kolko, *Railroads and Regulation, 1877–1916* (Princeton, Princeton University Press, 1965), pp. 153–154.
[41] William Allen White, "The Progressive Hen and the Insurgent Ducklings," *American Magazine*, LXXII, 3 (January 1911), p. 394.
[42] Kolko, *Railroads and Regulation*, pp. 153–154.
[43] Quoted by La Follette in *La Follette's Autobiography*, p. 293.

La Follette had refused to withdraw even after the Pinchots, Medill McCormick, and others in the Progressive League had urged him to do so,[44] Roosevelt had to bide his time in the hope that La Follette would provide him with an opportunity to move openly. La Follette was not long in doing just that.

The occasion was a speech at the Periodical Publisher's Association dinner on February 2, 1912. Exhausted by his campaign and anxious about his daughter who was to have a serious operation the next morning, La Follette was in an irascible mood. His speech, a severe criticism of the trusts and their control of the daily press, was interrupted at several points by antagonized listeners, which caused the annoyed La Follette to repeat sections of it for emphasis. At the end, which was not until 1:00 A.M., La Follette was in a state of near collapse. The Roosevelt forces then declared that La Follette had broken down, that his candidacy was at an end, and that Roosevelt was in the race. Of course, as the *Cleveland Leader* admitted, La Follette had already been out of the race before he showed "signs of illness." [45]

Actually, the content of La Follette's Philadelphia speech isolated him from those whose support he sought much more effectively than did his physical condition. In that speech, La Follette had defined his view of the emergent great corporations, their role in American society, and their relation to the newspaper and periodical press. Much of what he proposed was acceptable to the corporation liberals: when it came down to specific solutions, this was always true, since La Follette, like Roosevelt, Perkins, Brandeis, and Woodrow Wilson, looked to the federal government to act as regulator and social mediator of the existing system. Further, La Follette insisted that he "would not unjustly decry Wall Street or ignore the necessity of a great central market to provide capital for

[44] Amos Pinchot to Hiram Johnson, n.p., March 30, 1912, Box 10, Amos Pinchot papers.
[45] Quoted in *The Literary Digest*, XLIV, 7 (February 17, 1912), p. 319.

the large business undertakings of this country." Recognizing "the rights of capital and the service which capital can render to a great producing nation," he nevertheless argued that "this government guarantees equality of opportunity for all men" and must likewise guarantee "equality of opportunity for all capital." Corporations and combinations of corporations, "with their centralized banking and extending branch connections from state to state," should not be entitled to "special favors in legislation." Opposing the tendency of government to aid monopoly, La Follette proposed that the same government should regulate the corporations in the interest of the small businessman. It was, he said, claimed "on all sides that competition has failed." He denied it. "Fair competition has not failed. It has been suppressed."

La Follette then went on to attack the "rule of reason" enunciated by the Supreme Court in the recent Standard Oil case, not so much for distinguishing between reasonable and unreasonable restraints of trade, but because in drawing such distinctions the Court arrogated to itself a legislative power.[46]

It was not these comments that angered his listeners, but his presumption to examine the relation of the large corporations to the press. "One would think," La Follette began, "that in a democracy like ours, people seeking the truth" would find the press "their eager and willing instructors." Certainly that was true in the past. But since "the money power has gained control of our industry and government," it also controlled the press. This was true not only as regards the editorial sections of the newspapers, but "even as to news." The public was "fast coming to understand that whenever news items bear in any way upon the control of government by business, the news is colored." As if this were not bad enough, La Follette went on to say that while "cultured and able men" were still to be found on the staffs of all great dailies, "the public understands them to be hired men who no longer ex-

---

[46] *La Follette's Autobiography*, pp. 334, 335, 336, 337.

press honest judgments and sincere conviction"—men "whose judgments are salaried." The magazines, he added, were still free of this control, but even they were to be wary of the use of advertising and control of credit, lest they succumb as had the daily press.[47]

It was a courageous speech to have delivered to a magazine publishers association, but it laid bare La Follette's irresponsibility to the new system of large corporations. Don C. Seitz, business manager of the New York *World* (and toastmaster of the dinner), cried that La Follette had "foolishly, untruthfully and wickedly assailed" the daily press. *The Independent* intoned that his recent utterances "have been characterized by sensational exaggeration." It then compared La Follette's remarks to the Socialist charges that commercial newspaper editors were "servile and venal lackeys of the ruling class," and noted that the Socialists themselves thought La Follette had reached that fork in the road of opposition to the "trust" system where he might either go forward to socialism or take the reactionary path of an attempted return to free competition.[48]

La Follette's refusal to withdraw from the race after his disastrous speech at Philadelphia did not seriously hinder Roosevelt's campaign against Taft. In almost every state where contests took place for delegates to the Republican convention Roosevelt won over Taft and La Follette.[49] But La Follette's obstinate opposition to Roosevelt did cause confusion in the minds of many unsophisticated, and some fairly sophisticated, reformers. Even Amos Pinchot, in many ways the most radical of La Follette's original supporters, could not understand why La Follette did not withdraw. In a letter to Hiram Johnson, Pinchot complained that La Follette seemed

[47] *Ibid.*, pp. 340–341.

[48] "Senator La Follette's Disability," *The Independent*, LXX, 3298 (February 15, 1912), pp. 371–372.

[49] North Dakota was the major exception. There La Follette won the primary.

to have "forgotten that he entered the fight for principles rather than for personal ambition." [50] But Pinchot himself had recognized only a few weeks before that La Follette knew he could not win, but was remaining in the race to make the issues clear and define a platform for the convention.[51] Although Pinchot would soon come to understand La Follette's refusal to go along with Roosevelt and men like Perkins, Hanna, Willard, and Munsey, this confusion was not entirely his fault. Both La Follette and Roosevelt spoke about a need to return to popular government, both enunciated the necessity of an interstate trade commission (although, as Pinchot failed to note, each in his own image), both opposed socialism and spoke as true conservatives. In fact, Pinchot was closer to the Socialists than either La Follette or Roosevelt. As he told a correspondent, he believed "that economic exploitation by the privileged class was the trouble in this country," that "the control of national monopolies of production and distribution of necessities must be in the hands of the people." [52] But Pinchot was swept along in a desire to win. Soon enough he bristled at a progressive movement led by large corporation executives. Initially, he was elated with the Roosevelt movement.

Although lavishly financed by Perkins and his associates, Roosevelt could not overcome the advantage the presidency gave Taft in securing delegates to the convention. Roosevelt's hostility to Taft, and especially to the means by which Taft secured his renomination—through the manipulation of the Southern, organization-picked delegates—left him in a mood of defiance, but he knew he could not oppose Taft under another banner without massive financial support. That support

[50] Amos Pinchot to Hiram Johnson, n.p., March 30, 1912, Box 11, Pinchot papers.
[51] Pinchot to W. B. Colver, New York, February 2, 1912, Box 11, Pinchot papers.
[52] Pinchot to Frederick M. Kerby, n.p., October 19, 1912, Box 13, Amos Pinchot papers.

160

was forthcoming from Perkins and Munsey, who at the decisive moment of Roosevelt's defeat at the Republican convention assured him: "Colonel, we will see you through." [53] Significantly, the only thing Amos Pinchot could see to worry about after "the great act" of starting a new party had been accomplished was "the chance that the politicians will butt in and try to make this movement their own." [54] Two weeks later, Pinchot told Garfield he was concerned about the role of Perkins, Munsey, and Timothy Woodruff in New York—the latter because he was an oldline machine politician. Only Woodruff was really objectionable—Perkins and Munsey were seen by Pinchot as "good men"—but, he argued, "the public will not accept any of them as progressives." [55]

By then, Woodrow Wilson had won the Democratic Party nomination. Wilson's ideology closely paralleled that of the Roosevelt men, as Pinchot realized, and meant the loss of many Progressives from the Roosevelt camp. "We would," Pinchot wrote Medill McCormick, "welcome Wilson into our party and make much of him, and now we must *not* declare against him because he is in another party." [56] Pinchot, who agreed with Roosevelt on the need for an interstate trade commission, could justify opposition to Wilson only because he believed the prior principle was the establishment of a party "which is purely a progressive institution." Even so, he did not see "any real issue to fight on," other than the formation of a clean new party.[57]

As the campaign developed, Roosevelt spoke of the need

[53] Garraty, *Right Hand Man*, p. 263.
[54] Amos Pinchot to W. J. McGee, n.p., June 25, 1912, Box 12, Amos Pinchot papers.
[55] Pinchot to Garfield, Milford, Pa., July 8, 1912, Box 12, Amos Pinchot papers.
[56] Pinchot to Medill McCormick, New York, July 3, 1912; Thomas Shipp to Amos Pinchot, Indianapolis, July 6, 1912, Box 12, Amos Pinchot papers. [Emphasis added.]
[57] Pinchot to Medill McCormick, New York, July 3, 1912; Pinchot to Norman Hapgood, n.p., July 20, 1912, Box 12, Amos Pinchot papers.

to recognize and regulate monopoly and Wilson countered that it was competition which must be maintained and regulated. The differences were largely rhetorical. As Martin J. Sklar has shown, Wilson's position on the trust question in 1912 was a synthesis of the positions of Taft and Roosevelt. Acknowledging the demise of individual, entrepreneurial competition, Wilson affirmed and insisted upon reasonable intercorporate competition. At the same time, he looked with favor on "reasonable" combination and intercorporate arrangements consistent with the "public interest" or "general welfare," these to be regulated by the government on the basis of common law precedents, whether enforced by the courts (as Taft would have it), or by an administrative commission (as Roosevelt—and La Follette—preferred).[58] Like Roosevelt, Taft, and La Follette, Wilson recognized that "Business underlies everything in our national life, including our spiritual life." Nobody who really cared for the welfare of America, Wilson insisted, could "wish to upset business or interfere with any honest and natural process of it." [59]

That "natural process" had led to the emergence of the large-scale industrial corporations as more efficient and suitable to modern conditions than a state of unrestricted competition. "Modern business," Wilson observed, "is no doubt best conducted upon a great scale, for which the resources of the single individual are manifestly insufficient. Money and men must be massed in order to do the things that must be done for the support and facilitation of modern life." To Wilson, it was "plain enough that we cannot go back to the old competitive system under which individuals were the competitors." There were—and there still are—those who

---

[58] Martin J. Sklar, "Woodrow Wilson and the Political Economy of Modern United States Liberalism," *Studies on the Left*, I, 3 (1960), pp. 17–47, specifically p. 25.

[59] Wilson's speech to the Economic Club Dinner, New York, May 23, 1912, as reported in the *New York Evening Post*, May 24, 1912.

understood Wilson to stand with the small businessman against the large corporations, but that error was not encouraged by Wilson. In the speech accepting his nomination to the presidency, in August 1912, Wilson repudiated his own party's platform, which denounced the Rule of Reason decision of 1911—a position representing the Bryan wing of the party. Instead he identified with the views of Roosevelt, Garfield, and the Bureau of Corporations. "I am not," he said, "one of those who think that competition can be established by law against the drift of a worldwide economic tendency; neither am I one of those who believe that business done upon a great scale by a single organization—call it corporation, or what you will—is necessarily dangerous to the liberties, even the economic liberties, of a great people like our own." He was, Wilson insisted, "not afraid of anything that is normal. I dare say we shall never return to the old order of individual competition, and that the organization of business upon a great scale of cooperation is, up to a certain point, itself normal and inevitable." [60]

Wilson's specific campaign proposals for regulating competition were vague. In what Arthur S. Link calls his most precise speech on the subject, Wilson proposed that the government prevent corporations from fixing prices, tying contracts between manufacturers and retailers, controlling sources of raw materials, engaging in espionage and cutthroat competition. Such a program was apparently what Wilson meant when he spoke of eliminating monopoly. He claimed it would force such overcapitalized trusts as the Steel corporation to reorganize on a more efficient basis.[61] The main evil that Wilson saw was unnatural overcapitalization, or watering of

[60] Acceptance Address, August 7, 1912, *Official Report of the Proceedings of the Democratic Party National Convention*, 1912, p. 407.

[61] Arthur S. Link, *Woodrow Wilson, The Road to the White House* (Princeton, Princeton University Press, 1947), p. 514.

stock, which forced such corporations to charge unnecessarily high prices in order to pay the going rate of return on the public's investment. The International Harvester Company, on the other hand, was not attacked by Wilson, possibly because of the heavy financial support he received from the McCormicks, but also because its stock was not watered: fixed assets had been overvalued by only 15 percent when the corporation was organized, as compared to 100 percent overvaluation in the Steel corporation. Yet the Harvester corporation accounted for 90 percent of domestic production of grain binders and about 80 percent of mowers, the two major types of harvesting machines,[62] while the Steel corporation accounted for only 53 percent of the nation's output of ingots and castings in 1912, compared with 63 percent at the time it was organized in 1901.[63]

Indeed, the Steel corporation's need to charge high prices created a favorable climate for the continued existence of smaller manufacturers. As James R. Garfield noted, "a return to the old days of killing competition means necessarily the failure of many of the weaker concerns." [64] Even in the harvester field, where overcapitalization was no issue, previously existing small manufacturers lived harmoniously with the new giant. One such farm equipment manufacturer wrote to Seth Low that he had never been subjected to unfair competition by the trust. He did not say so, but apparently he benefited from the rise in the price of farm equipment that followed the organization of the corporation.[65] Regulated competition,

[62] Helen M. Kramer, "Harvesters and High Finance: Formation of the International Harvester Company," *The Business History Review*, XXXVIII, 3 (Autumn 1964), p. 297.

[63] Kolko, *Triumph of Conservatism*, p. 37.

[64] Garfield to Amos Pinchot, n.p., October 27, 1911, Container 18, James R. Garfield papers.

[65] A. B. Farquahar to Low, York, Pennsylvania, February 27, 1913, Box 106, Low papers.

since it did not mean a return to "cutthroat competition," simply meant regulation to prevent unreasonable practices. This, of course, was what Roosevelt meant when he talked about regulated monopoly.

As Gabriel Kolko has pointed out, Wilson's ideas about the corporations began to differ from Roosevelt's—or, rather, appear to differ—only after he had gained the Democratic nomination in 1912 and found himself in need of differentiating himself from the Progressive. In 1910, after favoring local initiative, he began to favor federal regulation, but opposed trustbusting. George Perkins found these views satisfactory and wrote Wilson on his election as Governor of New Jersey that his "views on the business questions of the hour" were "absolutely sound." Efficiency and big business seemed inseparable to him. Therefore, he told the American Bar Association in 1910, "If you dissolve the offending corporation, you throw great undertakings out of gear . . . to the infinite loss of thousands of entirely innocent persons and to the great inconvenience of society as a whole." Regarding the corporation "as indispensable to modern business enterprise," he was "not jealous of size or might." [66]

In early 1912 Wilson aggressively called for the cultivation of foreign markets and the development of a powerful merchant marine (policies he would pursue vigorously when he was in office, particularly during the war). In this, as in his views on the corporations, Wilson was criticized for sounding like Roosevelt. "When I sit down and compare my views with those of a Progressive Republican," he responded, "I can't see what the difference is, except that he has a sort of pious feeling about the doctrine of protection, which I have never felt." After his nomination Wilson was under pressure to accommodate himself to the antitrust sentiment among the Bryan Democrats. He solved the problem by condemning the methods

[66] Quoted by Kolko, *Triumph of Conservatism*, pp. 205–206.

used in organizing the giant corporations, but then going on to say that he observed "a new spirit" among "influential men of business" in the last year or two.[67]

Wilson did insist on freedom of entry for the small businessman, but in this he did not differ from the Supreme Court's position in the Standard Oil Case in 1911, or from most Progressives. "I admit that any large corporation built up by the legitimate processes of business, by economy, by efficiency, is natural; and I am not afraid of it, no matter how big it grows." No legitimate arrangement was to be disturbed, Wilson insisted, "but every impediment to business is going to be removed, every illegitimate kind of control is going to be destroyed. Every man who wants an opportunity and has the energy to seize it, is going to have a chance." [68] Stripped of the rhetoric, Wilson was merely reasserting the common law doctrine of unreasonable restraint of trade, a principle by then accepted by most business leaders, and certainly by Roosevelt and his Progressives.

The general business community was uneasy over the situation in 1912. Although none of the major candidates was antibusiness, no party clearly represented the corporations as a group. Taft's turn back to litigation under the Sherman Act and his attacks on Roosevelt's detente policies with United States Steel lost him the support of several Morgan men, including Willard Straight, Elbert H. Gary, Perkins, Munsey, and Hanna, as well as men such as Daniel Willard and some of the McCormicks. Wilson received his greatest support from Charles R. Crane, Cleveland H. Dodge, Jacob Schiff, Samuel Untermeyer, Jacob Ruppert (the brewer), Thomas and David Jones of the Harvester Company and Cyrus McCormick. But Frank Vanderlip of the National City Bank, who a year later would write to J. P. Morgan, Jr., that he had "never seen so

[67] *Ibid.*, pp. 206–207. On Wilson's policies during the war, see Chapter Eight, pp. 214–254, below.
[68] Kolko, *Triumph of Conservatism*, pp. 209–210.

166

much power wielded by any administration as Wilson seems to have, and if he can keep up his present pace he will truly be a wonder," remained aloof. He did so, presumably, because he feared other sections of the Democratic Party—the Bryan wing. Later, Vanderlip wrote Lyman Gage that the "prospect of Wilson having another four years is not particularly disturbing," since in a second term he "would have no politics to play." [69]

Despite Roosevelt's position on the trusts, the Progressive Party did not get a predominance of support from big business, partly because of the stand he took on the recall of judicial decisions, but also because of distrust of Roosevelt's personal methods or of the mixed character of the Progressive Party. Seth Low, for example, believed the idea of the recall of judges or of decisions endangered the constitutional separation of powers. [70]

Charles G. Dawes, a Chicago banker, thought that the Progressive platform was "an advance on both the Democratic and the Republican platforms" on the trust question. But the party "associated with it such a lot of dangerous principles" that it became "impossible as a permanent rallying point for the conservative constructive thought of the country." [71] Frederick A. Delano, Franklin D. Roosevelt's uncle, soon to be appointed to the Federal Reserve Board by Wilson, also thought Theodore Roosevelt was right on the corporations; he disagreed only with "the method of practice of control," which he saw as "that of a benevolent despot who decides what corporations should be destroyed and what left alone." [72]

[69] Frank A. Vanderlip to J. P. Morgan, Jr., n.p., November 13, 1913; Vanderlip to Lyman J. Gage, n.p., August 31, 1915, Vanderlip papers, Columbia University.

[70] Low to the Editor of *The Outlook*, n.p., October 15, 1912, Box 120, Low papers.

[71] Charles G. Dawes to George W. Perkins, Chicago, February 2, 1915, Box 26, Perkins papers.

[72] Frederick A. Delano to Seth Low, Chicago, March 4, 1913, Box 106, Low papers.

The Progressive Party *was* too mixed to serve as a rallying point for constructive conservative work. As the Socialists pointed out, the "mixture of interests in the Progressive Party of necessity determine[d] its policies." As a party, it sought to "maintain the existing order with such improvements" as were called for "to secure its permanency." The aim of the big business supporters was "business under government regulation," which in practice would mean that "business shall govern." However, the chances of reliability were slight in a party the bulk of whose membership consisted "of middle-class people rebelling against the dominating influence of the powerful 'interests.' " [73] As it turned out, one of the least reliable Progressives from the large corporation point of view, was Amos Pinchot. In October 1912, even before the election, Pinchot complained to Louis D. Brandeis about the role of Perkins and Munsey in shaping party policy and its public image. In December, Pinchot appealed to Roosevelt to remove Perkins as titular head of the party because of his identification with the Steel and Harvester companies. Attacking the labor policies of these corporations, Pinchot wrote that the party was not out for political victory alone, "but to establish social and economic justice." As Lincoln freed the chattel slave, "so we are going to free the industrial slave." [74]

Roosevelt, of course, sided with Perkins and attacked Amos Pinchot as a dangerous radical. Pinchot's rhetoric had been tolerable when he accepted the original hierarchy of the party and its implicit bias in favor of the large corporations. Perkins, as well as Pinchot, viewed the Progressive Party as an educational instrument for the new view of the trust problem; but better than Pinchot, Perkins knew the underlying thrust of Roosevelt's rhetoric. As Elbert H. Gary commented to

[73] "The Progressive Party and Its Elements," *The Issue*, III, 2 (New York, 1912). Copy in Subject file 45, Amos Pinchot papers.
[74] Pinchot to Brandeis, n.p., October 10, 1912, Box 13, Pinchot papers; Pinchot to Roosevelt, New York, December 3, 1912, Box 23, Perkins papers.

Perkins, Roosevelt was "generally right and therefore strong." His great value to these corporation leaders was his ability to capture "the sentiment of a large majority of the voters throughout the United States, including *all sections*." [75] But Perkins also understood the inherently unstable nature of the party. His loyalty was to the principles enunciated by Roosevelt, not to the party or the man. "In my judgement," Perkins told William Allen White, "there has been altogether too much of the practice in this country of being for a man" because he was attractive, "regardless of what he stood for." To Nicholas Murray Butler, Perkins was more direct: "Anyone who had the notion that" his course in politics had "been governed by my personal devotion to Colonel Roosevelt," had "entirely misunderstood" his position. He had supported Roosevelt "only because I believed that he more nearly than any other of our leading statesmen represented the forward-looking policies so necessary to the preservation of the Republican party and its traditions." [76]

The politics of 1912 served to bring into popular debate, in a manner ultimately satisfactory to most business leaders, the question of the relation of the state to the large corporations. In eliminating La Follette from the race and preventing the consolidation of an organization under his leadership, and then in drawing a sharp line of distinction between socialism and social reform under the leadership of such men as Perkins and Roosevelt, the Progressive Party circumscribed the danger to the system both of the "irresponsible" neopopulists and the "dangerous" revolutionaries. Before the election, Albert Bushnell Hart (a Harvard historian) wrote that "Millions of people in the United States find it hard to think that anything is seriously the matter in so prosperous and comfortable a

[75] E. H. Gary to Perkins, aboard HMS *Aquitania*, July 6, 1914, Box 24, Perkins papers.
[76] Perkins to W. A. White, n.p., February 2, 1917, Box 28; Perkins to N. M. Butler, n.p., January 24, 1918, Box 29, Perkins papers.

country." Yet, he warned, "a large minority of the American people, which is likely soon to be a majority, feels dissatisfied and resentful and is bound to make things different. Unless that movement'is checked, within sixteen years there will be a Socialist President of the United States." The only way to avoid that, Hart advised, was to support the party that would "take over the reasonable part of the Socialist programme"— the Progressive Party.[77] After the election, as Ralph Easley (who did not vote for Roosevelt) told Anne Morgan, the Progressive Party, if it did nothing else, "accomplished a great piece of work in forcing a clear line of demarcation between 'Social Reform' and 'Socialism.' "

As Easley further observed, "Thousands of social reformers voted for Debs" in previous years and "counted themselves Socialists because they wanted social reform and saw no other party platform that gave them any hope." In 1912, however, he estimated that at least 300,000 Socialist votes had been lost to Roosevelt.[78] For their part, some Socialists understood full well what 1912 signified. The *International Socialist Review* also looked upon Debs' 901,000 votes that year as a rock-bottom Socialist core from which the Progressive Party had successfully scraped the "decayed organic matter." [79] In addition, they understood that Wilson's victory meant that more reforms were coming.[80] Although the public, and possibly even men like La Follette, may have seen genuine distinctions between the New Freedom and the New Nationalism, the more sophisticated both among businessmen and Socialists understood that except for Debs' campaign the real politics of 1912 had taken place before the campaign officially began. Jeremiah W. Jenks, a professor of economics at Cornell University and a leading Civic Federation consultant, made this point force-

[77] Letter to the *New York Times*, September 30, 1912.
[78] Easley to Anne Morgan; Easley to Theodore Roosevelt, both New York, November 18, 1912: Box 82 and 83, respectively, NCF papers.
[79] "Editorial," XIII, 7 (January 1913), p. 561.
[80] "Editorial," XIII, 6 (December 1912), p. 495.

fully at the Fourteenth Annual Meeting of NCF. During the last campaign, he observed, the two words continually in the mouths of public speakers were "competition" and "combination." "Should we regulate competition or monopoly was the way it was put." Now, however, the campaign was over and it was time to get on with the constructive work of stabilizing the system. If, therefore, "we are to understand this question in the proper way," Jenks urged, Federation members needed "more than almost anything else" to free themselves from "the tyranny of words." [81]

[81] Jeremiah W. Jenks to the 14th Annual Meeting of the NCF, Morning Session, December 12, 1913, Minutes folder, Box 187, NCF papers.

CHAPTER SEVEN

THE FEDERAL GOVERNMENT AS SOCIAL INVESTIGATOR: THE COMMISSION ON INDUSTRIAL RELATIONS, 1913–1915

IN POLITICS THROUGHOUT the Progressive Era a primary concern of corporation and financial leaders associated with the National Civic Federation, as well as of almost all major political figures, was the promotion of social responsibility. In relation to the unions this meant, of course, the strengthening of conservative trade unionism as epitomized by Samuel Gompers against the challenges of Socialists within the AFL and of Socialists and IWW's on the outside. Among businessmen it meant the espousal of social reform and negotiation with responsible representatives of labor, farmers, and liberal intellectuals and social workers. In their commitment to these principles, on this level of abstraction, there was little difference among Theodore Roosevelt, William H. Taft, and Woodrow Wilson. In practical politics differences between these men were more apparent; in some cases these appearances were real.

The history of the United States Commission on Industrial Relations illustrates both the continuities and the divergences imposed by practical political considerations in the progressivism of Taft and Wilson. Until very recently, when the Commission has been remembered at all it has been treated as a Wilsonian innovation. In fact the Commission was sponsored by Taft, and the enabling legislation passed while he was still in office.[1] In choosing the Commissioners, also, the historical stereotype was violated. Taft (who got to choose a Commission, but whose choice was not confirmed) named a panel satisfactory to the small businessmen. Wilson (who owed nothing to the NAM) selected a panel ultimately much more advantageous to leaders of the large corporations represented in the NCF. Yet the United States Commission on Industrial Relations did do more to conciliate workers and radicals than any previous presidentially appointed federal body; for this Wilson was responsible.

The Commission was established in response to the general spread of radical discontent in 1911. But its creation was the direct result of one incident that year that shocked the nation and focused attention on the related problems of industrial warfare and Socialist politics. The occurrence was the destruction of the *Los Angeles Times* building by two professional union dynamiters.

The *Los Angeles Times* explosion was a classic case of union violence against an open shop employer. It took on special significance because of the man against whom the dynamite was directed and because of the political situation in the city. The *Times* was owned and edited by Harrison Gray Otis, leader of the open shop employers in Southern California and of the Los Angeles Merchants and Manufacturers Association (M and M), a group that had succeeded in keeping Los Angeles the only major open shop city on the West Coast. Labor costs were so much lower in Los Angeles than in other cities that new business and investment rushed there. In San Francisco, a tightly organized union town, wages were 30 percent higher. This condition helped spur the drive to

[1] Graham Adams, Jr., *The Age of Industrial Violence, 1910–1915* (New York, Columbia University Press, 1966) corrects the prevailing misconceptions, although even he exaggerates the differences between Taft's unconfirmed appointees and those finally chosen by Wilson.

organize Los Angeles, for the San Francisco employers had warned local unionists that if conditions were not equalized they faced collapse. The result was substantial aid from San Francisco's tough business union men to the Los Angeles unions and an all-out drive against Otis and the M and M.[2]

The initial impetus for the organizing drive came in May 1910 when the Los Angeles Brewers announced their intention not to renew their contract with the Brewery Workers (it was the only closed shop industry in the city). This led to a strike in the industry, quickly followed by strikes in the metal trades, among leather workers, laundry workers, railroad electricians, telegraph employees, construction workers, and others. In June 1910 a General Strike Committee was formed and unions from all over the state contributed funds; San Francisco unions alone gave $50,000.[3]

The dynamiting of the *Times* plant was part of the secret strike strategy. The plan was to blow up the *Times* and make it appear as if the explosion were the result of leaking gas and management unconcern with the safety of its workers. But when the charge went off it ignited secondary explosions and unexpectedly killed twenty workers. This happened at 1:00 A.M. on October 1, 1910. All top management personnel had gone home. Otis was out of town, on his way back from a trip to Mexico. Despite the destruction of the plant the *Times* came out in the morning proclaiming "Unionist Bombs Wreck the Times." The issue was printed in an auxiliary plant two blocks away. Otis explained he had expected to be dynamited.[4]

Immediately, of course, Otis and the M and M launched a campaign to find the "Unionite murderers." Organized labor countered with angry denials of guilt and with accusations

---

[2] *Ibid.*, p. 3; Louis Adamic, *Dynamite* (New York, Viking, 1934), Chapter 19.

[3] Adams, *Age of Industrial Violence*, p. 5.

[4] Adamic, *Dynamite*, p. 210.

against Otis. Had not the *Times* had trouble with leaking gas in its plant the month before the explosion? There had been many complaints of employees getting sick from inhaling gas fumes. Had not Otis anticipated the bombing? "What led him to expect it?" asked the *International Socialist Review*. "The *Times* and its crowd of union-haters," Eugene V. Debs asserted, "are themselves the instigators" of the murder of the twenty workers who perished in the explosion. Union men, Samuel Gompers insisted, could not have been guilty. "The greatest enemies of our movement," he argued, "could not administer a blow so hurtful to our cause as would be such a stigma if the men of organized labor were responsible for it." [5]

For six months the investigation dragged on. Then William J. Burns, the M and M's private detective, arrested James B. McNamara and Ortie McManigal in Detroit. They were registered at a hotel under assumed names and were found with timing devices similar to those used in the Los Angeles explosions in their possession. They were on a job for the Bridge and Structural Iron Workers (BSIW). Next Burns arrested John J. McNamara, James' brother and Executive Secretary of the BSIW, at the International's headquarters in Indianapolis. McManigal confessed to the *Times* "stunt" and to dozens of dynamitings at sites of nonunion construction around the country. James B. McNamara was reported by Burns to have said, "I'd blow up the whole damn country if I thought it would get us rights." [6] Because of legal complications in extraditing the McNamaras and McManigal, Burns took them illegally to California, where they were placed in jail.

Then the uproar began. John J. McNamara was a high union official, a conservative trade unionist, and, according to Victor Berger, a member of the Militia of Christ. [7] Yet he had

[5] Adams, *Age of Industrial Violence*, pp. 8–9.
[6] *Ibid.*, p. 11; Adamic, *Dynamite*, pp. 214–215.
[7] Karson, *American Labor Unions and Politics*, p. 197.

been "kidnapped" in much the same manner that Big Bill Haywood, Charles H. Moyer, and George A. Pettibone had been taken from Colorado to Idaho to stand trial for the murder of ex-governor Frank Steunenberg five years earlier. Haywood's acquittal in 1907 had defeated that attempted "frame-up," but only after a tremendous outcry from labor and the Socialists, climaxed by massive May Day demonstrations and a warning by Debs that if Haywood were convicted "not a wheel shall turn in this country" until the verdict be set aside.[8] Now Gompers cried that the arrest of McNamara was "a frame-up and a plot," and that Burns had "lied through the entire case." Debs charged that the "secret arrest" of John McNamara by a "corporation detective agency has all the earmarks of another conspiracy." Unionists in general, and, as it turned out, many others, suspected that the Los Angeles incidents were what Debs suggested. And labor, the Socialists, and others rallied to the McNamaras' defense. At its June meeting the Executive Council of the AFL created a McNamara Ways and Means Committee to organize support from local, national, and international unions and to coordinate fund raising. The San Francisco Building Trades Council alone pledged to raise $100,000.[9]

In Los Angeles, labor's support for the McNamaras strengthened the growing alliance of local unions with the Socialists that had begun with the organizing drive in May 1910. Job Harriman, a Socialist lawyer who had helped found the party in 1900 and was Debs' vice-presidential running mate that year, was chief attorney for the strikers and an attorney for the McNamaras. He had worked closely with the San Francisco labor men in planning the strikes that preceded the bombing of the *Times*; when he became the Socialist nominee for mayor in the spring of 1911 he received widespread labor support. Even Gompers endorsed Harriman, the

---

[8] Adamic, *Dynamite*, p. 150.
[9] Adams, *Age of Industrial Violence*, pp. 12, 13.

first time he had ever supported a Socialist for public office (and the last).[10]

The McNamara trial began on October 11, 1911, three weeks before the primary election, which quickly became a test of public sentiment about the case, a gauge of the relative persuasiveness of the open shop M and M and the union men. Three candidates entered the primary to vie for the two positions in the nonpartisan runoff to be held on December 5. The favorite was George Alexander, a Good Government man backed by the Merchants and Manufacturers Association and committed to their theory of union guilt. Harriman was expected to run second, and W. C. Mushet, the Republican, third. Even the most optimistic of the Socialists were surprised by the result. Harriman polled 20,137 votes; Alexander 16,790; Mushet 8,009. In addition, two Socialist-supported Constitutional amendments—woman suffrage and the initiative, referendum and recall—were carried after a campaign in which the Socialists had made clear their intention to use the recall to remove the McNamara trial judge, the same man who had earlier signed an antipicketing injunction against the strikers.[11]

The McNamaras were, of course, guilty. The Bridge and Structural Iron Workers had long used dynamite against open shop employers, and Burns had gathered much evidence of this, as well as of other bombings in Los Angeles following the destruction of the *Times* plant. But employers had also frequently initiated violence and been guilty of provocation and frame-ups against the unions. Otis and the M and M were ruthlessly anti-union—so much so that the majority of the population in Los Angeles apparently believed it more likely that Otis was responsible for the explosion than that the unions were. The city was faced both with a Socialist vic-

[10] *Ibid.*, p. 6.

[11] Ira Kipnis, *The American Socialist Movement, 1897–1912* (New York, Columbia University Press, 1952), pp. 352–353; *New York Call*, November 2, 1911.

tory at the polls December 5 and with the success of the organizing drive.

Clarence Darrow had reluctantly agreed to defend the McNamaras despite his certainty that they could not be acquitted. He did so only in response to Gompers' personal plea and the guarantee of a very large defense fund.[12] But by the time the trial began Darrow knew that Burns had an airtight case. He was convinced that both McNamaras faced the death penalty if the trial went on. Only one way to save their lives was open.

The trial could not possibly be over by Election Day. Harriman seemed certain to win. After that even a conviction would not necessarily convince most people of the McNamaras' guilt. It seemed just as likely that the brothers would simply become martyrs and the organizing drive would go on to success with the new Socialist mayor's aid. Only a confession of guilt by the brothers could stop Harriman and the unions. In exchange the business leaders in the M and M could spare the McNamaras. On December 1, at the urging of Darrow and muckraker Lincoln Steffens—and just in time—the McNamaras confessed. In return James B. received a life sentence, his brother John fifteen years. Harriman lost the election 87,000 to 50,000. The organizing drive was smashed and Los Angeles remained a bastion of the open-shop movement.

The confessions ended the case, but throughout the United States people confronted the fact that labor—the conservative unions—had systematically resorted to violence to achieve their ends. What was the cause of this? What could be done? Lincoln Steffens, who had been instrumental in arranging the deal that saved the McNamaras' lives, tried to use the case to establish the principle of the Golden Rule in labor relations. In an address to the City Club of Los Angeles, Steffens sug-

---

[12] According to Frank Morrison, of the AFL, Darrow received a fee of $50,000, plus $200,000 for expenses. Adamic, *Dynamite*, pp. 218–219.

gested that the way "to Beat the Socialists" was "to find a finer plan, a nobler ideal, a higher vision." [13] Violence against labor, the refusal to share the benefits of developing technology with the workers, Steffens argued, bred counter violence. He proposed to "assume that organized labor has committed the dynamiting and other crimes charged against it, and raise the question: Why?" Steffens hoped also to get labor's explanation and state it so that "anybody, even an employer, can comprehend it." He told his sister that the "big labor leaders" agreed to his making this assumption in print, "and then expressing their defense of crime." [14] He hoped that in exchange for the confessions (and Harriman's defeat) Los Angeles businessmen would recognize the unions and thereby institute a new era of labor relations.

Steffens' hopes proved futile. There was one meeting of representatives of the Chamber of Commerce with the Central Labor Council, but with no result. No further meetings were held and labor lost all its major objectives in the organizing drive. Otis continued his attacks on the unions and, according to Steffens, was one of the instigators of the businessmen's attempts to suppress free speech in San Diego in March 1912. The action of what Steffens called "a mob of businessmen" there was so brutal that San Francisco merchant Harris Weinstock, a Progressive appointed Special Commissioner by Governor Hiram Johnson to investigate the situation, confessed that "it was hard for him to believe that he was not sojourning in Russia, conducting his investigation there instead of in this alleged 'land of the free and home of the brave.' " [15]

[13] Steffens to Laura Steffens, Los Angeles [November 29, 1911], in Ella Winter and Granville Hicks, eds., *The Letters of Lincoln Steffens* (New York, Harcourt, Brace, 1938), pp. 280–281.

[14] Steffens to Laura Steffens, Los Angeles, November 17, 1911, in *ibid.*, p. 280.

[15] Adams, *Age of Industrial Violence*, p. 17; Steffens to Laura Steffens, Los Angeles, May 17, 1912, *Letters*, I, p. 293; William Preston, Jr., *Aliens and Dissenters* (Cambridge, Harvard University Press, 1963), p. 52.

But the McNamara case did cause many progressive businessmen and reformers to act. The nationwide concern was reflected in a symposium in the December 1911 issue of *Survey* on the "Larger Bearings of the McNamara Case." William B. Dickson, a former vice president of United States Steel and then president of Midvale Steel and Ordinance saw the source of the problem in labor's lack of statesmanship. "Some day," Dickson predicted, "a real statesman will arise out of the ranks of labor" who will accept leadership only on condition that the unions would "pledge their entire resources" to "stamping out the anarchistic element which has made the very name of union labor a reproach in the eyes of the American people." When that day came, Dickson predicted, "nothing on earth can prevent the enactment of legislation preventing any discrimination against employees because of their membership in labor unions." [16] Dickson's attack was misdirected (it was not the anarchists who had been responsible for the *Times* dynamiting), but the principle he laid down turned out to be correct even though it took twenty years to be acted upon. With the disappearance of socialist unionism in the 1930's—that is, once even the "radicals" accepted the idea of labor unions as bargaining agents within the corporation system—exactly the legislation that Dickson predicted was enacted, first as part of the National Recovery Act (section 7A) and then as the National Labor Relations Act.

The Boston merchant (and close friend of Steffens), Edward A. Filene, had a more practical remedy for violence. Filene argued that it would be to the advantage of every employer "to encourage the better and stronger class of his employes not only to join the labor organizations, but to take an

[16] "Larger Bearings of the McNamara Case," *The Survey*, XXVII (December 30, 1911), p. 1416. Dickson later became an outstanding critic of U.S. Steel's paternalistic labor policies and an advocate of unionism in the steel industry. See David Brody, *Labor in Crisis* (Philadelphia, Lippincott, 1965), pp. 82, 83, 109–110.

active and effective part in their work." From such unions, "much help will come" for settling issues between employer and employee "in the most lawful way." Many of the social workers participating in the discussion stressed the role of the state in mediating between the classes. The headworker at the University of Chicago Settlement House "of course" believed "that the machinery of the state must stop violence." But it must "also put peaceful weapons in the hands of labor" to enable them to protect themselves "and secure a living wage." [17]

Some argued along the same line as Steffens. "The workers," Paul Kennady of the New York Association for Labor Legislation contended, "have been driven until at last they are turned." Now that they saw "how easy it is, after all, to avenge their wrongs," there would be "more murder and arson before we have less." Economist (and active member of the National Civic Federation) E. R. A. Seligman saw the McNamaras as typical of those who had "begun to despair of equality and economic opportunity," and were "driven into violence" because of a conviction that "no other kind of action is possible." Socialist reformer Florence Kelly wrote that men commit such desperate acts "as the cornered rat bites" —in "wrath and despair of baffled effort and vain struggle." [18]

But exhortations would not solve the problem, particularly since there was not even agreement on its nature. Louis Brandeis therefore suggested that "our statesmen and thinkers" should "seek to ascertain the underlying causes of this widespread deliberate outburst of crimes and violence" through an impartial investigation. This line of thought was supported by John M. Glenn of the Russell Sage Foundation, who insisted that "only the government can get at the whole truth." He proposed a federal version of Wisconsin's fact-finding industrial commission.[19]

[17] *Ibid.*, pp. 1417–1418.
[18] Quoted in Adams, *Age of Industrial Violence*, p. 28.
[19] *Ibid.*, p. 29.

The same issue of *Survey* that discussed the implications of the McNamara case also contained what Steffens called a memorial by a "big committee of prominent reformers" for "a national inquiry by a commission like that of the Interstate." [20]

A petition addressed to President Taft was signed by social workers and other reformers, among them Jane Addams, Lillian Wald, Rabbi Stephen S. Wise, and the Reverends John Howard Melish and John Haynes Holmes. It asked for the formation of a federal commission with wide powers of investigation into trade unions, trade associations and the economic and social costs of strikes. The issues that were exposed by the McNamara case, the petition asserted, had struck "the social conscience of the nation," and exposed a "profound restlessness" among large groups of workers. Concerned that a "larger lawlessness" lay beyond the view of criminal courts, the reformers talked of the need to examine the effects of injunctions, evictions, and industrial spy systems. "Today as fifty years ago," they warned, "a house divided against itself cannot stand. We have to solve the problems of democracy in its industrial relationships and to solve them along democratic lines." [21]

Taft greeted the delegation that presented this petition warmly, promised to request Congress to create a Commission on Industrial Relations, and did so in his State-of-the-Union message on February 2, 1912. On February 29 a bill to establish the Commission was introduced in Congress. In mid-August the Commission bill passed both houses and was signed into law the next day. Support for the measure had been widespread and nonpartisan. Gompers and the AFL endorsed the Commission idea after Gompers had won assurance

[20] Steffens to Laura Steffens, New York, December 18, 1911, *Letters*, I, p. 283.
[21] *The Survey*, XXVII (December 30, 1911), pp. 1430–1431. Adams, *Age of Industrial Violence*, pp. 29–30, includes the quotations above.

from the sponsoring committee that labor would be represented on the Commission. Ralph Easley of the NCF was not particularly happy about the idea of a federal commission, since he viewed many of the original petitioners as "radical preachers and charity workers" and had just begun organizing NCF's own Industrial Survey. Easley saw the two as rivals; but both Gompers and Taft were on the NCF's Executive Council, and many other important Federation members supported the Commission, so Easley acquiesced.[22]

Significantly, only the National Association of Manufacturers reacted negatively—and even the NAM did not deem it prudent to oppose the Commission in Congress directly. Instead, NAM lobbyists concentrated on attempts to limit the power and appropriations of the proposed Commission. They managed to whittle the initial appropriation from $500,000 to a beginning grant of $100,000; experts' salaries were limited to $5,000 per year and the Commissioners were given an honorarium of $10 per day.[23]

The process of choosing the members of the new Commission on Industrial Relations revealed the extent to which NCF ideas had permeated both major parties. Composition of the Commission followed the principle established by NCF: of the nine members there were to be three each from capital, labor, and the public. The labor members proposed by Gompers and the Railroad Brotherhoods were appointed by Taft. They were James O'Connell of the Machinists, John B. Lennon of the Tailors, and Austin B. Garretson of the Order of Railway Conductors. All three were members of NCF. The business members were satisfactory to both the NAM and the NCF. Ferdinand A. Schwedtman, an NAM vice president, had been active in the movement for workmen's compensation legislation and was acceptable to NCF. Adolph Lewisohn, a banker, copper magnate, and important financial sup-

---

[22] *Ibid.*, pp. 33–36.
[23] *Ibid.*, pp. 39–40.

porter of the Commission legislation, had earlier been viewed by NAM counsel James A. Emery with some suspicion as "not really an employer but a banker"; but the Association did not object to his appointment. Frederick A. Delano, president of the Wabash Railroad, was an NCF member and acceptable to all. Among the public members chosen by Taft were Senator George B. Sutherland, as chairman, a conservative from Utah who was active in NCF affairs, particularly on workmen's compensation, and entirely satisfactory to the NAM; and Charles S. Barrett of Georgia, president of the Farmer's National Union and active in NCF.[24]

Both Easley of NCF and Emery of the NAM were pleased with Taft's choices. Emery was the more cautious, but gleefully noted that the "college element is utterly without recognition"—which must have disturbed Easley and the NCF.[25] The group of reformers who originally proposed the Commission were furious. They not only objected to the conservatism of the three representatives of the public, but also attacked the labor panel as "wholly reactionary" and suggested that it was "impossible" to "dismiss lightly the Socialists or the Industrial Workers of the World."[26] The criticism was not unreasonable, particularly as both O'Connell and Lennon had recently been replaced as presidents of their unions by Socialist rivals.

Taft's nominations had been made after he was a lame duck President, about to be replaced by Woodrow Wilson. Because of this, after a filibuster by the Democrats, the Senate failed to confirm his nominees; the final choice of the Commissioners fell to Wilson.

Like Taft, Wilson excluded Socialists and radicals. Like Taft's nominees, Wilson's were satisfactory to the AFL and

[24] *Ibid.*, pp. 44–45, 46.
[25] *Ibid.*, pp. 45–46.
[26] *Ibid.*, pp. 47–48.

the NCF—seven of Taft's men were members of the Civic Federation, eight of Wilson's were. But Wilson's chairman was markedly different from the conservative Sutherland. Originally, Wilson offered the chairmanship to Louis D. Brandeis, an ardent advocate of ameliorative social legislation and responsible unionism—and anathema to the NAM. When Brandeis declined, Wilson chose Frank P. Walsh, a Kansas City attorney and social worker. Walsh shared Brandeis' views on social reform, but was less committed to rationalizing and stabilizing the corporate system and more concerned with simple social justice. Wilson's two other representatives of the public were also concessions to the "college element"; they were John R. Commons of the University of Wisconsin and Mrs. J. Borden Harriman, socially prominent social worker. Reformers had preferred a woman like Jane Addams or Florence Kelly, but Mrs. Harriman was at least a woman. Commons was thoroughly acceptable. Easley of the NCF was pleased with the nominations. He told Gompers that he did "not see many of the IWW or in fact the Socialist promoters of the movement on the line," and also that he preferred Walsh to Brandeis, whom he accused of "trying to get the President to put an Industrial Worker on the Commission." [27]

The labor commissioners remained unchanged: it was the "responsible" labor leaders in the AFL and the Brotherhoods who were to be strengthened. On the business panel Wilson retained Delano, but substituted Harris Weinstock (the California Bull Mooser who had investigated San Diego's free speech fight) for Adolph Lewisohn, and S. Thruston Ballard, a Louisville, Kentucky, flour miller for the NAM's Schwedtman. All in all, Wilson's Commission satisfied labor, was accepted by the reformers, and disarmed the radicals. Only the NAM had clearly been edged out—but they represented in the business world what the Socialists and IWW's did in labor:

[27] Easley to Gompers, New York, July 3, 1913, Box 50, NCF papers.

the radical irresponsibles. It was they, primarily, who were to be investigated.[28]

Wilson's nominations for the Commission on Industrial Relations were shrewd and bold. By far the most important was the choice of Walsh, which was truly brilliant. A man acceptable to Easley, Walsh was also a very close friend of George L. Creel and many other reforming journalists and social workers who were despised by the NCF leader as a "crazy bunch of Socialists."[29] Walsh had no loyalty to the corporations and little to their system as such. As he told Irwin St. John Tucker, editor of the *Christian Socialist*, he was an independent in politics and "so far as social and economic effort is concerned" he was "ready to go with any person or group traveling in the direction of human justice." He was not sure whether that made him a Socialist or Tucker a Democrat; he did not care.[30] Easley's trust in Walsh probably came from his knowledge of Walsh's relationship with John R. Commons, with whom Walsh had discussed and worked out a plan of action for the Commission before accepting the nomination.[31] Commons was close to Easley, had worked for the Civic Federation in conciliation work before going to the University of Wisconsin, and was a pioneer, along with Charles V. McCarthy, in social engineering in that state.[32] In the course of the hearings over the next two years it would become clear that Walsh had serious differences with both Commons and McCarthy, precisely over the social engineering concept; in 1913 these were still beneath the surface of a common purpose to reduce social tensions and ameliorate social conditions.

---

[28] See Adams, *Age of Industrial Violence*, p. 74, for the opposite view.

[29] Easley to E. R. A. Seligman, N.Y., n.d. [1915], Box 51, NCF papers.

[30] Frank P. Walsh to Irwin St. John Tucker, Kansas City, September 16, 1915, Box 144, Frank Walsh papers, New York Public Library.

[31] Walsh to Boyd Fisher, Kansas City, June 30, 1913, Box 142, Walsh papers.

[32] John R. Commons, *Myself* (Madison, University of Wisconsin Press, 1964), pp. 81 *et seq.*

This purpose was compatible with the desires of the large corporation executives. The danger was that being abstractly committed to social reform, rather than seeing it as a means of stabilizing the existing social structure, might lead to radical proposals. The views of L. A. Halbert, general superintendent of the Kansas City Board of Public Welfare (for which Walsh had been attorney) bore this out. Halbert hoped the Commission would not spend much time examining specific problems such as health, safety, and comfort in factories, or industrial education, but would "go directly at the question as to how much voice the laborers should have in determining the conditions under which they will earn their living." He told Walsh that the Commission had "a glorious opportunity to marshal the arguments in favor of industrial freedom and a real democracy" based on "the sense of brotherhood." Halbert believed that "cooperation is the ultimate ideal in industry," rather than "a general competitive system." But he also wished "to give the people power over industry and not be hindered by the ancient fetish of the rights of private property." He realized that such a purpose "cannot be avowed in the beginning," but hoped Walsh would gather "the data to establish this position so that it can become the dominant idea for all time." An investigation which did this, Halbert concluded hopefully, could "change the base of industry." [33]

If rigorously pursued, Halbert's ideas could lead to socialist concepts; it was just such "theorists" that a practical man like Easley feared and shunned. But Walsh seems never to have thought one way or the other about the underlying social structure: he simply fought for human justice. Since he was permitted to do so within the existing system he saw no need to seek fundamental changes in social relationships. His great value to Wilson was precisely his ability to maintain friendship with men like Halbert, and others more radical, while

[33] L. A. Halbert to Walsh, Kansas City, June 13, 1913; Halbert to Walsh, Seattle, July 8, 1913: both in Box 142, Walsh papers.

remaining loyal to the President and to the Democratic Party through which he gained personal influence.

Not that Walsh was unaware of the more general questions about existing society. He confided to Creel that he viewed the Commission's investigation as likely to result in "placing our whole industrial system upon trial," and he was not sure whether the outcome would be endorsement or condemnation. Yet when Walsh proposed solutions there was never a hint of transforming existing social relations. Creel quoted Walsh, with his enthusiastic prior approval, in an article in *Collier's* as suggesting that a "larger measure of paternalism," carrying with it not only minimum wages, workmen's compensation, and industrial insurance, but also social security was desirable. "The fate of the nation, the success of our experiment in democracy," Walsh concluded, lay "in determining and removing the causes of industrial unrest that is eating the heart of our society." [34] This followed the spirit of remarks—endorsed by Walsh—of Paul U. Kellogg, an editor of *Survey* and Henry R. Seager, a professor of political economy at Columbia University. Kellogg wrote that the purpose of the Commission should be to survey the relations which a "free, self-governing people" bear "to corporate forms of work." It was "on these industrial relations" that "the progressive development of our manufacturing resources" depended and upon which the happiness of Americans—who looked to "these new and massed forms of employment for their livelihood"—rested. Seager warned labor against violence and wrote in favor of the kinds of reforms advocated by Walsh in *Collier's*.[35]

[34] Walsh to Creel, Kansas City, August 18, 1913; Walsh to Creel, Kansas City, September 3, 1913: both in Box 142, Walsh papers; George Creel, "Why Industrial War?" *Collier's*, DII (October 18, 1913), p. 33.

[35] Paul U. Kellogg, Henry R. Seager, "The Constructive Work Before the Industrial Relations Commission," *Survey*, XXX (August 2, 1913), 571–588. Walsh's endorsement in Walsh to Bert St. Clair, Kansas City, August 18, 1913, Box 142, Walsh papers.

These men shared with Walsh a vision of a socially responsible society in which cooperation and genuine accommodation between social classes would be possible. A man like Halbert, who perceived a conflict between private property and "real democracy," was exceptional. Most emphasized cooperation and social responsibility, ideas that were dominant in the Civic Federation. Seager, a frequent consultant for the NCF, favored regulation of corporations, rather than trust busting, and argued for reform as a substitute for socialism. In discussing minimum wages, he suggested that there was "quite as much logic in the contention that this and other needed social reforms tend to make outright socialism undesirable and unnecessary as in the other view that the adoption of any policy that socialists happen to advocate must lead to socialism." He found "more weighty" the objection that "a state which decrees that its citizens shall not be employed for less than the living wages" was logically bound to see that such citizens be given employment at such wages or be maintained in some other way." Seager agreed that a minimum wage did "commit organized society to a more responsible attitude toward the whole labor problem" than any American state had yet adopted; he welcomed this development.[36]

Perhaps the central difference between Walsh and reformers such as Seager, Commons, and Charles McCarthy was Walsh's insistence on publicity about conditions as a means of increasing political awareness and political action by labor and its friends. Walsh sought to strengthen the hand of reformers in the political arena by exposing the immorality and hidden power of such men as John D. Rockefeller over public officials. Commons and McCarthy sought reform through the removal of issues from politics and their solution by private conference or through representative bodies of

[36] Garraty, *Right Hand Man*, p. 276; Minutes of the 16th Annual Meeting of the NCF, January 17, 1916, Box 187, NCF papers.

experts. In the course of the hearings this difference occasionally boiled to the surface, and always underlay the decisions and actions of the Commission.

In preparation for the Commission's work, Walsh and Commons agreed on a division of labor. Walsh would conduct a series of public hearings; Commons would be responsible for research. To confirm this plan, Walsh discussed it with the social reformers in New York—he told Creel he would come East to "call a meeting of 'conspirators'" and to "map out a line that I believe you know I will stick to." [37] When the Commission met for the first time in the fall of 1913, it confirmed the Commons-Walsh plan and agreed that its work was meant to be "interpretive and remedial." As Walsh put it: "It's *causes* that we are after, not *symptoms*." [38]

Walsh's radicalism, his genuine hostility to big business, gave the Commission a public image of a liberalism that was anti-business. Graham Adams, Jr., historian of the Commission, writes that its composition was a triumph for small business and conservative labor: that at this time "Wilson's New Freedom excluded both big industry and radical unionism." [39] But while there was no big businessman on the Commission (politically it was not possible; even Taft's nominees included only one moderately big businessman, Adolph Lewisohn), all the members but Walsh belonged to the Civic Federation and shared its basic orientation. The two ideological currents absent on the Commission were precisely those against which Ralph Easley constantly railed: the hard-line open-shop "business anarchism" of the NAM and the anticapitalism of the Socialists and IWW. The main function of the hearings was to present the case for responsible unionism and to expose the inhumanity and danger of what Walsh's Final Report called the "industrial feudalism" of those communities "in which the

[37] Walsh to Creel, Kansas City, September 3, 1913, Walsh papers.
[38] Adams, *Age of Industrial Violence*, p. 73.
[39] *Ibid.*, p. 74.

employees are unorganized." As his actions and his Final Report showed, Walsh was pro-labor and not at all hesitant to attack and expose the brutality and social irresponsibility of even the biggest of big businessmen; yet Walsh was not anticapitalist; nor did his framework of thought on social matters conflict fundamentally with that of the NCF.

"Political freedom," the Final Report stated, "can exist only where there is industrial freedom; political democracy only where there is industrial democracy." Walsh saw "almost infinite gradations marking the stages of evolution which have been reached" in different communities "between conditions of industrial democracy and industrial feudalism." But most significantly, he was satisfied that industrial democracy had been established "in certain American industries" and "for certain classes of employees." The main difference between Walsh and Easley was that while Easley constantly congratulated himself and his "important" friends on the progress that had been made, Walsh was outraged by continuing malpractices (as he would have defined them) and militantly agitated for change.[40] Yet, although Easley and his business friends in the NCF came to distrust and even despise Walsh, the only effect of the Commission's hearings that could be complained of was legitimately that they improved the public image of conservative, responsible unionism, and, therefore, labor's relative strength in a consensus in which the large corporations remained dominant. Given existing social tensions, anything less would have failed to meet the political need that had created the Commission.

The conflicting approaches and Walsh's courage and integrity stood out most clearly in the hearings on the Colorado coal strike of 1913–1914. The most important single coal firm involved in the strike was the Colorado Fuel and Iron Company, which exerted a commanding influence over its smaller

[40] Commission on Industrial Relations, *Final Report and Testimony* (Washington, D.C., 1916), I, p. 17.

competitors and completely controlled those sections of the state in which it operated. Colorado Fuel and Iron (CFI) was a Rockefeller-controlled company which was not only anti-union, but ran its mines and mining camps with a medieval despotism. Every aspect of the miners' lives in the CFI camps was controlled by the company. The miners were forced to live in company housing that its own social worker described as "hovels, shacks, and dugouts that are unfit for the habitation of human beings." Until a law forbade the practice, they were paid in scrip which had to be spent at company stores that overcharged for everything. School teachers were selected and dismissed by mine superintendents and company officers, who also censored movies, books, and magazines so as to "protect our people from erroneous ideas." Election precincts coincided with company property; polling places were located on CFI land; registration lists were hidden in private offices in company buildings. Political control by management led to lax inspection of the mines, which had a death rate twice that of any other state. In addition coroners' juries were company controlled and almost invariably ruled that accidents had been the fault of the laborer, not the company. Since 1900 these conditions had sparked union activity, but it had always been smashed by management.[41] In 1913 the union opened its biggest push in history and succeeded in enrolling a substantial portion of the miners in the United Mine Workers Union.

The union now demanded of the coal operators an eight-hour day, enforcement of safety regulations, removal of armed guards, abolition of company scrip, the right of the men to elect their own check-weighmen (to supervise the weighing of each man's coal), and the right to choose where they would live. Colorado statutes already guaranteed these conditions, but the operators ignored the laws. In addition, the union asked for a ten percent increase in wages and recognition of the UMW as bargaining agent, as had been agreed to in nine other

[41] Adams, *Age of Industrial Violence*, pp. 148–151.

coal-mining states. The operators not only refused to meet the union demands: despite conciliation efforts by Colorado's governor, they would not even meet with union representatives.

With no compromise possible, the strike began in September 1913 with 40 to 100 percent of the miners leaving their jobs in the various mines. In a drenching sleet and snow storm 10,000 miners and their families trudged down Colorado canyons into camps provided by the unions. There they dug themselves into tent colonies for the winter.[42]

Strike tactics on both sides resembled preparations for war. Under CFI direction, sheriffs recruited large numbers of guards and deputies from out of state; they were armed and paid by the company, deployed in trenches around mining properties, and equipped with huge searchlights and machine guns. In turn the union openly bought weapons for miners without their own revolvers or shotguns. These were stored at spots where strikebreakers could see them on their way to the mines. Violence began immediately and grew in intensity, with the union retaliating for each killing perpetrated by the company and its sheriffs. Individual killings soon developed into pitched battles involving hundreds of strikers and company police; the miners held their own in widespread guerrilla warfare.[43]

As the fighting spread, Governor Elias M. Ammons called out the National Guard to restore order. He instructed Guardsmen to protect all property and men at work, but not to give help in bringing in strikebreakers. The Guard was welcomed by both sides and peace prevailed as long as Ammons' initial orders stood. But then he announced that he had gone beyond the law in ordering his men not to protect strikebreakers. This, he explained, was an interference with production. From that

---

[42] *Ibid.*, pp. 151–152. The account of the strike presented here is taken largely from Adams.

[43] For details see *ibid.*, pp. 152–155.

time on violence increased on both sides as Guardsmen aligned themselves more and more openly with the CFI. According to union sources they not only protected scabs, but induced strikers to return to work and participated in robberies, lootings, and holdups against adamant strikers.

The clashes between strikers and the Guard culminated in a pitched battle at the miners' Ludlow tent colony. There, after a day-long battle, Guardsmen burned the colony to the ground, killing two women and eleven children who were trapped under the burning tents. This was the famous Ludlow massacre, which called national attention to the events in Colorado, and which also set off open warfare. State Federation of Labor officials now called every miner in the state to arms. Union men seized possession of Ludlow and Trinidad and attacked one mine after another in a 250 mile radius. One group stormed the Empire mine, killed three guards, and left the property in ashes. A few days later, 300 strikers attacked the Walsen and McNally mines, engaging in a fifty-hour gun battle that ended with the dynamiting of the property. At Forbes hundreds of union men ambushed strikebreakers and policemen, killing nine and setting fire to company buildings thirty miles around. Other hands burned and pillaged CFI property at Delagua, Aguilar, Hastings, and Black Hills. "For ten days," Graham Adams writes, "a workers' army which controlled vast areas of territory clashed with state and company forces. Exactly as in war, each belligerent issued communiques, reported casualties, and boasted of victories. Newspapers discussed grand strategy, exulted in triumphs of their own side, and belittled claims of the enemy." [44] This was too much for the Governor, who finally called upon President Wilson to send in troops. On April 28, 1914, several regiments of federal troops intervened to restore peace.

The events in Colorado, and particularly Rockefeller's connection with them through his controlling interest in the

[44] *Ibid.*, pp. 155–161. Quotation is from pp. 160–161.

CFI, were made to order for Walsh and the Commision. First Walsh held hearings in Denver, where reforming Judge Ben B. Lindsey charged that CFI "owned judges on the bench as they have owned their office boys," that they had controlled district attorneys, and even governors. They "not only make the law to suit their own wishes," he added, but prevent the enforcement of laws for the protection of human rights—such as the eight-hour day—that did pass. "This," Lindsey asserted, "is violence." It was a "condition of terror which the industrial government of Colorado, backed by the industrial government of this country with its seat in New York City," had shown "against the political government in Colorado." Lindsey's point was that this great power of capital had become "superior to the President of the United States" (unless the President were "willing to exert himself in spite of it"), that it was both arrogant and "irresponsible." If federal power were not now used to compel arbitration, Lindsey warned, the "republican form of government will not be possible." [45]

Two weeks or so later, in New York, the Commission heard John D. Rockefeller, Jr., heir to America's greatest fortune, deny any responsibility for the conduct of the strike or the refusal of the CFI to meet with the union. Pleading almost total ignorance of the policies pursued by the coal company, Rockefeller insisted that he did not shape the firm's managerial policies or its attitude toward the union. He had been responsible only for CFI's financial affairs, although the strike had made him realize that there was "something fundamentally wrong" in a situation that caused such bitterness and suffering. Beyond this, Rockefeller testified that he was not opposed to trade unions, or to collective bargaining to obtain higher wages and improved conditions; in fact, he said, "I favor them most heartily." [46]

Rockefeller's appearance disarmed almost all in the audi-

[45] *Final Report*, VII, pp. 6401–6403.
[46] Adams, *Age of Industrial Violence*, pp. 162–163.

ence and on the Commission. Commissioner Garretson (a labor member) was persuaded that "Mr. Rockefeller is not the kind of man the laboring men thought he was." Others shared this view, but not Walsh. He had originally been convinced that the hearings in Denver were "bringing a good deal of knowledge of these conditions to the doors of the real owners and managers of the property in New York." [47]

But during this time and in the months after the Denver hearings, Commission researchers had collected files of letters from Rockefeller to officers of CFI in Colorado that proved Rockefeller had lied at his first appearance. Walsh carefully prepared these and then called Rockefeller to a second hearing in Washington, D.C. There Rockefeller again insisted he was ignorant of company strike strategy and reaffirmed his belief in collective bargaining. Walsh, however, now had evidence that Rockefeller had been fully informed of CFI plans and policy and had endorsed them fully in correspondence with the company president and its executive board chairman. At the very beginning of the strike, chairman L. M. Bowers had outlined the issues and situation in detail and had told Rockefeller that CFI would hold out against union recognition "until our bones were bleached as white as chalk in these Rocky Mountains." To this, Rockefeller had replied that "what you have done is right and fair"; Bowers' position on the union was, Rockefeller proclaimed, "in the interest of the employees of the company." "Whatever the outcome," he assured Bowers, "we will stand by you to the end." [48]

The most damning thing that Walsh uncovered was evidence of Rockefeller's complicity in coercing Governor Ammons to rescind his initial decree to the militia not to aid the strikebreakers. It was that order that had led to the worst violence, and to the Ludlow massacre. Bowers wrote Rocke-

[47] Walsh to Charles McCarthy, Denver, December 4, 1914, McCarthy papers, Wisconsin State Historical Society.
[48] Adams, *Age of Industrial Violence*, pp. 165–166.

feller that he had mobilized Colorado bankers, the real estate exchange, the Chamber of Commerce, and editors of fourteen of the most important newspapers to force "our little cowboy governor" to use the militia to help the coal companies. "We used every possible weapon to drive him into action," Bowers boasted. "There probably has never been such pressure brought to bear upon any governor of this state." Rockefeller was delighted, and so, he told Bowers, was his father, who had "followed the events of the past few months . . . with unusual interest and satisfaction." Rockefeller also supported the CFI policy against Secretary of Labor William B. Wilson's plea for informal talks with the union. In a telegram to the Secretary that Bowers showed to his executive board, Rockefeller affirmed that CFI's inflexible anti-unionism "meets with our cordial approval, and we shall support them to the end."

Walsh's final triumph, proof that "industrial feudalism" led to "political feudalism," was his revelation that Rockefeller, with the assistance of his new public relations man, Ivy L. Lee, had personally written a letter for Governor Ammons to send to President Wilson. Lee had been hired by Rockefeller and paid out of his personal funds to conduct a pro-management publicity campaign under the name of the Coal Mine Operators Committee. Rockefeller expressed great confidence in his ideas, which were indeed forerunners, if somewhat overly frank and crude, of modern corporation concepts of public relations. Lee believed that "crowds were led by symbols and phrases" and was obsessed with analogies between Rockefeller's position and those of such leaders as Henry VIII and Napoleon. "We know," Lee wrote, "that Henry the Eighth by his obsequious deference to the forms of law was able to get the English people to believe in him so completely that he was able to do almost anything with them." [49] The analogy was clear; the *forms* of democratic government must be maintained. Behind those forms, Rockefeller

[49] *Final Report*, IX, pp. 7830–7831.

could dictate his letter to the President presenting a completely pro-company and anti-union view. But it must appear that the "little cowboy governor" had done it himself.

Walsh, of course, was outraged by such manipulation of public opinion. His concept of democracy rested on a belief in the possibility of knowledge of all sides of industrial questions being freely available to the American people, and of allowing them to choose on that basis. This meant an observance not only of forms of law (even that had been violated by CFI in Colorado), but also the settling of social questions publicly—that is, politically. But this, of course, also implied an increase in class politics because it meant that each class or group in society should promote its own interests in the public arena. Or that the state should be neutral, or, at least, represent what the voters thought it did. Ammons had been elected governor with labor support and was considered a friend of the unions, but the secret pressures brought to bear on him had forced him to aid the coal operators. It was experiences such as this that led workers to lose faith in democracy. In exposing Rockefeller's role in this perversion of democratic processes, Walsh was strengthening the political hand of labor; he was also renewing the faith in the existing social system of countless workers and liberals, and even of some Socialists.

But Walsh's lack of respect for what Rockefeller represented, his "agitation" of class feelings, sharply distinguished him from such progressives as Commons and Charles McCarthy—not to mention men like Easley. There were two implicit objections to Walsh's approach to social questions, one generally valid, the other not. The first was that such frontal attacks on men of great wealth, even those admittedly as irresponsible as Rockefeller, would make cooperation and compromise with others difficult, if not impossible. The second was that such exposés so disillusioned workers and middle-class Americans as to make them lose faith in the system —make them into radicals or socialists. But the key question here, as President Wilson no doubt understood (even if Walsh did not), was who did the exposing. A revelation such as Walsh's, if made by the Socialists, might indeed be damaging; when made by an official government agency its main effect was the opposite. The Commission hearings had the effect of winning almost unanimous support from labor as well as widespread support from Progressives and admiration from Christian Socialists and even from Eugene V. Debs.[50] The praise went to Walsh, but behind Walsh stood the President.

Yet on the Commission there was a serious split between Walsh and McCarthy (who had become director of research in 1914) over how to conduct the investigation and whether to concentrate on hearings—"agitation" as Walsh called it— or on model bill drafting and informal conferences with the principals in order to reach agreements on legislative reforms in those areas where conflict was least. The initial form of the conflict was over the Commission's budget, which was subject to renewal by Congress each year. In 1915 Congress allocated only $100,000 to finish the work by August (when the Commission expired). McCarthy complained that this was "a mere fragment such as not to allow us to do decent

[50] See, for example, letters to Walsh from George W. Bills (Bloomington Illinois Trades and Labor Assembly) to Walsh, May 25, 1915; Ben B. Lindsey to Walsh, Denver, June 2, 1915; Herbert S. Bigelow (an Ohio Progressive who had been chairman of the state Constitutional Convention in 1912) to Walsh, Cincinnati, June 1, 1915; John Fitzpatrick and E. N. Nockels of the Chicago Federation of Labor to Woodrow Wilson, June 28, 1915; Kansas City Allied Printing Trades Council to Wilson, June 30, 1915; Socialist Party of La Grande and Union County, Oregon, n.d.; Gompers to Walsh, Washington, D.C., July 13, 1915; Amos Pinchot to Walsh, New York, August 4, 1915; J. Louis Engdahl (editor of the *American Socialist*) to Walsh, Chicago, August 7, 1915: all in Box 143, Walsh papers; Debs to Walsh, Terre Haute, October 9, 1915; Marion Wharton of The People's College to Walsh, Fort Scott, Kansas, September 24, 1915: Box 144, Walsh papers.

work." He had hoped to be able to present "a great legislative program to the President which all progressives in America could get behind." But Walsh advised McCarthy not to say anything about the appropriation, and McCarthy believed he did so under orders from Wilson. Walsh wanted to use all the remaining money for hearings; McCarthy wanted to suspend the hearings—this before the second Rockefeller confrontation—and spend the money on bill-drafting.[51] Walsh fired McCarthy, but all research did not stop. McCarthy's successor, Basil M. Manly, continued to work with a small staff. The reduced appropriation apparently was in line with very heavy pressure from Southern senators not to hold hearings scheduled in the South.[52] Perhaps Walsh agreed to forego the Southern hearings at Wilson's request, while gaining Presidential approval of his plans to expose Rockefeller.

In any case, Walsh's firing of McCarthy revealed the underlying differences between the former's neopopulism and the latter's corporate liberalism. As Walsh saw it, both Commons and McCarthy believed that investigations and recommendations should have prior approval of "so-called advisory committees of employers and workers." This was part of the "Wisconsin Idea," which also involved "interminable bill-drafting" by "countless employees, experts and the like, 'of scientific training,'—the very thought of which should throw the legal profession into spasms of delight, and the proletariat into hopeless despair." McCarthy and Commons, Walsh added, were "well thought of by the philanthropic trust in New York," who had made "strenuous efforts to apply the methods of scientific philanthropy to the work of this Commission." Walsh's resistance, he noted gleefully, caused these gentle-

[51] McCarthy to John S. Murdock, Madison, February 27, 1915; McCarthy to Joseph E. Davies, Madison, February 25, 1915; McCarthy to Redmond S. Brennan, Madison, March 1, 1915; McCarthy to John Fitch, Madison, March 1, 1915: all in Box 20, McCarthy papers.

[52] Adams, *Age of Industrial Violence*, pp. 207–208. One hearing was held in Dallas in 1914.

men to reach "a state of irritation which would seem impossible for such cool scientific beings." [53]

McCarthy had given full expression to his views in testimony early in the Commission hearings. His central concerns were to have the law change in accordance with changing conditions, and with increasing the efficiency of the American political economy. In discussing social tensions and antagonisms, McCarthy pointed out that "other countries have had unrest" and had dealt with it. Germany was to him "a wonderful example to the rest of the world as showing what a country can do." In fact, she had become a model of efficiency and was "now importing foreign labor." All that was needed was good planning. "Bismarck did a great deal of that planning, and the men around him, Wagner and other university men were brought in by him," McCarthy observed. England, too, was "simply imitating Germany," McCarthy continued. "Lloyd George told me himself that he had constantly gone to Germany" to study "the methods of the German Government." In Wisconsin, McCarthy had drawn heavily on his knowledge of what Bismarck had done. "Take for instance the great industrial commission act, which is after all based upon the suggestion of the German Act," McCarthy said. "After all," he added, "where does your Workmen's Compensation Act come from? It came to England and from Germany. The Wisconsin Act has as much German stuff in it as it has English."

Like Germany, Wisconsin had a Socialist problem. "The labor unions up there have been Socialists and they have come into the legislature, and not withstanding the fact that we have had some very severe, harsh men at the head of our affairs up there," McCarthy went on, "still Wisconsin has gone right on and it has been building up something which has not destroyed capital." McCarthy was then asked what

[53] Walsh to Marion Reedy, Kansas City, April 17, 1915, Box 143, Walsh papers.

he considered the backbone of his thought on political economy. "The backbone here," he replied, "is that the state must invest in human beings in the same way as you invest in cattle on a farm. . . . You have got to have better human beings." Commissioner O'Connell then asked: "Your idea is to build people up physically?"

"Yes," replied McCarthy, "using the word 'physical' in a big sense; physically, mentally, and all those things. A man will produce more, and the employer will get more for his money, and the state will get more out of the man, and my idea is that the state ought to invest in the health, strength, intelligence, and ability of the people who make up the state." [54]

It was not this ideological perspective to which Walsh objected—he hired McCarthy after this testimony was given —but the elitist and manipulative techniques that such a view implied. McCarthy and Commons, as much as Walsh, genuinely wished to help the workingman and farmer improve his lot. The difference was that while Walsh sought to restore a condition of bargaining—or contesting—in the political arena, McCarthy and Commons followed the more "practical" path of seeking to adjust public policy to the needs of the giant corporations that now pervaded every aspect of American life. As Commons put it when dissenting from Walsh's final report, the issue was "whether the labor movement should be directed toward politics or toward collective bargaining." [55]

In practice, the differences meant that Walsh acted to strengthen the political power of labor and the neopopulists so as to force concessions from the corporations and to remain in a position to enforce them, while Commons and McCarthy sought to convince representatives of the business community of the need to improve conditions in the common interest.

[54] *Final Report*, I, pp. 379–387.
[55] Quoted in Adams, *Age of Industrial Violence*, p. 215.

Neither perspective directly challenged the domination of the corporations, but Walsh's approach was inherently more dangerous as long as the Socialists were seriously contesting for the consciousness of the workers. In the Commission's work these contrasting approaches were most clearly apparent in relation to the investigation of John D. Rockefeller.

McCarthy, so he said, had reluctantly agreed to come on the Commission only under tremendous pressure from the President himself. This had been exerted after "grave circumstances arose over the Colorado strike," because of the "bitter opposition to each other" of capital and labor. At a meeting in Washington, McCarthy was told that he was "the man upon whom all parties could agree," and that if he "acted merely as a buffer between contending parties" he could "straighten the whole thing." [56]

If this were so, it was perhaps because McCarthy had been a classmate and friend of Rockefeller's at Brown University, and had remained on good terms with him in later years. After the Ludlow massacre and the storm of indignation against Rockefeller that followed it, Rockefeller had set up his own Industrial Relations Department as a division of the Rockefeller Foundation. The Canadian William Lyon McKenzie King had been appointed director of this division, and Jerome D. Greene, a Rockefeller aide, explained to McCarthy that while the "apprehensions excited in certain quarters both on the side of capital and on the side of labor" were "not unnatural under the circumstances" surrounding the strike, he hoped that they might be reduced and that under King's direction, the Rockefellers might "gradually convince the public both of our disinterestedness and of our strictly scientific method." [57]

[56] McCarthy to M. S. Dudgeon, Madison, December 9, 1914, Box 17, McCarthy papers.

[57] Jerome D. Greene to McCarthy, New York, October 14, 1914, Box 17, McCarthy papers.

To this, McCarthy replied that he thought Rockefeller would "make no mistake" if he tried to "keep in touch with the industrial commission" and kept "explaining to them what you are trying to do." The more Rockefeller kept explaining and the "more approach you make to the American People," McCarthy advised, "the better they will understand your motives." "You may think this is a nuisance," McCarthy told Rockefeller, "but take my advice to you and get some machinery for making constant explanations. Every statesman in the past has had to do that in order to insure any support from the people, and an organization like yours, it seems to me, will gain support for its work if your motives are right and the people thoroughly understand them. You are a student of history," McCarthy reminded his old classmate, "and it is needless to say that democracy will always be suspicious, and it will often make mistakes and sometimes cause bitterness." But "in the end if you are right and honest in your motives, it will give you credit." [58]

Walsh found this "cooperation" with Rockefeller "extremely repugnant" and viewed McCarthy's activity as "a plan little short of espionage over [the Commission's] work by representatives of those forces in the country which the great majority of workers, at least, believe to be the principle despoilers of their rights and the most notorious exploiters of their kind." [59] When he confronted McCarthy with the letters to Rockefeller (they were among Rockefeller correspondence subpoenaed by the Commission), McCarthy explained that he did not support a directed Industrial Survey by Rockefeller, but had argued that the money should have been given with no strings attached to a "democratically controlled" group. "I thought," he elucidated, "it would be a great good

[58] McCarthy to Rockefeller, Madison, October 17, 1914, Rockefeller file, McCarthy papers.
[59] Walsh to Marion Reedy, Kansas City, April 17, 1915, Box 143, Walsh papers.

for this country if this hundred million dollars was given outright to a committee entirely outside the Rockefeller foundation which would be composed of capital and labor." [60]

But Walsh had a very different view of the Rockefeller Foundation, even as it regarded purely scientific research. He challenged "the wisdom of giving public sanction and approval to the spending of a huge fortune through such philanthropies" and viewed such "philanthropic trusts" as a "menace to the welfare of society." The possession of such enormous fortunes meant "arbitrary power over the lives and destinies of other men," Walsh wrote, adding that "the forms of political democracy avail nothing when the lives of the many are controlled by the few who wield arbitrary economic power." Walsh insisted that "even in the power to do good, no one man, or group of men, should hold a monopoly." The setting up of scientific or social work foundations, Walsh warned, must lead to a condition of "loyalty and subserviency" to men of wealth and their "interests from the whole profession of scientists, social workers and economists." Already there were "thousands of men in these professions receiving subsidies, either directly or indirectly, from the Rockefeller Estate." These men were in a position where to "take any step toward effective economic, social and industrial reform" would bring them "directly counter to the interests of their benefactor." No sensible man can believe, Walsh insisted, "that research workers, publicists and teachers can be subsidized with money obtained from the exploitation of workers without being profoundly influenced in their points of view and in the energy and enthusiasm with which they might otherwise attack economic abuses."

As an example of this, Walsh pointed to McKenzie King, who had testified that he had been given a free hand when hired by Rockefeller to investigate the Colorado situation. The result was King's suggestion that Rockefeller need not

[60] McCarthy to Walsh, February 15, 1915, Box 20, McCarthy papers.

greatly modify his "arbitrary and undemocratic" policies "because unemployment and distress resulting from the European war would weaken the power of labor and force labor to take about what the employer cared to give it." It was the author of this "masterpiece of frank and unashamed selfishness to whom the world is asked to look for a way out from the problems which have arrayed employer and employee in hostile front." This "scholar of the highest repute," Walsh added, "apparently drew no line, in lending his cooperation, between the Rockefeller philanthropies and the Rockefeller exploiting industries." From this Walsh concluded that "Mr. Rockefeller could find no better insurance for his hundreds of millions than to invest one of them in subsidizing all agencies that make for social change and progress." [61]

In regard to Colorado, King had been hired, so he testified at the Commission hearings, to work out a plan to set "an example to the rest of the world" by making the Rockefeller holdings "better industries than they had been, and to improve the relations between labor and capital in them." But Rockefeller had made plain that he would under no circumstances recognize the union in the Colorado Fuel and Iron holdings, and King took the assignment with this proviso.[62] In fact, the plan derived from King's suggestion to Rockefeller to make numerous concessions to the workers in regard to working and living conditions, and the CFI loosened its more obvious political controls in Colorado. But the union was not recognized and labor remained hostile. Both UMW officials and Gompers attacked the Rockefeller-King investigation, and Walsh noted happily to Gompers that their "combined efforts have put an end to that particular activity." [63]

Rockefeller's reforms in Colorado succeeded in ameliorat-

[61] "The Great Foundations," typescript, n.d., Box 144, Walsh papers.

[62] Final Report, IX, pp. 8789, 8793.

[63] Walsh to Gompers, Kansas City, August 27, 1915, Walsh papers; Adams, Age of Industrial Violence, p. 172.

ing conditions there somewhat, and, therefore, in reducing immediate tensions in the area, but his adamant refusal to meet with the union only further irritated class feelings in a broader sense. Even Ralph Easley, who in July 1915 had done his best to help McKenzie King bring Gompers and Rocke-feller face to face, criticized Rockefeller privately. Easley was outraged by Walsh's handling of the Rockefeller hearings, but he confided to Seth Low that after "reading the history of their proposed industrial investigation and hearing Mr. Lee talk about conditions, I almost agree with Mr. Walsh that the wealth in the hands of these rich young men ought to be taken away from them and given to somebody who has some responsibility and brains." The only trouble with that, Easley concluded, was that "giving it to the Government would not meet that situation but would turn it over to the salary grab-bers and grafters." [64] As Easley's letter implied, the Commis-sion had in at least one respect done the Civic Federation view of consensus a service. In stigmatizing Rockefeller as the archetype of irresponsible employers, Walsh was within the tradition of both Theodore Roosevelt and the NCF.

The Rockefeller hearings and the firing of McCarthy had revealed substantial, though not basic, differences among the Commission members. These had first arisen in regard to Commons who, of course, supported McCarthy and who was less active and interested in the Commission's work after he was removed. The next indication came during Walsh's piti-less cross-examination of Rockefeller, when both Mrs. Harri-man and Harris Weinstock objected. These differences were later reflected in the writing of a final report, with the result that not one, but three reports were submitted. Walsh's re-port was signed by the three labor members; Commons and

[64] Easley to Low, New York, July 2, 7, 1915, Box 52, NCF papers; Easley to Low, New York, September 3, 1915, Box 146, Low papers; W. L. Mc-Kenzie King to Easley, Ottawa, July 8, 15, 1915, NCF papers; Easley to King, New York, July 12, 19, 1915, *ibid.*; Easley to Vincent Astor, New York, July 8, 1915, *ibid.*

Mrs. Harriman filed one together, and Harris Weinstock wrote one for the business members. The main report was the staff report, written by Basil M. Manly and signed by Walsh, Garretson, O'Connell, and Lennon. It contained the findings of fact, which were undisputed by the other Commissioners according to Walsh.[65] Both Mrs. Harriman and the business members, particularly Weinstock, condemned the staff report as partisan to labor. The Commons-Harriman report advocated a vast extension of labor-capital commissions, a la McCarthy, to draw up legislation. It also advocated an advisory council composed of the Secretaries of Commerce and Labor and delegates from trade associations and trade unions.[66] In short, it proposed an extra-political council of different economic groups to establish codes of behavior and negotiate social and economic reforms. For labor, as Commons would have had it, this "collective bargaining" would substitute for political action. Since these bodies would be advisory, however, and since they would be ultimately under the control of the federal executive, politics would be left to an amorphous "public," to be manipulated and ultimately controlled by the corporations.

Commons' thinking on the subject of capital-labor relations was similar to much that would later underlie New Deal legislation, including the National Recovery Administration and the Wagner National Labor Relations Act. In this respect, Commons was in tune with other Commissioners and staff members who suggested programs that would later take such form as the Works Project Administration and the Civilian Conservation Corps. William M. Leiserson, an economist on the Commission staff (and a close associate of McCarthy), proposed another idea later adopted during the New Deal. He suggested the creation of a "state fund for public improve-

[65] Walsh to John R. Lawson, Kansas City, August 20, 1915, Box 143, Walsh papers.
[66] Adams, *Age of Industrial Violence*, p. 217.

ments which would be a sort of insurance fund for industrial depressions." This could be used to build roads, schools, and state institutions, and for reclaiming waste land and for reforestation. Leiserson proposed that the money should be allocated by state boards of employment, which would also be charged with the establishment of state employment services. As part of his plan, the federal government would "offer to the states federal aid for equal amounts that the state would spend" on such projects. It was essential, Leiserson concluded, that "the problem of unemployment should be considered a problem of industry which it really is, and not a problem of charity." [67] This view, of course, was completely compatible with the idea that the solution of "industrial problems" was the business of the state and federal governments, that it was the government's function to maintain favorable market conditions and a favorable climate for investment.

S. Thruston Ballard submitted a comprehensive report on industrial unrest and its solution that reflected his own enlightened policies as an employer. Ballard's mill was the largest winter wheat refinery in the world and the first to institute the eight-hour day. In discussing this reform, Ballard pointed out that he had been able to change from two twelve-hour shifts of 22 men to three eight-hour shifts of 15 men, for an increase of only one employee. Workers were now paid the same for eight hours' work as they had been for twelve, but they worked harder, produced more, and most important, their rates of turnover and absenteeism were lower.[68] In his report Ballard listed five causes of industrial unrest, of which the first two were low wages and unemployment. For low wages, Ballard saw three causes: large-scale immigration; the lack of training and industrial education; the increase in the

[67] William M. Leiserson to McCarthy, Chicago, December 15, 1914, Box 18, McCarthy papers.

[68] S. Thruston Ballard, "Eight-Hour Shifts in the Milling Industry," *American Labor Legislation Review*, IV (1914), pp. 117–118.

number of unskilled workers. His solutions were: 1) to restrict immigration after the War (which had already temporarily eased the problem); 2) to establish vocational, trade,
and continuation schools as part of the public school system;
and 3) to enact for the unskilled, "a national minimum wage
law."

Unemployment had two causes: seasonal work and depression. For these Ballard advocated a federal employment
service, public works, and if these were insufficient, "Government concentration camps where work with a small wage
would be provided, supplemented by agricultural and industrial training." Unemployment because of sickness or accident
was to be cured by workmen's compensation and sickness insurance. For long hours and unsanitary conditions, Ballard
proposed mandatory factory inspection laws and a federal
eight-hour, six-day law.[69] All in all, Ballard's report and the
other staff reports were, as Walsh told the United Mine
Workers' leader John R. Lawson, "more radical than any
report upon industrial subjects ever made by any governmental agency." Ballard was pleased that Walsh considered his
report favorably and told his "chief" that he "was really anxious to go on record, not only now, but for all times, as being
heartily in sympathy and fellowship with the working man,
and especially with the common, or so-called, unskilled laborer." "The more I think of our Commission, the more I
feel that the world will be better for its existence," Ballard
added.[70]

Walsh's staff report was even more advanced and more
in sympathy with the workers than Ballard's. It stressed the
importance of the right of labor to organize into unions and
declared "industrial feudalism" to be "the rule rather than

[69] Copies in Box 82, NCF papers and Box 14, Walsh papers; *Final Report*,
p. 249.
[70] Walsh to Lawson, Kansas City, August 20, 1915, Box 143, Walsh
papers; Ballard to Walsh, Louisville, August 19, 1915, *ibid.*

the exception" in those places where labor was unorganized. Manly wrote that workers had not shared proportionately in the increase in wealth from 1890 to 1912—that wealth was up 188 percent but wage earners' income was up by only 95 percent, that one third to one half of the families of wage earners lived below the level of comfort and decency, that farm tenancy had increased by 32 percent in the last twenty years, and that 37 percent of working class mothers were forced to work to supplement family income. The staff report recommended among other things a steeply graduated income tax, the proceeds of which should be used for education, federal social services, and public works.

The report was critical of the antilabor record of the federal judiciary. It called for legislation to protect the right of labor to organize and of workers to belong to unions, and to give the Department of Labor power to prosecute corporations for infringement of these rights. It recommended that the Bureau of Labor Statistics gather and publish information on wages and hours of work,[71] and that state and federal laws establish an eight-hour day and six-day week in industry. It advocated equal pay for women and a child labor law. It called for a national mediation commission with power to recommend solutions to labor disputes, but not to enforce solutions. And it called for federal sickness insurance.[72] Taken together with Ballard's and Commons' reports, the *Final Report* fairly well laid out the New Deal of 1933–1938, and like much of the

[71] During the course of the hearings, William M. Leiserson, assistant Director of Research for the Commission, informed Royal Meeker of the United States Bureau of Labor Statistics that the Commission would recommend a national system of labor exchanges in the form of employment offices to be "established and maintained by the states and cities." He also urged the Bureau "to take up gathering and publication of statistics of unemployment throughout the United States," since "no one is doing it now." The need, Leiserson suggested, was for a permanent organization and monthly reports. Leiserson to Royal Meeker, Madison, Wisconsin, September 30, 1914, Files of the Bureau of Labor Statistics, Record Group 257, National Archives.

[72] *Final Report*, pp. 17, 21–24, 35–36, 67–72, 121–126.

legislation in the New Deal, the proposals were made mostly by men whose conscious purpose was to help the working man, while stabilizing and strengthening the corporate system.

But if Walsh's report was to contribute to the transformation of the federal government into an agency of rationalization and stabilization of the existing industrial system, if it would aid the corporations in securing their hegemony in the United States, neither labor nor the Socialists noticed. Gompers wrote Walsh, upon seeing his report, that it was "impossible for one who has not been through the experience to appreciate the magnitude and the power of the influence exerted by vested interests in this country." Having been through that experience, Gompers could "appreciate all the more the splendid victory" Walsh had won in presenting "such a candid, fearless and suggestive report on industrial relations in the United States." Gompers thanked Walsh for exposing the "evils and burdens that have been heaped upon the wage earners of this country" and proclaimed that Walsh had thereby won "the confidence of the people of this country." [73]

For the Socialists, Eugene V. Debs added his praise of Walsh. Expressing his "increasing regard" for Walsh and the "great work" he had just completed, Debs averred that "the more I review your labors and the more I contemplate the results, the more extraordinary does the achievement seem to me." The Commission's work, Debs asserted, had "measureless value to the working class and to the cause of humanity." He believed it would be "recorded in living letters in the annals of labor's struggle and final emancipation." "Thank God," he concluded, for "your superb courage, amounting to genuine moral heroism." [74]

Debs' praise was eloquent testimony not only to Walsh's courage—which was real enough—but also to the value of the

[73] Gompers to Walsh, Washington, D.C., August 31, 1915, Box 143, Walsh papers.
[74] Debs to Walsh, Terre Haute, October 9, 1915, Box 144, Walsh papers.

Commission on Industrial Relations to the developing corporate order. Success could best be measured not in terms of the changes the Commission made in American life; these were few enough. Ironically, considering Walsh's motives, the main effect of the Commission was to win the support of workers and radicals to the Wilson administration and to the idea that unions and radical intellectuals possessed real power over social policy. The hearings and Walsh's Final Report, supplemented by the Adamson Act (which established the eight-hour day on the railroads) helped greatly to stop the growth of Socialism between 1912 and 1916. Beyond that, the Commission had set down a range of proposals for a liberal corporate order, almost all of which were adopted when conditions once again made social reform a pressing necessity. Few immediate reforms came from the Commission hearings or recommendations because preparedness and then American entrance into the World War followed so quickly upon the end of the Commission's work. During the war, as we shall see, many of the ideas developed on the Commission, but also current in the debates of the NCF were put into effect, even if only temporarily.

CHAPTER EIGHT

WAR AS FULFILLMENT

THE ENTRANCE OF THE UNITED STATES into the First World
War in April of 1917 provided a full-scale testing ground for
the new liberalism and for the new liberals. Out of the war
came striking proof that the ideas and institutional reforms
developed in the prewar days by the National Civic Federation, as well as by such diverse reformers as John R. Commons, Louis D. Brandeis, Frank Walsh, and George Creel,
served the interests of the new corporate giants and their political economy of corporate liberalism. The wartime experience also laid bare, for those few who dared look, the essential
powerlessness of the reformers, social workers, and social engineers who joined the crusade to save democracy. Some of
these crusaders shared Walter Lippmann's belief—or hope—
as the war began that under Woodrow Wilson the United
States stood "at the threshold of a collectivism which is greater
than any as yet planned by the Socialist Party." The war,
Lippmann believed, had "already carried us beyond the stage
of merely national socialism." [1]

But at war's end many liberals, and even a few pro-war
Socialists, quickly became disillusioned. The Treaty of Ver-
sailles and American intervention against the Bolsheviks convinced many who had earlier viewed the war as one for
Democracy and against autocracy that the war was in fact a

[1] Walter Lippmann to J. G. Phelps Stokes, New York, May 1, 1917, Box
26, Stokes papers, Columbia University.

commercial war, even simply an imperialist war.[2] During the war, most intellectuals and reformers had taken the lead in attacking those who condemned it as an imperialist venture. Yet, in so doing, and particularly in rushing into government service in the various wartime agencies, they had—in what Randolph Bourne called the "vain hope of conscious guidance and control"—accepted "almost every program that the bigoted unsocialized patriot has demanded." Although men like Walsh and George Creel may have had different motives, Bourne wrote, their actions had served simply to give "their reactionary opponents a rationalization for war." The "real control" had been taken over by the "reactionaries who pull the strings of power."[3]

Bourne's understanding of the role of the liberal reformers was accurate enough, but his characterization of those who held the strings of power was misleading. It was not the reactionaries—small businessmen in the National Association of Manufacturers and in various local boards of trade—who ran things. Rather, it was such men as William Gibbs McAdoo, Secretary of the Treasury and Director General of the United States Railroad Administration, Daniel Willard, who headed the War Industries Board when it was part of the Council of National Defense, and Bernard Baruch, who headed the WIB when it became the most powerful of all independent wartime agencies. In the WIB other progressive businessmen were also important—men such as Robert S. Lovett, chairman of the board of the Union Pacific Railway, Alexander Legge, general manager of the International Harvester Company, and Robert Brookings, founder of the Brookings Institute. These men were not reactionaries in any acceptable sense of the term. The

[2] See Warren I. Cohen, *The American Revisionists* (Chicago, University of Chicago Press, 1967), Chapter 2.

[3] Randolph S. Bourne to Van Wyck Brooks, n.p., March 27, 1918, Bourne papers, Columbia University; Max Lerner, *Ideas for the Ice Age* (New York, Viking, 1939), p. 130.

215

historian of the War Industries Board, himself the Director of the Council of National Defense, wrote of Baruch: "A conservative at twenty-five, he was a liberal at forty." [4] The description fit most of these men, many of whom, like Baruch, had been supporters of Roosevelt and then of Wilson. To the extent that various independent liberals deceived themselves —and most of them seemed better to know what they were doing than they would later admit—it was in confusing their own pragmatic or problem-oriented liberalism with that of the corporate liberalism of the highly ideological business and political leaders. If they allowed themselves unwittingly to be used, it was because they had the conceit to consider their intelligence and social values equal to the influence of the industrial and financial institutions that were the heart and muscle of American power. When the chips were down it became clear who ultimately held power, and on what terms it would be exercised.

The war presented two major problems to the Wilson administration: organizing the vast industrial capacity of the United States for efficient modern warfare and winning the cooperation and support of workers, farmers, and political dissidents for the war. The first of these tasks was carried out through such wartime agencies as the Food and Fuel Administration, the United States Railroad Administration, and the War Industries Board. The second was handled primarily by George Creel's Committee on Public Information, and such subsidiary groups as The American Alliance for Labor and Democracy, supplemented by the punitive measures of the Attorney General and the Postmaster General. The primary approach in both areas was to conciliate business and pro-war unions, and, failing that, to use the power of the federal government to attempt to coerce uncooperative businessmen and

[4] Grosvenor B. Clarkson, *Industrial America in the World War* (Boston and New York, Houghton Mifflin, 1923), p. 67.

216

to destroy anti-war unions (particularly the IWW) as well as Socialist organizations and newspapers.

The control and direction of production for full-scale war concerned President Wilson as early as 1915. With his approval, the Industrial Preparedness Committee was organized as a semigovernmental organization to survey industrial capacity and plan for wartime production.[5] In 1916, chaired by Howard E. Coffin, vice president of the Hudson Motor Company, the Committee conducted an inventory of manufacturing plants capable of making munitions. By September the various state committees, composed of members of the five leading engineering societies of the country, had canvassed twenty thousand manufacturers. Most of them believed that the United States would enter the war. As Grosvenor B. Clarkson, director of the Council of National Defense observed, these men, "stimulated as the result of Allied contracts, cheerfully cooperated in the census of preparedness.[6]

Before Coffin's canvass had been completed, Congress had established the Council of National Defense (CND), out of which the War Industries Board was to grow. Created as a peacetime body to prepare the country for an emergency,[7] the Council itself consisted of the Secretaries of War, Navy, Interior, Agriculture, Commerce, and Labor. But its real work was done by an Advisory Commission, appointed by Wilson, whose proposals were usually approved by the Cabinet mem-

[5] The Industrial Preparedness Committee grew out of the Industrial Preparedness Committee of the Naval Consulting Board in response to a growing feeling among businessmen that the United States would enter the war. See Clarkson, *Industrial America in the World War*, pp. 10–13.

[6] *Ibid.*, p. 13.

[7] The Council of National Defense was created in a section of the Military Appropriations Act in August 1916. The National Defense Act, passed at the same session of Congress, authorized the President to appoint a board of industrial mobilization at his discretion. Wilson never did appoint such a board, but worked through and with the CND to evolve the powers of the War Industries Board.

217

bers. In appointing the Advisory Commission in late 1916, Wilson asserted that the country was best prepared for war when thoroughly prepared for peace. "From an economical point of view," Wilson wrote, "there is now very little difference between the machinery required for commercial efficiency and that required for military purposes. In both cases the whole industrial mechanism must be organized in the most effective way." Or, as the legislation establishing the Council stated, it was to create "relations which will render possible in time of need the immediate concentration and utilization of the resources of the nation." The two main purposes of the Council, Wilson said, were coordination of transportation and preparation for the mobilization of industry. For that purpose, he claimed, the Council's advisory members, appointed without regard to party, marked "the entrance of the nonpartisan engineer and professional man into American governmental affairs on a wider scale than ever before." [8]

Wilson's words were, no doubt, most gratifying to the social engineers. But his appointments contradicted his words. In charge of transportation on the Advisory Commission, Wilson appointed Daniel Willard of the Baltimore and Ohio Railroad; in charge of munitions, Howard E. Coffin; in charge of supplies, Julius Rosenwald of Sears, Roebuck and Company; in charge of raw materials, Bernard Baruch; in charge of labor, Samuel Gompers. The only engineer on the Commission was the president of the Drexel Institute of Philadelphia, Hollis Godfrey, who was responsible for engineering and education. The clear implication of the language of the act creating the CND, and of Wilson in announcing the personnel of the Advisory Commission was that cooperation and coordination would replace competition in planning for the war—and possibly even for simple peacetime "commercial efficiency." Thus, in 1918, with Wilson's approval, Congress passed the Webb-Pomerene Act, which permitted manufac-

[8] Quoted in Clarkson, *Industrial America in the World War*, pp. 21–22.

218

turers to organize associations to conduct export trade without coming under the restrictions of the Sherman Act. Wilson had long approved the principle embodied in the Webb-Pomerene Act, but for political reasons had hesitated to include such a provision in the Federal Trade Commission Act in 1914.[9] At war's end he and members of the War Industries Board would consider the elimination of the Sherman Act even as it applied to domestic trade, but as we will see, political considerations intervened to make this impossible.

In its early discussions before the United States entered the war on April 6, 1917, the Council of National Defense laid out many wartime policies. Between December 1916 and March 1917, the Council devised a system of purchasing war supplies, planned for press censorship, designed a system of food control with Herbert Hoover as its director, and developed a daylight-saving plan. The Council also insisted that there be universal military service and arranged for the exemption of skilled labor. As Howard E. Coffin told the Executive Council of the NCF on February 6, 1917, there was "no one in the official family in Washington who is not heartily in favor of" universal service. In 1919, in reviewing the early work of the Council, a Congressional critic observed (and the Director of the CND agreed) that "there was not an act of the so-called war legislation afterwards enacted that had not before the actual declaration of war been discussed and settled upon by this Advisory Commission." [10]

Yet, while this was generally true, the problems of coordinating industry for the total mobilization of resources during the war had not been solved by the CND in its early deliberations, or by the War Industries Board in its initial form as a subsidiary agency of the CND. In part this failure was the

[9] Kolko, *Triumph of Conservatism*, pp. 275–276.
[10] Clarkson, *Industrial America in the World War*, pp. 24–25;· Howard E. Coffin to the Meeting of the Executive Council, February 6, 1917, Box 189, NCF papers.

result of the views of Wilson's Secretary of War, Newton D. Baker, a former protégé and successor of Cleveland's reform mayor, Tom L. Johnson. In Cleveland, Baker had stood firmly for home rule; in Washington he still opposed centralization of power. The advisory board of the CND pressed Baker for real authority and for overall control of purchasing and the establishment of priorities. Baker resisted. The result was that by the end of 1917 "A jerry-built array of 150 committees was associated helter-skelter with various army bureaus." [11] Production and the labor market were in incipient states of chaos.

Several of the civilians on the advisory board pushed for the creation of a single agency with more than advisory power to establish priorities in purchasing for the various government and Allied bodies. They were opposed consistently by Secretary Baker, but gradually the President moved to support the demands for centralization of men such as Baruch and Frank A. Scott, a Cleveland industrialist who headed the munitions board. The first step was a compromise suggested by Wilson that established a War Industries Board on July 28, 1917, designed primarily to coordinate, rather than direct industrial efforts. Its lack of final power, which remained in the hands of Secretary Baker, pleased Baker and the Army but it annoyed the businessmen. Secretary McAdoo, a strong supporter of Baruch, complained that he was "genuinely discouraged that such a complicated piece of machinery has been set up." [12] By December the supply problem had become extremely bad and pressure increased for a centralized and powerful civilian agency to direct production and distribution of war materiel. In the face of this pressure, and a congressional investigation, Baker made concessions in the direction of greater civilian control over purchasing. He appointed a new

[11] Daniel R. Beaver, "Newton D. Baker and the Genesis of the War Industries Board, 1917–1918," *The Journal of American History*, LII, 1 (June 1965), p. 46.

[12] Quoted in *ibid.*, p. 48.

Director of Purchases and a Director of Storage and Supplies, and then brought Edward R. Stettinius, a partner in J. P. Morgan and Company, and Samuel McRoberts of the National City Bank, into the War Department to work with them.

But Baker had moved too little and too slowly. In the congressional investigation both Daniel Willard and Baruch insisted that efficiency could be achieved only if authority to purchase all supplies were vested in one man, in a civilian agency independent of the War Department. Writing to Colonel Edward M. House, Louis Brandeis supported this approach. He urged that the War Department be relieved of all responsibility for purchasing, production, and transportation of military supplies; that an administration be established to handle these problems, and that all powers be vested in a single head with full powers of delegation. He also recommended separate departments to handle labor and transportation.[13]

Despite Brandeis' suggestion that a new agency be created, Wilson decided that the existing War Industries Board should simply be given real power over purchasing and the setting of priorities. Baker suggested John D. Ryan, President of Amalgamated Copper, or Stettinius as the head of the new board, but Colonel House, McAdoo, and Wilson's private secretary, Joseph P. Tummulty, were opposed to Ryan and were afraid that appointing Stettinius would (in House's words) make it "look too much like the Morgans are running things." Instead, Wilson chose Baruch, who had been urged upon him strongly by McAdoo. He did so over the persistent objections of Baker, who looked upon Baruch as a Wall Street speculator without executive ability.[14]

But Baruch was a near perfect choice to head what was to become the most powerful of all the wartime government

[13] Quoted in Mason, *Brandeis*, pp. 523–524.
[14] Beaver, "Newton D. Baker," p. 56.

agencies. His great wealth gave him stature in the eyes of corporation leaders, and had been acquired through an understanding of, and sharing in, business principles. Yet he had no attachment to particular corporations or financial groups. As Grosvenor Clarkson observed, the "nature of his acquisition made him independent of all bias or obligation to the 'interests.' The bigness of it put him on a plane of equality and familiarity with all comers." On the War Industries Board this gave Baruch a special ability to deal with manufacturers as they believed government should. "Poets," Clarkson noted, "esteem each other according to the merit of their verses; men of affairs measure each other by dollars." Baruch had earned his dollars by hardheaded business experience. "He was not saturated with theories lacking the heat treatment of practice." He dealt with facts. "Instead of preaching he traded, instead of commanding he bargained." [15]

In that description, Clarkson caught the essence not only of the War Industries Board, but of the entire relationship of business to government that Civic Federation and other business leaders had tried to establish during the Progressive Era. Government and business were to be partners in the common enterprise of an ever-expanding economy. Each partner had somewhat different immediate interests, but they shared a common goal. The same was true during the war, of course, and now much that had been only theory before the war could be tested in practice.

In setting up the War Industries Board, Baruch and his subordinates had one major aim: to secure maximum production with the least possible disruption of normal business routine and with the least political disturbance. The heads of the sixty commodity sections, which were the heart of the WIB, were themselves experienced in the respective industries for which they were responsible. They functioned under "a loose

[15] Clarkson, *Industrial America in the World War*, p. 70.

222

central control" whose purpose was "not to dominate, but to coordinate them." It was a system under which production was maximized by "businessmen wholly consecrated to Government service, but full of understanding of the problems of industry" facing "businessmen wholly representative of industry," but "sympathetic with the purpose of Government." [16] In summarizing the nature of the WIB, Clarkson wrote that Baruch's subordinates were "all well adapted to the central idea of industrial self-control for patriotic purposes." Being themselves from industry, "they would have resented dictatorial methods had they remained in it. They knew just how the men at home felt. They were also simple, democratic Americans." Therefore, they would, "naturally . . . have favored regulation of industry by consent rather than by rigid rule." Such men obviously "fitted admirably into the conception of industry imposing from its best judgement its own rules and regulations and self-administering them." In short the War Industries Board "was really the town meeting of American industry curbing, disciplining and devoting itself." [17]

Wilson asked Baruch to assume the chairmanship of the War Industries Board and granted him wide powers over procurement and conversion of existing facilities to war work on March 4, 1918.[18] Ten days later, under the chairmanship of Robert S. Brookings, The Price Fixing Committee of the War Industries Board held its first meeting. At it, Brookings laid down the guiding principles of this key section of the purchasing agency. He made it clear that while "a runaway market must be guarded against on the one hand, on the other hand it is absolutely essential that prices be fixed that will stimulate

[16] *Ibid.*, pp. 301, 303.
[17] *Ibid.*, p. 73.
[18] Wilson to Baruch, Washington, D.C., March 4, 1918, Archives of the War Industries Board, Record Group 61, 1-Cl, Box 73, National Archives. Although the WIB started functioning almost immediately, the executive order establishing it is dated May 28, 1918. Order No. 2868, *ibid.*

223

production." [19] The subsequent meetings of the Price Fixing Committee, held three or four times a week until after the war ended, were bargaining sessions in which industry representatives often implicitly threatened to withhold production if a suitable profit margin were not guaranteed. Yet the meetings were not entirely one-sided. Committee members did insist on relatively stable prices and relied on findings of the Federal Trade Commission to suggest reasonable price structures. The meetings were what Clarkson called them: bargaining sessions. And the representatives of industry, particularly the larger manufacturers, understood the need to avoid taking full advantage of the immediate market conditions.[20]

At a meeting to consider cotton goods (April 10, 1918) Brookings began by saying that the general feeling of representatives of the industry "was that the so-called runaway market in cotton goods was not a very good thing for the industry of the nation." The cotton goods committee, he added, thought it "quite worth their while" to "get together in a friendly way and talk over the situation and see whether anything ought to be done" to "stabilize the market." The cotton situation, he explained, was very much as the steel situation had been, and "no industry as large as cotton or steel" could "profit very much by a market such as we have today." Given the need for industrial peace—and the labor shortage—wage increases were unavoidable. "We all know that labor follows the market, in these times at least, almost as rapidly as the market advances," Brookings warned. Yet the manufacturer was the one who got "the full thud of the fall when it comes, to say nothing of the very great difficulty of getting labor down when it assumes a higher level." [21]

[19] Minutes of the Price Fixing Committee of the WIB, March 14, 1918, RG 61, 4-B1, Box 529, N.A.

[20] See Minutes of the Price Fixing Committee of the WIB, March 16, April 3, 10, November 27, 1918, and *passim, ibid.*

[21] Minutes of the Price Fixing Committee, April 10, 1918, *ibid.*

Control of prices and the market was possible despite the Sherman Act, Brookings explained, because in the cotton trade, "the government becomes a partner with you." Furthermore, "we avoid one phase of the antitrust law. We never fix but a maximum price," although in fact that "becomes a minimum price." If that could be done to the converter, manufacturer, and the jobber, Brookings mused, "I suppose that is as far as the industry could be controlled." Brookings then appealed to the social responsibility of the cotton goods men. Most say, he began, that the market is "very, very high." In that situation some manufacturers "have the feeling that it is wise to take all you can get when you can get it." But Brookings did "not believe that is the case with the larger manufacturers of this country. In the steel industry," he explained, "we met the men at two o'clock one afternoon and by nine o'clock that night we had fixed a price on steel." [22]

But, as E. H. Gary himself later told the members of the Price Fixing Committee, Brookings' policies hardly required sacrifice on the part of the larger manufacturers. "In order to secure the largest production of steel—to permit the operation of all the facilities of all the companies and firms" in the steel industry, Gary began, "it was necessary to arrive at a basis of price which, as applied to many of the corporations yielded large profits, yet at the same time did not permit an unreasonable profit to many of the high cost mills." Therefore, Gary went on, "we need not be especially grateful because you permitted profits which seemed to be large in many instances." If there was reason for gratitude, Gary pontificated, it was "because we know that your motives were right, that you recognized your obligation to your country, and still at the same time in the performance of your duties you were always considerate, friendly and fair, and were as liberal in your conclusions as your duty to the government you represented per-

[22] *Ibid.*

225

mitted." Patting the Board members on the back, Gary concluded by expressing his pleasure that the Board had "consisted of men who had not only the disposition but the intelligence to rise to a plane of action where exact justice could be done to all concerned." United States Steel, of course, had few high-cost mills. Its profits during the war were very large, even in the eyes of the corporation's own Finance Committee.[23]

While the War Industries Board permitted extraordinarily large profits for the more efficient producers, it and other wartime agencies, sometimes supported directly by President Wilson, also attempted to change the labor policies of various large employers. The presence of Gompers on the Advisory Commission of the Council for National Defense, and of Hugh Frayne of the AFL on the Price Fixing Committee of the WIB meant that "there were no dealings with 'big business' or any other kind of business in which labor was not consulted and represented." According to Clarkson "Frayne knew labor's point of view and how to manage it," and so when "prices were fixed at levels which yielded profits that would stimulate production, it was always provided that labor should have a share." [24]

At the hearings on the price of refined copper, for example, Hugh Frayne told Daniel Guggenheim of American Smelting and Refining that he could not agree to a price increase while a Guggenheim plant paid lower wages than those prevailing in the industry. "Your men have been paid 50 cents a day less," he reminded Guggenheim. "There has been a strike. There will be another one tomorrow or the next day. I have assured these men that this thing could be adjusted. This is the situation. These men must receive more money. I would oppose your getting an increase on a fixed price while your

[23] Minutes of the Meeting of the Price Fixing Committee of the WIB, December 11, 1918, Box 531, *ibid.* See, for example, George W. Perkins to Theodore Roosevelt, n.p., August 1, 1918, Box 29, Perkins papers.
[24] Clarkson, *Industrial America in the World War*, p. 92.

men are being paid less than those men who are doing like work in competing plants." [25]

In the lumber industry of the Northwest Administration intervention was direct. There, in order to insure production of Sitka spruce for airplanes as well as other essential lumber —and also to destroy the IWW which was conducting a highly successful strike in the lumber regions of Oregon, Washington, and Idaho—the government organized its own labor union and imposed drastically improved conditions on the industry.[26] This led to a special plea by representatives of the Douglas fir industry to the War Industries Board in November 1918. A. C. Dixon of the Booth Kelly Lumber Company told the Price Fixing Committee that last year "at the direct request of the President" the industry in the Northwest went on the eight-hour basis. "You know that no other place in the United States has the lumber industry on that basis," Dixon complained. "The competitive difficulties coming out of that you all realize without any explanation. Subsequent to that under the direction of the War Department, and General [Brice P.] Disque [in charge of the government's union], we went on a uniform wage scale" with the shipyards in Seattle.[27]

Dixon assured the Committee members that with the end of the war they did not propose to change from the eight-hour day or to reduce wages "until the cost of living is materially reduced." The problem was not the wage level, but that there were approximately 120,000 men in the woods and 80,000 in the shipyards, "and we do not know what to do with them frankly." Remembering the "riots, labor disturbances" and general unrest at the time the United States entered the war,

[25] Minutes of Meeting of the Price Fixing Committee, April 3, 1918, Box 529, *ibid.*
[26] See Robert L. Tyler, "The United States Government as Union Organizer: The Loyal Legion of Loggers and Lumbermen," *The Mississippi Valley Historical Review*, XLVII, 3 (December 1960), pp. 434 ff.
[27] Minutes of Meeting with the Douglas Fir Representatives and the Price Fixing Committee, November 27, 1918, Box 531, *ibid.*

Dixon told the Committee that he was "as much worried today about the danger of violence and absolute labor revolution in Oregon and Washington" as he was about the financial condition of his own business. "We can take care of the finances in some way with the help we will naturally get from the Government in adjusting these contracts," he said. But he did not know "how to take care of the labor, and we have not had any suggestions made to us that show us any way at all." [28] Nor were any suggestions forthcoming. Indeed, only two months later the labor situation in Washington erupted into the Seattle General Strike as the shipyards were cut back and lumber production was drastically reduced.

Attempts were made to impose a general eight-hour day in industry by Felix Frankfurter, chairman of the War Labor Policies Board, created by Wilson in April 1918. In September, Frankfurter called E. H. Gary to a meeting to discuss hours of work in steel. He told Gary that the Board had decided to press for a standard, or "basic," eight-hour day, under which all work done in excess of eight hours would be paid time and a half. Before ordering the reform he wanted to hear what Gary had to say. Gary, who understood that a "basic" eight-hour day would leave the twelve-hour day intact, replied that the proposal was a sham to get higher wages, not shorter hours. An actual eight-hour day would be an interference with production, Gary insisted. But Frankfurter persisted, reminding Gary of his responsibility in connection with the war, which he said "was equal to that of a Cabinet member." Gary admitted that he did have such responsibility, implying that he did not want to come into conflict with the government. Frankfurter then told him that Henry Ford, who had instituted an actual eight-hour day in his plant in 1916—but was using the "basic" eight-hour day as a war measure, had been made the War Labor Board umpire on this question. Gary shrugged and conceded that Ford would rule for the

[28] *Ibid.*

228

principle of the eight-hour day. Five days later the Iron and Steel Institute announced the adoption of the "basic" eight-hour day in the industry.[29] In doing so as a war measure, Gary must have understood that the Steel Company would later be able to return to the twelve-hour day and at the same time reduce pay without cutting nominal hourly wage rates. While the war was on, of course, the cost of the increase in wages due to the adoption of the basic eight-hour day could be passed on to the government.

On the issue of union organization in steel, little progress was made during the war, despite Frankfurter's probable desire to change labor policy in the industry. The positive attitude toward the unions of the War Industries Board, the United States Railroad Administration, the War Labor Policies Board, and other agencies, however, must have encouraged Gompers and others to support early postwar attempts to unionize steel. But these met with determined opposition from Gary and led to the Great Steel Strike of 1919. When the strike itself became identified with Bolshevism, in part because of the prominent role played by William Z. Foster, secretary-treasurer of the National Committee for Organizing Iron and Steel Workers, Gompers backed off. The Organizing Committee had never been adequately financed by the unions, perhaps because they expected a friendlier climate after their responsible behavior during the war. In any case, the internal weakness of the Organizing Committee, combined with the steel industry's success in utilizing postwar anti-radical hysteria against the strikers, led to the defeat of the organizing drive.[30]

After the strike, George W. Perkins urged Gary to institute an actual eight-hour day. In response, Gary began a study of

[29] Minutes of Meeting of the War Labor Policies Board, September 20, 1918, Archives of WLPB, Box 16, National Archives; Frankfurter to Baruch, Washington, D.C., September 25, 1918, *ibid.*, David Brody, *Labor in Crisis* (New York, Lippincott, 1965), pp. 58–60.

[30] For an excellent history of the strike see Brody, *Labor in Crisis.*

the possibility of three shifts instead of two, but the objections of the steel men in the production end of the Corporation impressed Gary more than Perkins' plea. It was not until 1923 that the Wilson administration's efforts to shorten the workday in steel were rewarded, and then at the urging of Secretary of Commerce Hoover and President Warren G. Harding. Hoover argued with Gary and Charles M. Schwab at a dinner in May 1922 for a reduction. When it was not forthcoming he drafted a letter for Harding, expressing Presidential disappointment with the steel industry. Public reaction forced the steel men to give in and in July 1923 the industry established an eight-hour workday and granted a compensating twenty-five percent wage increase.[31]

Within the War Industries Board the approach of peace led to consideration of the extension into normal times of the federally supervised cooperation that industry had enjoyed during the war. As an historian of the Board has observed, the agencies members "unhesitatingly supported the reconstruction policies for which the business community was agitating at the end of the war." [32] These included a "determination to sweep aside the prewar antitrust policy so that industry could without hindrance form a genuine cartel system in which the collective will of an industry—not the competitive market—would set prices and production levels." Such had been the underlying thrust of much prewar agitation by the large corporations: wartime experiences apparently convinced many smaller firms that such action was desirable. Through the National Association of Manufacturers, they too now became enthusiastic supporters of Sherman Act revision.[33]

If the Board's actions during the war had strengthened

---

[31] Herbert C. Hoover, *The Memoirs of Herbert Hoover* (New York, Macmillan, 1952), II, pp. 103–105; Brody, *Labor in Crisis*, pp. 177–178.

[32] Robert F. Himmelberg, "The War Industries Board and the Antitrust Question in November 1918," *The Journal of American History*, LII, 1 (June 1965), p. 59.

[33] *Ibid.*, p. 61.

confidence in government supervision of business, fear of the collapse of the wartime boom, and of the consequent postwar inflation led to early consideration of an extension of the WIB, or some similar agency. In the end nothing was done, partly because of the indifference of President Wilson, partly because the members of the WIB, particularly the Board Counsel, Albert C. Ritchie, believed legislation further relaxing the Sherman Act to be politically impossible in the postwar situation. But, as Robert F. Himmelberg has observed, the Board "was convinced that revision was a necessity and seriously considered playing the part of lobbyist for the emasculation of the antitrust tradition." This is clearly apparent in the legislation proposed and commented on by Board members and advisors. One bill, supported in principle by Baruch and Secretary of Commerce William C. Redfield, would have permitted manufacturers "to cooperate in the adoption of plans for the elimination of needless waste in the public interest" under the supervision of the Federal Trade Commission. Another more direct approach would simply have allowed a majority of a given industry's firms to set production quotas for all firms in that industry.[34] Priorities Commissioner Edwin B. Parker, whose bill this was, told Ritchie that he had discussed the bill at length one evening at Baruch's house with Commissioner of Finished Products, George N. Peek, and a number of other businessmen and government officials. "Without exception," Parker reported, "they have expressed themselves as believing that such a measure would be distinctly in the public interest, especially at this time." [35]

Still another bill, by Mark L. Requa, Assistant Administrator of the Fuel Administration, proposed the creation of a United States Board of Trade. A WIB memorandum on this

[34] *Ibid.*, pp. 70–71.
[35] Edwin B. Parker to Albert C. Ritchie, Washington, D.C., November 25, 1918, RG 61, 1–A5, Box 41, N.A. Cited partially by Himmelberg, "WIB and the Antitrust Question in 1918," p. 71.

bill commented that in the war emergency the Sherman and Clayton acts had proven to be hindrances, and had to be suspended in practice. "With the return of peace," it went on, "these methods of securing the greatest efficiency on the part of the several industries will cease to exist." Yet "with our enormous national debt and the international competition which must be met it is impossible to return to the old system if we are to maintain successfully our place among the nations." The whole theory of "controlling and supervising industry by means of penal statute, whatever its previous justification" was now "no longer tenable." Instead, "there must be a spirit of mutual cooperation between government and industry. They must be partners in a common enterprise, and may no longer occupy the position of the lawbreakers and policeman." The appeal of Requa's proposal for a Board of Trade was that it left intact the antitrust laws while providing a method whereby acts or agreements which "promoted the national welfare" might be entered into and carried out. The law would make no attempt to define these precisely; the Board of Trade would be impowered to do that.[36]

Even though President Wilson had decided to dissolve the WIB on January 1, 1919, and had indicated by late November that he would not push legislation for a National Readjustment Commission (for which he had requested suggestions in early November),[37] individual members of the Board seemed to believe such legislation was possible and desirable. Nevertheless, Ritchie insisted that the proposed bills could not be passed because they departed too radically from what "wisely or unwisely, has become our fixed policy in dealing with business." Furthermore, Ritchie feared that the public would react negatively to suggestions for the weakening of the

[36] Memorandum on a bill by M. L. Requa, initialed "N.B.B.," Box 42, 1–A5, RG 61, N.A.

[37] Memorandum from Harold T. Clark (assistant to Baruch) to Albert C. Ritchie, November 14, 1918, Box 42, *ibid.*

antitrust tradition emanating from the War Industries Board in its closing moments. He warned against the cry that would be made if "Mr. Baruch's last act, before he went back to business, was to try to have the antitrust laws, to which business has generally been opposed, suspended." This was apparently the telling point. In any case, after Ritchie's argument the Board decided to take no action.[38] With that decision the wartime experiment in government coordination of business temporarily came to an end.

To Grosvenor Clarkson of the CND, as to many others, this was unfortunate. The War Industries Board, he wrote, "literally brought business into the business of Government. If we had a Government business manager with a free hand to run the business side of Government, as free as Baruch had in the War Industries Board, we should have a successful Government of business." Some day, he mused, "it may occur to some President to apply the organization scheme of the War Industries Board to Government." [39] Fourteen years later, in the crisis of the Great Depression, Franklin Roosevelt turned to Baruch, and to men like Gerard Swope, Hugh S. Johnson, and George N. Peek, all of whom had worked under Baruch on the WIB, for guidance. The results included the National Recovery Administration and the Agricultural Adjustment Administration, administered respectively by Johnson and Peek.

The happy relationship of government to business during the war did not extend to other social classes. Support for the war among workers and farmers was spotty, and necessitated a dual policy of concessions to pro-war organizations, such as the American Federation of Labor, and suppression of antiwar organizations and periodicals. John Hays Hammond had com-

[38] Quotations and conclusions are from Himmelberg, "WIB and the Antitrust Question in 1918," pp. 71–72.
[39] Clarkson, *Industrial America in the World War*, p. 312.

mented on the extent of opposition and indifference to American participation before April 1917;[40] after the declaration of war that sentiment remained largely unchanged. Activity against the war was greatest in rural areas, both North and South, and in factory towns and larger cities in the North. In the South, such agitation reached its height in the Eastern part of Oklahoma, in early August 1917, where about 1,000 farmers took to arms in the Green Corn Rebellion. In general, as the secretary of the Atlanta, Georgia, Chamber of Commerce told George Creel, the situation was "very serious regarding the rural population and it is going to take an extraordinary effort to reach them." [41] Charles S. Barrett (who had been one of Taft's appointees to the Commission on Industrial Relations) told the League for National Unity that on his trip through the South in August 1917 he had found antiwar sentiment to be prevalent. In New Orleans, Barrett attended a state Farmers Union convention where the 350 delegates had condemned the war with only nine dissenting votes. A few days later, at a convention of 2,000 farmers in Dallas, Barrett observed that only one man in fifty supported the war. "There is," he added, "a great deal of indifference in North Carolina," and "a great deal more in Virginia than I thought." [42]

In the North, too, farmers expressed their anger over what they considered to be betrayal by President Wilson. During the summer of 1917 Socialist antiwar meetings in Minnesota drew crowds of 5,000, 10,000, and even 20,000 farmers to protest the war, conscription, and profiteering. In Wisconsin one small city newspaper (the *Plymouth Review*) commented

[40] See Chapter Five, pp. 136–137, above.

[41] Walter G. Cooper to George Creel, Atlanta, Georgia, March 18, 1918, Archives of the Committee on Public Information, Record Group 63, 12–A1, National Archives. For a detailed account of antiwar activity and sentiment see James Weinstein, *The Decline of American Socialism*, Chapter III.

[42] Minutes of the League for National Unity, September 12, 1917, Washington, D.C., Box 168, NCF papers.

that "probably no party ever gained more rapidly in strength than the Socialist party is just at the present time." Expressing the opinion that the Socialists could "carry Sheboygan county by three to one against the two old parties together," the *Review* reported that "thousands assemble to hear Socialist speakers in places where ordinarily a few hundred are considered large assemblages." [43] Similarly, in Ohio the conservative *Akron Beacon-Journal* commented that there was "scarcely a political observer whose opinion is worth much but what will admit that were an election to come now a mighty tide of socialism would inundate the Middle West" and "maybe all other sections of the country." The *Beacon-Journal* believed that the United States had "never embarked upon a more unpopular war," and that "the vast majority of the people" had "never been convinced that war was necessary either to sustain our honor or to protect our interests." [44]

Until war had been declared many nonsocialist pacifists and a sizable number of major party politicians had expressed their opposition to involvement, but after the declaration the Socialist Party was the only nationally organized group that continued its agitation. At its Emergency Convention in St. Louis, meeting only one day after the United States entered the war, the Socialist Party branded the declaration "a crime against the people of the United States," and proclaimed allegiance to the principle of international working class solidarity. Characterizing the war as one of capitalist interests fighting over colonial markets, the resolution adopted at St. Louis called on workers to stand in opposition to it, and pledged "continuous, active and public opposition" to the war and to conscription.[45] The strong stand taken against the war made the Socialists highly vulnerable to attack from the

[43] *Plymouth Review*, August 29, 1917.
[44] *Akron Beacon-Journal*, September 7, 1917.
[45] "Special Convention on War," *International Socialist Review*, XVII. 11 (May 1917), pp. 670 ff.

235

government, but it also presented the party with an unprecedented opportunity to rally the various antiwar elements under its banner. The party, of course, was unable to mobilize all opponents of the war, partly because of its consistently socialist analysis of American motives and partly because of its limited resources. Yet in many states Socialists were "in evidence almost everywhere," speaking against continuation of the war and against conscription.[46] This agitation was carried on at first through a series of mass meetings and parades. These were attacked by various governmental agencies and by mobs of men organized by local chambers of commerce and boards of trades in dozens of small cities and towns. The focus of antiwar action then shifted to the municipal elections of 1917, in which Socialists made substantial—in many cases amazing—gains.

The most important of these elections took place in New York City, where Morris Hillquit polled 22 percent of the vote, almost five times the normal Socialist vote there. In addition, in New York, Socialists elected ten assemblymen, seven aldermen, and a municipal court judge. In some sixty other cities from Boston to Minneapolis similar gains were made. In Chicago, for example, the party increased its vote from 3.6 percent in 1915 to 34.7 percent; in Toledo, Ohio, from 5.9 in 1916 to 34.8; in Cleveland from 4.5 to 22.4; in Buffalo from 2.6 to 30.2; in Hagerstown, Maryland, from 1.6 to 15. Most of these gains were in industrial cities, and in the working class wards of them. The small towns and cities in which Socialist mayors were elected were factory towns or industrial suburbs of cities like Pittsburgh and St. Louis.[47]

The Wilson administration met the problem of opposition to the war in two ways. The first was to attempt to destroy Socialist and IWW organizations and publications. The second was to make concessions to labor and to organize pro-war

[46] *Dayton* (Ohio) *News*, August 18, 1917.
[47] Weinstein, *Decline*, Chapter III.

liberal groups to win the confidence of rank and file pro-socialist workers and reformers. Traditionally, Wilson is portrayed as being deeply upset by a fear that once the United States entered the war Americans would quickly "forget there ever was such a thing as tolerance." But Wilson also believed that "to fight you must be brutal and ruthless," [48] and he had from the beginning acted accordingly. At his direction the "loyalty" plank of the Democratic Party platform in 1916 condemned every organization tending "to divide our people into antagonistic groups and thus destroy that complete agreement and solidarity . . . so essential to the perpetuity of free institutions." [49] Immediately after war was declared, Wilson promoted a series of security measures including the Espionage Act of June 15, 1917. In Congress debate on this bill centered around his demand that it include a section authorizing direct press censorship. This would have given the President power to proclaim certain information useful—or possibly useful—to the enemy, and to provide heavy penalties for the publication of such material. Congress, and the press, balked at this provision and despite Wilson's firm stand, finally dropped it. But the President achieved his purpose through another provision of the Espionage Act granting the Attorney General the right to withhold from the mails matter urging "treason, insurrection, or forcible resistance to any law of the United States." [50]

Even before Wilson signed the Espionage Act into law, his Postmaster General, Albert Burleson, began removing Socialist publications from the mails. His first victim was the Halletsville, Texas, *Rebel*, which had exposed the eviction of tenant farmers and their replacement by unpaid prison labor on land

[48] Quoted in H. C. Peterson and Gilbert C. Fite, *Opponents of War, 1917–1918* (Madison, University of Wisconsin Press, 1957), p. 11.

[49] See Harry N. Scheiber, *The Wilson Administration and Civil Liberties, 1917–1921* (Ithaca, New York, Cornell University Press, 1960), pp. 8–9.

[50] *Ibid.*, pp. 18–19.

237

Burleson owned in Texas.[51] But Burleson quickly demonstrated that he could be equally strict where his immediate personal interests were not involved. In the weeks after June 15 he seized dozens of antiwar publications, including the *Masses*, *The Appeal to Reason*, and the *International Socialist Review*. These seizures dealt a particularly heavy blow to the Socialist Party because of its heavy dependence on its press as a means of communication with thousands of small locals in states like Oklahoma, Texas, Washington, Montana, and Nevada. *The Appeal to Reason* had a circulation of over 500,000 in 1917, for example. It had 38,000 subscribers in Oklahoma alone. Its readers were entirely dependent on the mails for delivery, as were the readers of most Socialist periodicals. The loss of these links to the party made the many small town and rural locals much more vulnerable to wartime pressures against dissenters. And yet, as the November elections demonstrated, the removal of Socialist papers from the mails was not enough to halt the spread of the Party's influence.[52] Thus after the fall elections of 1917 the most serious repression was initiated; thousands of Socialists, IWW's, and other antiwar radicals were indicted and were almost invariably convicted under the Espionage Act. As a result of these two Administration tactics the Socialist Party was reduced from 5,000 locals at the beginning of the war to 3,500 at its end, while the IWW had virtually its entire leadership put in prison.

Not all Administration leaders favored such direct repression. George Creel, who headed the vital committee on Public Information, and Frank Walsh, who became co-chairman with William H. Taft of the War Labor Board, dissociated themselves from such attacks. When the *International Socialist*

[51] Oscar Ameringer, *If You Don't Weaken* (New York, Henry Holt and Company, 1940), pp. 318 ff.; Halletsville *New Era*, June 12, 1917. The editor of the *Rebel*, E. R. Meitzen, had cooperated closely with Frank Walsh during the Dallas hearings of the Commission on Industrial Relations in 1915.

[52] Weinstein, *Decline*, Chapter III.

Review was suspended from the mails Charles H. Kerr and Mary Marcy wrote to the pro-war ex-Socialist, William English Walling, asking for help. Marcy explained that she and the magazine were pro-Ally but antiwar, and Walling in turn told Creel that Kerr and Marcy were "honest" and that it would be best to allow publication of the *Review*—"even though their radicalism more than counterbalances their pro-ally sympathy." Creel understood. He explained to Walling that before the passage of the Espionage law he had been able to prevent such action, but that now there was nothing he could do as the Attorney General's office felt that its duty was plain. But, he added, suppression was "unwise." [53]

Whether, in fact, suppression was unwise from the Administration's point of view is a moot question. The extent of antiwar sentiment and the Socialists' demonstrated ability to rally it behind an ideologically unacceptable critique of the war indicates that suppression may have been necessary to prevent the rapid growth of the Party. But even if suppression was necessary, Creel's attitude, as well as Walsh's, was useful to the Administration. It allowed radicals to believe they had real support in high Administration circles. Reports to the Attorney General's office, for example, indicated that in Minneapolis the Socialist mayor and local labor organizations had "confidence in the federal War Labor Board" because of Walsh's co-chairmanship and were probably observing wartime regulations. There was unrest in Minneapolis, but according to a Special Assistant Attorney General this was the result of attacks on unions by local employers and of the failure of local officials to enforce laws against vigilantes attacking the Non-Partisan League in Minnesota.[54]

[53] Mary Marcy to William English Walling, Chicago, June 26, 1917; Walling to George Creel, New London, Connecticut, June 29, 1917; Creel to Walling, n.p., July 17, 1917: Records of the Committee on Public Information, Tray 43, 1-A1, RG 63, National Archives.

[54] John Lord O'Brian to Albert C. Ritchie, Washington, D.C., October 24, 1918, Records of the WIB, 1–A5, RG 61, N.A.

The major attempt to win labor support for the war was made through the American Alliance for Labor and Democracy (AALD) with Walsh's active participation and under Creel's direction. Creel secretly assumed control of the AALD in his capacity as chairman of the Committee on Public Information, an agency created by Wilson under his emergency powers on April 14, 1917. The need to "unify sentiment in the nation" in support of the war had been explained by Howard E. Coffin of the Council of National Defense two months before the United States entered the conflict. Speaking to the Executive Council of the National Civic Federation, Coffin emphasized the "need for an independent fund for publicity work," as congressional limitations made it impossible for the CND to give publicity to anything.[55] Immediately after war was declared Secretaries Baker, Josephus Daniels, and Robert Lansing wrote Wilson suggesting that "censorship and publicity can be joined in honesty and with profit, and we recommend a Committee on Public Information." Acting on this advice, Wilson created the CPI, assigned funds for its operation from his emergency reserve, and appointed Creel as administrative head. Until the passage of the Espionage Act two months later, Creel organized voluntary self-censorship of the press; thereafter the CPI became primarily a propaganda agency.[56] As such, its main function was to mobilize journalists, artists, speakers, and others to convince Americans that Germans were violent beasts, that all opposition to the war or conscription was a German plot and that Bolsheviks were German agents. This was done through press releases and the nationwide organization of speakers bureaus. But Creel also understood the need for ostensibly independent pro-war organizations, particularly of workers and pro-war Socialists.

The American Alliance for Labor and Democracy was just

[55] Coffin to the Executive Council of NCF, February 6, 1917, Box 189, NCF papers.

[56] Scheiber, *The Wilson Administration*, pp. 15–16.

such an organization. The original plans for the AALD were worked out by Samuel Gompers and Ralph Easley in early July of 1917. As Easley saw it, the AALD was to be "made up entirely of wage earners and socialists who have left the party on account of its capture by the German 'Hillquits.' " For that purpose Easley advanced the first $700 to the AALD and suggested that Gompers call Creel and "put the situation before him and let him take it up with the President." "Of course," Easley added, Creel's bureau "could have nothing to do with it but they could furnish the funds for both the publicity and organization work." [57]

Gompers followed Easley's advice and a few days later Creel let him know that he was "ready to get behind you and the Central Federated Union in your attempt to Americanize the labor movement." But, Creel added, "I must insist that the entire movement be governed and directed by organized labor." Then he suggested that AALD offices be located on the Lower East Side of New York and informed Gompers that he wanted "the meaning of America, and the purpose of America, to be put before the foreign born in all their languages." [58]

Robert Maisel, a former Socialist, was appointed director of AALD by Gompers, who became president. J. G. Phelps Stokes, another pro-war ex-Socialist, was asked by Maisel to be treasurer. He agreed to serve in that capacity, but explained that because of his financial commitments to the Social Democratic League, a new pro-war Socialist group, and other organizations he could not assume any responsibilities for AALD debts. If Gompers would "explicitly agree to protect me financially," Stokes wrote Maisel, he would accept the position of treasurer. Maisel replied the next day, assuring Stokes that the

[57] Easley to Vincent Astor, New York, November 14, 1917; Easley to Gompers, n.p., July 12, 1917: both Box 54, NCF papers.

[58] Creel to Gompers, Washington, D.C., July 26, 1917, CPI papers, 1–A1 RG 63, N.A.

241

position entailed no financial responsibilities. We have, Maisel announced, "sufficient money to carry out our work." [59]

Actually, Stokes served only as a figurehead. Creel kept tight control both of AALD activities and finances.[60] In his first report to Creel, Maisel wrote that he had acted on Creel's "instructions" to rent an office on Canal Street. In the following reports and correspondence it was clear that Creel made all final decisions on the publication of pamphlets and other printed material of the Alliance. In September, after the AALD had been formally organized at a convention in Minneapolis, Creel told the League for National Unity that the CPI had "formed an alliance for labor and democracy by Mr. Gompers, and the Government is behind it to the limit of its power." [61]

In July of 1918, after Congress had cut the CPI appropriation almost in half, Creel told Gompers that he could no longer extend financial aid to the AALD. He then offered the organization to Roger Babson of the Department of Labor, informing Babson that "we organized the American Alliance for Labor and Democracy, with headquarters in New York, and with branches in 164 cities." In addition to the organiza-

[59] J. G. Phelps to Robert Maisel, n.p., August 22, 1917; Maisel to Stokes, New York, August 23, 1917: both Box 27, J. G. Phelps Stokes papers, Columbia University.

[60] See, for example, Creel to Maisel, n.p., August 28, 1917 CPI, 1–A1, RG 63, in which Creel sent a voucher to be signed by Stokes, and returned for payment by Creel. In the letter Creel lectures Maisel on the need to file his expense account in detail. In particular, there was an item of $200 payable to Gompers the purpose of which was not listed. Creel wrote that it should have been put down as a return to Gompers, presumably for money he advanced when the AALD was organized.

[61] Minutes of the League for National Unity, September 12, 1917, Box 168, NCF papers; Report of Robert Maisel, September 27, 1917, CPI, 1–B1 RG 63. See, also, other reports in the same file, and letters between Creel and Maisel in CPI 1–A1, Tray 26. In one such Maisel asked permission to publish a report on the AALD given to the AFL convention. Creel replied: "Before giving any such consent I must see what the proceedings are. Please send them to me and I will answer at once." Maisel to Creel, New York, October 22, 1917; Creel to Maisel, n.p., October 23, 1917.

tion work done by the Alliance, Creel boasted, "it has operated a most intelligent labor publicity service yet devised by anyone, and has built up a tremendous following not only in the labor press but in the press as a whole." "I am," Creel concluded disingenuously, "entirely willing to turn this over to you, in fact, I have decided that it is no longer a valid part of our work, and I would suggest that you get in touch with Maisel." [62]

Although less actively involved in the operation of the AALD, Frank Walsh lent his name and his prestige among radicals to it and its attempts to win the loyalty of workers and Socialists to the war. Walsh attended the founding conference of the Alliance in Minneapolis at the beginning of September 1917. Working closely with Creel, he tried to get Midwestern pro-war Socialists to the AALD conference and cooperated with John Spargo and others in framing resolutions at Minneapolis. In particular, Walsh asked a Fort Scott, Kansas, Socialist to speak at the Minneapolis convention because he was "strong with the Socialist crowd and labor movement in Kansas and Oklahoma," and was connected with the *Appeal to Reason.*[63] After the conference, Walsh wrote Creel that it had been a great success and that he had gotten Creel's letter and suggestions, "and you probably noticed that they all went into the resolutions." In addition, Walsh reported, "Spargo's epitome of the President's expressed war aims and peace terms was a masterpiece. I took it to be the joint work of all of you." Now, he concluded overhopefully, "we have an organization which, if worked out properly will put an absolute quietus on all supposed spokesmen for labor and the radical element. They will continue to look cheaper and cheaper every day until they finally disappear." [64]

[62] Creel to Gompers, n.p., July 17, 1918; Creel to Babson, n.p., July 17, 1918, *ibid.*

[63] Walsh to Creel, Kansas City, August 30, 1917, Box 17, Walsh papers.

[64] Walsh to Creel, Kansas City, September 10, 1917, *ibid.*

243

But to Scott Nearing, a Socialist economist who had been fired from the University of Pennsylvania in 1915 and from Toledo University in 1917, it was Walsh who looked cheap. "You knew about Paterson and Ludlow," he wrote Walsh. "You knew who was behind them." "You know that these same forces are throttling democracy in America today—in the name of liberty in Europe." Nearing then reminded Walsh of Bisbee, Arizona, where over a thousand striking copper miners had been ruthlessly deported into the desert, of Tom Mooney, and of Frank Little, an IWW organizer who had been lynched at Butte, Montana, in August 1917. It was to such things that Walsh was lending his name and influence, Nearing charged. "The plutocrats are using your power to rivet the chains," he cried. "How can you do it?" [65]

Like Randolph Bourne, Nearing understood that Walsh's participation in the wartime Administration would make it easier for radicals to support the war. The AALD provided a means of involvement that could be rationalized by pro-war socialists and radicals, both in and out of the labor movement, as consistent with their earlier principles. Creel understood this very well, and one must assume that Wilson did too.[66] Gompers, on the other hand, was slower to understand the value of apparent ideological diversity. Indeed, he had to be lectured by W. J. Ghent, another pro-war socialist, on the value of radicals to the Administration.

At the time of the organization of the AALD in early September of 1917 Ghent, Stokes, John Spargo, Upton Sinclair,

[65] Scott Nearing to Walsh, n.p., September 6, 1917, *ibid.*

[66] Easley's changing attitude toward Creel is interesting on this point. In November 1917 Easley wrote Vincent Astor about the AALD and added, "Incidentally, speaking about Creel, I want to tell you that he is a wonder! I had him in my mind as a 'blatherskite,' a freak socialist, an anarchist, a syndicalist, and every other 'ist' that is possible—and at one time I was right. . . . He is in closer touch with the President than is any other man I know of, not excepting Colonel House, for he sees him every day and has the most confidential relations with him." Easley to Astor, November 14, 1917, Box 54, NCF papers.

and others were ready to launch the Social Democratic League. Since many of the SDL initiators were also delegates to the AALD convention in Minneapolis, they decided to use that opportunity to meet and to organize formally. At Minneapolis, in accordance with earlier plans, the leaders of the new SDL also decided to meet with leaders of the Prohibition Party and the remnants of the Progressive Party a month later in Chicago to launch the ephemeral National Party, which they hoped would replace the pro-war Socialist Party as a rallying point for radicals.[67]

When Gompers got wind of these activities he was furious. In a letter to Maisel, copies of which he sent to Stokes, Spargo, Ghent, and others, Gompers complained that he could not understand the purpose of "another Socialist political party." A political party, he wrote, "exists essentially to support the administration and government of the country or to oppose it, and, by opposing, wrest the power from the existing administration and government." But since the purpose of the new party was to support the administration it was superfluous. "Such a party already exists and therefore a creation of a new party for that purpose is unnecessary, and it must necessarily prove abortive." Gompers then charged that the organization of a new party would have a "baneful influence" on the AALD and was "violative of the purpose and spirit" of it. Furthermore, the pro-war socialists had taken advantage of his hospitality, Gompers charged. They represented no one but themselves, he reminded them, and yet he had given them full delegate status at the AALD convention along with representatives of unions with tens of thousands of members. It was a cruel way for the Socialists to reward him for legitimizing them, he concluded.[68]

[67] John Spargo to C. E. Pitts, Old Bennington, Vermont, July 18, 1917; Spargo to all delegates, Old Bennington, September 13, 1917; Stokes to William E. Walling, n.p., September 11, 1917: Boxes 27, 28, Stokes papers.

[68] Gompers to Maisel, Buffalo, September 29, 1917, Copy "F," Box 28, Stokes papers.

Gompers was correct in his prediction that the new party would prove abortive, but he was brought up sharply by Stokes, Spargo, and W. J. Ghent about the legitimacy of their action and its effect on the AALD. Stokes, who at this time did not know who was paying the AALD's bills, and Spargo both reminded Gompers that the AALD had been promoted as a nonpartisan organization, rather than an arm of the Democratic Party. Ghent also made this point, adding that had he known "that attendance at the Alliance convention laid a delegate under obligations to give an unquestioning support to the Democratic party" he would have had "nothing to do with the convention." Then he lectured Gompers on how to build a successful front organization. Agreeing that the Alliance could be made "a powerful factor in support of the government," Ghent added that "a partisan interpretation of its scope and mission" would "destroy it before it has had a chance to get started." More important, Ghent noted the implication in Gompers letter "that some special favor was granted the Socialists and radicals in admitting them to participation in the Alliance convention." But, Ghent insisted, "had it not been for their participation the convention would have been a complete failure. The press would have ignored it as an Administration 'plant.' " [69]

In fact, the AALD was not a success. Rank and file working class support for the war remained lukewarm and the overwhelming majority of Socialists continued to oppose American participation. The direct activities of the Committee on Public Information—those of propaganda—were much more effective. But, as one historian has observed, as a result of the CPI's campaigning, "the loyalty of the innocent enemy alien was undoubtedly impugned, and excesses

[69] Spargo to Gompers, Old Bennington, October 9, 1917; Stokes to Gompers, n.p., October 6, 1917; Ghent to Gompers, Los Angeles, October 10, 1917: all Box 28, Stokes papers.

were probably encouraged." [70] A special assistant Attorney General, writing shortly after the war, believed that "no other one cause contributed so much to the oppression of innocent men as the systematic and indiscriminate agitation against what was claimed to be an all-pervasive system of German espionage." [71] The CPI was the leading initiator of such agitation, and its effect was to weaken all radical or critical groups, whether Socialist or of the La Follette variety. Recognizing this, at the end of the war, Walsh resigned from the AALD and its Executive Committee. The occasion was an anti-Bolshevik article written by the former Socialist Gustavus Myers, which the AALD published. Explaining his move, Walsh wrote that "without attempting to pass in any way upon the Russian situation, the article, it seemed to me, was a vicious onslaught on a great body of people, fighting valiantly to control their own destiny, whether right or wrong." But to Samuel Gompers he was more forthright. He had, he told Gompers, "very grave doubt" as to the AALD's "utility now that hostilities are over." [72]

Walsh's postwar awareness of the limitations of the AALD paralleled his resignation as co-chairman of the War Labor Board. Writing to a friend in the labor movement, Walsh said that he had resigned from the Board because it "has come to the point where it cannot be anything but a disappointing mirage to the working people of the country." The WLB's announced principles, and the few good decisions it rendered, had created the hope in the minds of "many thousands of workers that it is some sort of forum in which justice may be found." But Walsh now believed that "by some sort of agreement" employers were "holding things back," and

[70] Scheiber, *The Wilson Administration*, p. 16.
[71] Quoted in *ibid.*, p. 17.
[72] Walsh to Frank E. Wolfe, New York, December 30, 1918; Walsh to Gompers, New York, December 30, 1918: both in Box 26, Walsh papers.

that if the Board does anything "it will be along the line of strangling the aspirations of the workers rather than fulfilling them." The employing members of the Board had, "without exception," sat "like hawks" to "pounce down upon any person making an effort to ameliorate the conditions of workers anyplace." That they had not succeeded, he added, had been because of the "really fine spirit of honest cooperation of Mr. Taft," and of Basil Manly.

But as a liberal defender of the system, Walsh had changed his view of the large corporation. He now saw only one possible solution to the Board's weaknesses. It was that it should be reconstituted by Wilson "commandeering" the biggest employers in the country to serve. Specifically, Walsh mentioned his former nemesis, John D. Rockefeller, Jr., Ogden Armour, Jacob H. Schiff, Samuel Insull, and Francis S. Peabody of the Peabody Coal Company (and chairman of the Coal Production Committee of the CND), on the business side, and Gompers and other labor leaders on the labor side.[73] It was a suggestion that would have won hearty approval from Ralph Easley.

Unlike Walsh, Creel never even partially repudiated his wartime activities, but in an amazing letter to Wilson just after the heavy Democratic losses in the congressional elections of 1918, Creel did reveal a more complex view of American participation than he had expressed in 1917. Creel wrote that although Wilson had indeed made the war one to "make the world safe for democracy," it was "not that sort of war when we entered it." American entrance, Creel reminded Wilson, "had its chief impulsion from our most reactionary and least democratic elements." The "Republican representatives of big business made a clear record of patriotic support of what was then, in outward appearance, a reactionary trade-imperialist war." Of course, Creel added, Wilson had successfully raised the war "to the level of a war for democracy," and

[73] Walsh to Victor Olander, n.p., December 4, 1918, *ibid.*

248

in so doing had won over "all progressive and democratic elements." But because the reactionaries had been the leading interventionists they had been able to use the war to attack and destroy liberals and their political machinery.[74]

It should surprise few that Wilson was neither as simpleminded or naïve as Creel's letter implies. In fact both Wilson and his Secretary of the Treasury (and son-in-law) were as acutely aware of the commercial implications of the war as were the bankers—and not only in regard to trade with Europe, but also as these related to the position of the United States in the colonial world. Some two months before Wilson called for a declaration of war, Secretary of the Treasury McAdoo had summoned Thomas W. Lamont to Washington to discuss Allied war credits and the prospects for gaining control of certain Latin American investments from Britain and France as a result of their increasing financial dependence on the United States. When he returned to New York, Lamont wrote a long letter to McAdoo explaining the position of J. P. Morgan and Company and the other leading banks. Lamont assured McAdoo that the banking group led by Morgan and Company had "been steadily working to the same general end as you have in mind" in regard to Latin American securities. Lamont then explained what the banking group had done. It had already acquired fifteen million dollars of six percent notes of the Central Argentine Railroad. This acquisition had transferred control of the railroad to American investors, since the railroad simultaneously called in an equivalent amount of its sterling issues in England. The American banking group had also bought three million dollars of securities of the Antofogasta Railway on the West Coast of South America, thereby "converting into dollars sterling securities formerly held by English investors."

[74] Creel to Wilson, n.p., November 8, 1918, Creel papers, Woodrow Wilson Letterbooks, Library of Congress.

McAdoo, so Lamont said, had "very properly" asked him "why Great Britain does not force her holders of South American securities to sell them outright" to the Morgan group, "instead of putting them up as collateral to loans." The answer Lamont gave was that Britain was willing to do just that, but that there was not much of a market for such securities in the United States and the banks found it unprofitable to hold the securities themselves. "Here, as I say," Lamont went on, "we are holding in our portfolios two of the highest class South American railway issues, which as yet we have been unable to dispose of. With that situation there is not much encouragement to force out larger British holdings." "I mention this," Lamont added, "in connection with your query as to whether such action would not be wise to enable this country to gain a foothold in South American industries that will be valuable when war is over." In fact, "for months we have been negotiating with reference to an issue of thirty million dollars of San Paulo Railway securities, but we have been unable to make much definite progress because of the difficulty of putting the proposed issues into a form both safe and salable in the United States. In the same way, he added, "we have been figuring on the securities of the Brazil Railway held by French investors."

Lamont then reviewed the problems in conducting this kind of business, which included "the extreme difficulty of dealing with the South American governments in a form that will enable us to offer their securities according to American financial usages." Concluding, Lamont told McAdoo that he had "gone very fully into this matter" because he was "anxious to have you get a complete picture of it and to have you understand how fully our own desires coincide with yours as to the development of South American business. We have been well aware of the desire of the present Administration and of yourself personally to cultivate our relations with our friends in

South America," Lamont explained, "and we have been doing our utmost along this line." [75]

The war, then, provided Wilson with the opportunity to show the business community that a liberal administration could be sensitive and responsive to the "natural" requirements of business without being antilabor, and even allowing reformers and an occasional radical to sit on some government boards. Through representation on the War Industries Board and its subsidiaries, on the War Labor Board, and on other federal agencies, labor gained official recognition on a scale that would not have been tolerated before the war. Despite that, many businessmen had lost their former suspicion of government intervention and regulation by the end of the war. The idea of government-business partnership had, in fact, gained considerable ground. At the beginning of the Progressive Era most businessmen, whether large or small, saw little need for government interference in business affairs. Of course, government had been expected to defend business activity, whether from threats to Americans doing business in Latin America, Asia, or Africa, or from strikes and other forms of social upheaval. And government had been expected to subsidize those industries that were commonly needed but were insufficiently profitable, or too risky, to attract the necessary private capital. But government had not generally been seen as being responsible for regulating business in the interest of the corporate community, or for creating or maintaining a favorable climate for investment. Nor, although state and federal governments had on occasion assumed the role of arbitrator between classes, had they been expected to accommodate the trade unions in the interest of social peace. In short, at the turn of the century, few expected government to manage society—business was expected to function freely, and the free operation of the market, both in goods and

[75] Thomas W. Lamont to William Gibbs McAdoo, New York, February 21, 1917, McAdoo papers, Library of Congress.

labor, was expected to produce satisfactory conditions for society at large.

The changes in the concept of the proper role of government and in the techniques of maintaining political and social stability reflected the end of "free" competition and the rise of a new corporate oligarchy. In the rhetoric of the new liberals, these concepts represented a growing concern for the welfare of the public (and many ordinary liberals and probably some corporate liberals were so motivated). In fact, the increasing centralization of power and the expert management of business and social life by federal and state governments met the needs of corporations whose scale of operation was national and international. Day to day power centered more and more in the hands of administrators and experts who thought primarily in terms of increasing the efficiency of the existing system, were constrained to do so in a manner to win the approval of corporation leaders. Workers, farmers, and small businessmen, in other words, had less and less real power, even though, in a formal sense, they had gained recognition as legitimate social forces.

That recognition went, of course, to the conservative leaders of the more conservative labor and farm organizations. But even if this had not been so, the form of the new administrative agencies so delimited labor's real influence that the result would have been little different. The concept of the tripartite body which the Civic Federation had developed was inherently biased in favor of the large corporations, since it began with the assumption that the existing system was to be ameliorated and made more efficient. Further, business was doubly represented, once on the business side and again on the "public" side, which was usually made up of corporation lawyers, philanthropists (such as Andrew Carnegie), politicians like Oscar Straus (Roosevelt's Secretary of Commerce and Labor) or William H. Taft, or academic leaders with close ties to the great philanthropists. Of course labor representation, even if on a basis of less than equality, was not a bad thing in itself. But the price that had to be paid was a process of the erosion of politics—the gradual imposition of administrative and judicial control in place of independent political action. This, over the years, has been reflected institutionally most clearly in the decline in the importance of Congress and the increasingly dominant role of the executive and judicial branches of the federal government.

The great success of the liberal defenders of the new corporate order has been made possible by several factors. The first was the sophistication of men like George W. Perkins, Mark Hanna, Samuel Insull, Frank A. Vanderlip, John Hays Hammond, Seth Low, Ralph Easley, Jeremiah Jenks, Bernard Baruch, Theodore Roosevelt, Woodrow Wilson, and many others who helped formulate the new liberal concepts or who came to accept and support them. Developed openly in the meetings of the National Civic Federation and other organizations in the early stages, the new concepts were later refined and new programs planned more quietly and informally through a number of more specialized organizations.[76]

The second factor was the favorable position of the United States with respect to Europe and the colonial world which made possible a process of rapid and sustained industrial expansion, supported in the nineteenth century by a vast internal (continental) empire, and in the twentieth by the penetration of the old empires of Europe, facilitated by the growing dependence of the Allied powers on the United States as the result of two world wars. This circumstance made available the material affluence that made possible many of the welfare programs of the new liberal state.

[76] On the role of the various research foundations in developing the new corporate liberalism, see David W. Eakins, "The Development of Corporate Liberal Policy Research in the United States, 1885–1965" (unpublished Ph.D. dissertation, University of Wisconsin, 1966).

Equally important has been the absence of any serious competition from the left or the right since World War I. The right has been sustained as a minor political force by its appeals to the individualism of the free market, but lacking major corporate support has never been a potent challenger to the new liberals. The socialist movement collapsed as a serious opposition after the split of the old Socialist Party in 1919. In the absence of a revolutionary party with a comprehensive critique of the existing society and a comprehensive vision of a new one, all reformers, no matter how radical they thought themselves to be, could be (and have been) caught up in reform structures whose underlying purpose is to reduce the inharmonies of the existing social system. Either that, or, as has happened to some radicals more recently, they have been forced to abstain from participation in the larger society, to "drop out," and become truly irrelevant. The new liberals, starting with the National Civic Federation, presented radicals and socialists with a challenge that undercut many of their criticisms. The new liberals, both in the Progressive Era and later in the New Deal, the New Frontier, and the Great Society, have demonstrated that when faced with immediate threats they can make the necessary adjustments to restore at least a façade of social harmony. So far, for many reasons, socialists and radicals have been unable to meet that challenge, or, by and large, even to face its implications.

INDEX

Accidents, industrial: rates in U.S., 40–41; defenses for employer, 41–42
Adams, Charles Francis, 8, 112
Adams, Graham, Jr., 190
Adamson Act, 213
Addams, Jane, x, 127, 182, 185
Agar, John G., 24
Agricultural Adjustment Administration, 233
Akron *Beacon-Journal*, 235
Aldrich, Nelson, 28, 74, 140
Alexander, George, 177
American Alliance for Labor and Democracy (AALD), 240–243; effectiveness of, 246
American Anti-Boycott Associations, 80
American Association for Labor Legislation, 7, 48
American Federation of Labor (AFL), 4, 5, 21, 172; and Socialist Party, 23; and Catholics, 118; and NCF, 120
Ammons, Elias M., 193, 196, 197, 198
Anarchists, 4
The Appeal to Reason, 238, 243
Arkell, Bartlett, 130
Armour, Ogden, 248
Astor, Vincent, 244n
Atlanta *Journal of Labor*, 59

Babson, Roger, 242
Baker, Alfred L., 151
Baker, Newton D., 220, 240
Baldwin, William D., 124
Ballard, S. Thruston, 185; report of, 209–210
Ballinger, Richard A., 142–143
Bancroft, Edgar A., 79, 81
Barrett, Charles S., 184, 234

Baruch, Bernard, 215, 216, 218, 220, 221–223, 231, 233, 253
Beard, Charles A., 112
Beck, James M., 78
Bell, John C., 129
Belmont, August, 9, 18, 48–49, 50, 52, 73, 77, 123; as president of NCF, 12, 38; on immigration, 26; and compensation legislation, 44–45
Berger, Victor, 120, 175
Berryhill, James G., 99, 109
Beveridge, Albert, 140
Black, Charles A., 105
Bolling, Raynal C., 46–47, 53
Bonaparte, Charles J., 8
Bourne, Randolph, 215, 244
Bowers, L. M., 196
Brandeis, Louis D., 24, 50, 89, 118, 157, 168, 181, 185, 214, 221; on unions, 17
Bristow, Joseph L., 11, 140, 146
Brookings, Robert, 215, 223, 224, 225
Brown, William C., 13
Buck's Stove and Range case, 16
Bureau of Corporations, 69
Burdett, Everett W., 124
Burleson, Albert, 237
Burns, William J., 175
Businessmen: small, 4–5; and workmen's compensation, 44–45
Butler, Nicholas Murray, 8, 75, 77, 119, 169

Cantrell, J. C., 32n
Capper, Arthur, 127
Carnegie, Andrew, 8, 17, 30n, 49, 56, 82, 150, 252; and Buck's Stove case, 16; on immigration, 26–27; and compensation legislation, 45; and Hepburn bill, 81

255

Index

Lovett, Robert S., 215
Low, Seth, 12, 17, 23, 24, 30n, 31, 32, 37, 48, 53, 74, 77, 79, 80, 81, 82, 85, 86, 88, 89, 134, 148, 164, 167, 207, 253; as NCF president, 38
Low, William G., Jr., 35
Ludlow massacre, 194
Lumber industry, 227
Lyman, Hart, 119

McAdoo, William Gibbs, 215, 249, 250
McCarthy, Charles, 25, 89, 186, 189, 198, 199; firing of by Walsh, 200–204
McCormick, Cyrus, 11, 30n, 84, 85, 127, 166
McCormick, Medill, 157, 161
MacDonald, Duncan, 22
McManigal, Ortie, 175
McMillin, Emerson, 33, 34, 35
McNamara, James B., 175–178
McNamara, John J., 175–178
McRoberts, Samuel, 221
MacVeagh, Franklin, 8, 17, 27, 31, 73
Macy, V. Everitt, x, 48, 134–135
Mahon, William D., 12
Maisel, Robert, 241, 242, 245
Manager government, 92–116; initiative for, 99–100; success of, 102–103; opponents of, 106–108; and minority groups, 110; and laissez faire, 113
Manly, Basil M., 200, 208, 248
Marcy, Mary, 239
Masses, 238
Mather, Samuel, 77
Maurer, James H., 121
Meeker, Royal, 211n
Melish, John Howard, 182
Mercer, Hugh V., 53
Mergers: and Sherman Act, 68
Metropolitan Magazine, 129, 130
Militia of Christ, 122–123
Miller, Charles R., 123, 124

Miller, John S., 73
Mills, Ogden, 126
Milwaukee Journal, 151
Minimum wages, 32; for women, 32–33, 44
Minority groups: and commission and manager government, 110
Mitchell, John, 8, 9, 12, 14, 21, 24, 31, 77, 120, 123
Monopoly, xii, 64–65
Mooney, Tom, 244
Moore, Joseph B., 32n
Moran, William J., 56
Morawetz, Victor, 29, 77
Morgan, Anne, 170
Morgan, J. Pierpont, 56
Morgan, J. P., Jr., 166
Morrison, Frank, 21
Morrissey, P. H., 77
Moyer, Charles H., 176
Municipal reform, 93–95
Munsey, Frank, 154, 155, 160, 161, 166, 168
Mushet, W. C., 177
Myers, Gustavus, 247

The Nation, 57, 151
National Association for the Advancement of Colored People, 119
National Association of Manufacturers (NAM), 92, 118; and laissez faire, 5; and labor unions, 14–15; history of, 15; and open shop, 18, 22; Committee of Employer's Liability, 47; and compensation, 47–48; and Sherman Act, 70; and Hepburn bill, 80; and Commission on Industrial Relations, 183
National Cash Register Company, 19
National Civic Federation (NCF), xv; organization of, 7–8; membership of, 8; and labor, 10, 120; and unions, 13–14, 17; Trade Agreements Department, 14; and NAM, 17; Welfare Department, 18–19; and welfare work, 18–20; and so-

Index

262

Index